D1645290

90710 000 202 172

WHILE WANDERING

While Wandering

Words on Walking

EDITED AND WITH AN INTRODUCTION BY
Duncan Minshull

FOREWORD BY
Robert Macfarlane

VINTAGE BOOKS
London

Published by Vintage 2014

2 4 6 8 10 9 7 5 3 1

Selection and Introduction copyright © Duncan Minshull 2000
Foreword copyright © Robert Macfarlane 2014
For copyright of contributors see pp.389–94

First published in Great Britain in 2000
with the title *The Vintage Book of Walking* by Vintage

Vintage
Random House, 20 Vauxhall Bridge Road,
London SW1V 2SA

www.vintage-books.co.uk

Addresses for companies within The Random House Group Limited
can be found at: www.randomhouse.co.uk/offices.htm

The Random House Group Limited Reg. No. 954009

A CIP catalogue record for this book
is available from the British Library

ISBN 9780099593362

The Random House Group Limited supports the Forest Stewardship
Council® (FSC®), the leading international forest-certification
organisation. Our books carrying the FSC label are printed on
FSC®-certified paper. FSC is the only forest-certification scheme
supported by the leading environmental organisations, including
Greenpeace. Our paper procurement policy can be found at:
www.randomhouse.co.uk/environment

MIX
Paper from
responsible sources
FSC® C016897

Printed and bound in Great Britain by Clays Ltd, St Ives PLC

For Ray Minshull, who got me going . . .

CONTENTS

It is good to collect things, but better to go on walks.

Anatole France

Foreword

Walking is our oldest means of motion, and footfall – along with heartbeat and breath – is one of the three first rhythms of human life. To the pace of the lifted and shifted leg we have set our ways, measured our memories, told our tales and given tempo to our thoughts. No surprise, then, that walking and writing should have been so long entwined: the footprint is our original letter, and the path our earliest story.

I have wandered the pages of Duncan Minshull's anthology of walking-writing for a decade now, and I still have not exhausted its excellence. My copy is foxed from miles in rucksacks, and dog-eared from hours in armchairs. Pressed into the index are a few blades of marram grass from a west Hebridean beach, in whose firm wet shell-sand I recall leaving tracks neat as pastry-cuts. Squidged onto a paragraph of Hazlitt is a yellow-brown stain that may have been a petal, but might also have been an unlucky fly. The margins of my copy are scribbled and starred in different inks: thick with ticks, and dense with exclamations of delight and insight.

Sauntering this book's byways and sidetracks, I have met old friends from the literature of the leg: Patrick Leigh Fermor, for instance, whose elaborately lawless prose (baroque-amok) never fails to set my feet itching; Walt Whitman, singing up the open road since 1856, or Bashō, whose three-thousand-mile walk 'to the deep north' is told in a voice both precise and mysterious. But I have made new acquaintances, too: without Minshull to guide me, I would never have encountered William Lithgow on his 'Rare Adventures and painfull Peregrinations', seen the 'slinky-hipped Colonel' of William Styron's *The Long March*, or witnessed the kit-list of the Chevalier de la Tocnaye for his walk through Ireland in the 1790s ('a sword stick . . . a powder bag made out of a woman's glove . . . Breeches, fine enough, when folded, not bigger than a fist'.)

The Chevalier was a dandy, but he was also wise to the fact that walking – especially over long distances – can be an uncomfortable business. And while this anthology gives full voice to the romantic tradition of enlightenment and epiphany on foot, it recognizes that bunions, blisters and hip-clicks are also part of the path (Bashō again, whose 'bony shoulders' are 'sore' by the end of each day, and whose 'paper coat' does so little to keep the cold at bay).

Here you will meet with some desperately serious walkers – such as Werner Herzog, who on hearing that his friend Lottie Eisner had suffered a stroke and was dying in Paris, set off from Munich on foot to reach her. 'I walked against her death', he wrote, 'knowing that if I walked she would be alive when I got there' (and so she was). But you will also cross paths with rakes, jokers and punsters, from Belloc to Wilde. Indeed, Minshull's anthologizing possesses its own dry wit, as when he juxtaposes in the same section Bunyan's progressive pilgrim, Milton's globe-striding Satan and Albert Speer, making his transcontinental dream-walk from his prison cell at Spandau.

But enough now, I think, with this pre-amble. One can spend all morning lacing up one's boots. What I mean in sum to say is that this is the best anthology I know about an activity I cannot live without. So – forwards from the foreword! Get up, get on, get going, get reading!

Robert Macfarlane
Cambridge, 2014

Introduction

Out alone, slightly tired, a walking mantra is what you need, and some lines of W. H. Auden will do: 'But I avoid it when I take/A Walker's Walk for Walking's Sake . . .' And they are simple lines to move along to, to keep in time to, as you make your way. Then again, they won't do at all. For its own sake might mean for pleasure's sake – and that's good enough – but what about the other reasons for going on foot? On your road, in your boots, thought overtakes recitation with – *why* do I walk?

Historically, and for many, walking has simply got us places; there was no other means, end of journey, end of story. Or other means were taken because you never liked to walk. Yet for those engaged in the activity, the whys and wherefores have always been numerous and complicated. You set off for reasons physical, geographical, intellectual, spiritual. Walks have allegorical and metaphorical significance. On your road, in your boots, ideas come to mind, you can justify this . . . You walk to stay fit; you walk to plot; you walk to enjoy nature; or unravel a city; your walk pleasingly snubs the car; and sometimes you head for dangerous ground – how good it looks, how nearly heroic.

So Auden describes a walk, and side-steps definition. After decades of continent-hopping, John Hillaby also holds back – explanations leave him 'perplexed'. Two singular voices in what is a tradition of articulating the need to 'foot it'. Writers on walking usually reveal an examined activity, transforming the impulses above, and others too, into accounts quite magical and strange. On your road, in your boots, you go for a hundred and one reasons – and I hope the following pages cast some light on these.

Walks are seamed into fiction and explored in all forms of non-fiction; they are held high in poetry and disputed in drama (interestingly, this last medium is home to the non-pedestrian). I have arranged the familiar and unfamiliar of these, tried to put them on well-marked paths. They come from British, European and American sources – areas best known to me – and are embellished with extracts from Africa, Asia and the Far East. And my focus is on *literary* matter; that is, walking in a context wider than the rucksack and rambling lines of guidebook or fitness manual. Extracts tend to run chronologically within sections, though early examples in mythology and religion reveal little to the reader. The journeys of Xenophon and Christ, for instance, are only outlined in original texts, never made specific – were details of how they went so incidental? Booted heydays came (with insight), the boots were put away, they came out again. Contemporary pieces are included – mainly travel tales, fewer philosophies – but it doesn't signal another walking age, no consensus follows. As always, it is a walking age for some.

The history of pedestrian literature is also diverse, and grouping the authors has been irresistible. So let's join the road again, which is starting to fill. With pilgrims and naturalists, commissioned to report. With countless essayists, turning things over, asserting the finer virtues of two feet. With the modern traveller, whose route inspires everything – local politics, environmental concerns, personal memoir. With professional marchers who have something to say. With the walker-poet stepping out a meter for his words, as his Romantic counterpart strides to the wilds. Then it's back on the gravel for some novelists, often indifferent movers who use the activity. Pedestrian scenes in stories serve as catalysts: on a path to somewhere something always happens, events move forward. (In much of Dickens, Hardy and D. H. Lawrence a network of walks is established, and on them people will engage, resolve or squander their futures. Austen's women shine on walks when they can't in the home. Others, often military men, hup into personal hells – comically so with *The Good Soldier Švejk,* in dread with William Styron's *The Long March.* And then certain walks become the subject: we follow Beckett's famous tramps as they merely tramp before us . . . *merely* tramp? Their trudgery glorifies an existential state.)

The pedestrians who record their journeys, the walking characters in fiction, these are about to move through eleven sections. They will take us into different places, into trouble, on the march, and towards an end of sorts. And, yes, before starting off, there is thought on the why. To properly 'see' and 'feel' the country or city, suggest Robert Walser and Iain Sinclair. To lose four pounds, quips Bernard Levin. Deeper psychological impulses echo through all ages – the desire to 'walk yourself into well-being', so sweetly put by Søren Kierkegaard, is important to Edmund Spenser in relieving court ennui and embraced six centuries later as film-maker Werner Herzog covers two countries in hope of curing a friend. Well-being leads to clarity of vision, to order and composition, to closeness to a god. On terra firma you will walk and talk, walk and woo, and it can be quicker by foot – past and present. But practical or personal, acceptable or odd, just know, says Henry Thoreau, that you belong to a special group – to the Order of Walkers.

And Thoreau's lot are keen on form; not only do primers and handbooks declare on etiquette and equipment, assorted literary pedestrians have their say on how to go. As far back as the 1300s even, with Dante precise on bearing in *Purgatory.* Then Petrarch considers logistics – which path for Mount Ventoux, who to choose for company. Taking company or going it alone pre-occupies Petrarch, as it does Robert Louis Stevenson in the 1870s when the walking-essay is ubiquitous. The walk as social ritual, the hike as manly test, these are perfect topics for the genre, and after Stevenson various Edwardians fuel the form. Secure and booted voices of Empire, stepping out to fill landscape and page, they are loud on footwear, on maps and stimulants, on our duties in rural areas. In the last fifty years, Ramblers have pamphleteered their views; the do's and dont's almost stifle. Now things have calmed, gone informal. Desultory concern about the state of our feet, something on spare socks. But perhaps the how has lost its zeal.

Why, how, and *where* do we go? Convention looks to countryside and city, and sections on both are central to the collection. Country/city comparisons occupy many niches in literature, in pedestrian literature they contrast those who hike the fields and those who stroll the pavements. More than a question of gait though, it is a state of mind. We perceive the committed nature walker as Romantic, a Wordsworth or Thoreau, followed by others with similar desires – George Borrow, Edward Thomas, John Muir. They take to field and wood to escape the crush of urban life; their excursions earn them space and freedom and oneness with Nature. Then re-evaluation will come. Then enlightenment. The course of this walk is reflected in passages with narrative sweep, with suggestions of start, middle and end. And other pieces, too, suggest that the urban walker seeks affinity with environment, yet his high-street saunter attracts all that the rambler avoids. He is characterised by Poe's man of the crowd and *in extremis* by the spirit of Charles Baudelaire: one who 'botanizes on the asphalt', who absorbs the crowds and their incessant side-shows. Another romantic perhaps – he is self-aware, he makes the mundane look magical – but here is no purposeful walker with a complete story. He wants to get distracted, often waylaid, before a drift into exhaustion and isolation. Buildings blur, pavements end, he is gone . . . His tales of city life – call them his internal walks – are fragmented and elliptical. The sum of a few steps here, a few steps there . . .

I have found these hikers in gentle meadow and on harsh moor, and many strollers are lifted from London, Paris and New York. Each has a wayward relation – the pedestrian adventurer – who is on every road, in every century, and occupies a section full of questions. For a start: why do so many walk into so much trouble? Why is there a higher ratio of women here? (These women probe the abstract difficulties ahead: Virginia Woolf and Merle Collins are vivid on dubious night-walks, not for them the standard bogs and ravines.) Recalling 'tough tracks' provides richer comedy than preceding chapters. And I can't accept a lot of experiences on offer: two early seventeenth century travellers – Thomas Coryate and William Lithgow – might be writing prototype novels, such are their outlandish encounters. But you can say this about any pedestrian story – like the fish that got away, his or her trek was *so* long, was *so* remarkable. And it keeps on growing.

Of course, the big adventure has you encircling the world, and wasn't this achieved a decade ago? The books have since been discredited, so it's back to imagined accounts for our walk of walks. It looks good going global, even in print. Milton realises this with his mock glamorisation of Satan: easy bounds take him beyond the 'barren planes', and he burns up countries and continents like no other on foot. 'Satan alighted walks' comes the familiar refrain, trying to sell us a dashing and eternal stride – but a stride, ultimately, into what? Into isolation (like our city flâneur), into perpetual darkness, and here is one we won't be travelling with. Then rather less flamboyant, somehow more appealing, is an attempt made during incarceration. Spandau Prison, 1955, and Albert Speer concocts a spectacular walk that repeats Kierkegaard – a dreamed walk into well-being. It keeps him sane, what a project! He wanders the prison garden and evokes Berlin to Heidelberg – '620 kilometers!' Second time out, his diary records the big one: Munich to Rome; Yugoslavia to Greece; Ankara to Persia; Aleppo, Beirut, Baghdad and across to Persepolis and Teheran. Much of this crosses desert – a 'long, hot tramp' – and is often off-course. Positive and unhindered Speer looks to be, yet also careful. He must avoid all Communist states.

Other types, however, detract from the ambitions of the adventurer. Little in the way of imagination here, yet they are strong in voice and due some space. Anti-walkers rarely get the point: you're going without horse, carriage or car, and you won't accept a lift – why not? To those approaching on foot, the inn is shut, the horn is beeped, the stones are chucked. Pedestrians will be robbed, kidnapped, arrested. They don't belong to a noble order; rather their status is viewed as odd and unfixed, out on the fringes of everyday life. Gypsy, tramp, Sunday rambler. There is a deep-rooted need to mistrust, and the road-side figure satisfies this. Mistrust and superstition are the interesting reactions, we are just as likely to find laziness and the seduction of wheels; and these wheels will tempt the most hardened – W. H. Hudson stands out. Perversely, Max Beerbohm takes a stroll to compose his complaint (one of the longest included, footing it 'rots the brain'), but the message is usually consistent. And timeless. For this antagonism sustains an ongoing debate. From William Congreve's couch-beau to Ray Bradbury's robotic police there is heard the same – 'You *walked*?'

Anti-walkers also miss out on a vibrant language; on choice words and phrases that evoke the journey by foot. Take our country hiker first, portrayed ahead in various ways: rambler, ambler, tramper, trekker, ranger, stomper, stumper, strider, trailer, backpacker; here is one who *leaps* and *skelps* and *swings* to a destination. His city cousin, the stroller, is also individualised; less actively so, less visceral-sounding. Saunterer, lingerer, loiterer, dandy, dawdler, strutter, scuffer, boulevardier, *flâneur*, hints at one averse to the great journey. Then, on your road, in your boots, Arthur Rimbaud's yell cum mantra inspires: 'Let's go! Route march, burden, desert, boredom, anger . . .' And certain writers champion their endeavours by humanising the tools of the trade. George Trevelyan refers to his legs as 'my two doctors'; and I wonder if Bruce Chatwin hasn't borrowed from this when, during his final bedridden weeks, he realises time has come to say 'goodbye to the boys'. In various passages, asphalt and gravel are celebrated; there is something all-enduring about 'roadsters' (definitely an Americanism here: John Burroughs and Thoreau argue for and against the type). Die-hard roadsters look for their special line snaking into the distance, which Stevenson sees as a 'white ribbon of possible travel'. He says he rejoices in *Sehnsucht*: 'the passion for what is ever beyond', the passion that will take us to the city gates . . . And then one walking verb actually changes meaning; you might say adapts. To *roam*. The soft, carefree connotations caught in Thoreau and Muir, and in the urban meanders of Baudelaire and James Thomson, tell half the story. It has been a politicised term for at least two centuries, with John Clare roaming in 1818 to denounce the effects of enclosure on England's common fields; another walker-poet, Andrew Young, invites us to roam restricted areas at the start of this century; and Julian Barnes's president of the Ramblers Association is currently funny in bespoke gear, yet serious in his intention to march across all lands. For roam now read the Right to Roam.

On his desert trek, John Hillaby isn't so much distracted by approaching sandstorms, as by a word new to him in the lexicon. He's still avoiding the why, but hooked on *festination*. A habit, it seems, of moving rapidly and relentlessly, with little hope of respite. You simply walk to drop (with Patrick Suskind's Mr Sommer an alarming case to come). And the word has some relevance in concluding this book – how best, that is, to complete the task? Is there ever completion? Well, I have looked to one of those metaphorical roads, which are at the heart of many texts. Just as the line starting out is a signifier of hope and freshness, so its end can denote the traveller's end. It is elevated in the literature *to* something like the Road of Life With the Walker On It (and sometimes with a dog at heel, thankfully mute). Thomas Hardy steers his characters on such a path, destinies mapped out, Tess the memorable leader. Others set off brightly at the start of the collection, only to reappear later as said Road converges with a final breath – Walser will locate his 'dark path' of the countryside, and a stroller will fall in the lines of Edwin Arlington Robinson. And Bashō, pilgrim of three thousand miles, pens an epitaph for those who cannot shed their boots:

> No matter where I fall
> On the road
> Fall will I to be buried
> Among flowering bush-cloves.

Bashō is at the tail-end of two hundred authors making tracks (twice this number might have been included, but there was a plan to follow); and he is one who takes up an age-old rhythm: walking gives rise to thought, which leads to expression. Easily and distinctly. And would the anthologist find in those other natural movers – the runners, climbers, swimmers – such vital celebration of their obsession, such a willingness to fix on reasons that go beyond the 'sake' of it. I think not. I think I have had it quite easy. Anyway, may the following suggest to all walker-readers where next, or where to dream of going next. And as for the anti-walkers, may the powers ahead persuade . . . Happy Festination.

Duncan Minshull
January, 2000

ONE

Why Walk

There's an old story about a centipede who was asked which particular set of legs he used to start walking. The question took him by surprise. What had seemed a perfectly normal means of progression became a wholly perplexing problem. He could scarcely move. I'm faced with a similar difficulty when I try to account for – not how I walk, but why.

John Hillaby

ONCE UPON A TIME IT WAS THE ONLY WAY

Along the roads of England five hundred years ago there moved a steady procession of foot-travellers, sometimes a constant stream, sometimes a solitary figure, all making their way purposefully and all resigned to walking, not riding. Most were engaged in basic trades or dealings: drug sellers, pedlars and chapmen, who bought and sold and bartered; jobbing workmen such as stone-masons or joiners; and entertainers – perambulating minstrels, singers, buffons and gleemen. A special breed were the messengers, bearers of letters or packets or verbal tidings, often the fastest of the foot-travellers and, though themselves of humble status, protected by the authority of those who had sent them. To these were added the religious, the preachers, pardoners, mendicant friars and pilgrims. And finally there were the people on the fringes of society, some utterly ignored by it – beggars, poachers, escaped peasants, robbers, bandits and general down-and-outs. On they went through the hours, keeping to the sides and out of the way of the horses and palfries and axle-creaking wagons on which rode the more fortunate; and for the purpose of the journey there were but two classes – those who walked and those who rode.

Miles Jebb, *Walkers*, 1986

IT IS QUICKER ON FOOT

The lady, having finished her story, received the thanks of the company; and now Joseph, putting his head out of the coach, cried out, 'Never believe me if yonder be not our parson Adams walking along without his horse!' – 'On my word, and so he is,' says Slipslop: 'and as sure as twopence he hath left him behind at the inn.' Indeed, true it is, the parson had exhibited a fresh instance of his absence of mind; for he was so pleased with having got Joseph into the coach, that he never once thought of the beast in the stable; and, finding his legs as nimble as he desired, he sallied out, brandishing a crabstick, and had kept on before the coach, mending and slackening his pace occasionally, so that he had never been much before or less than a quarter of a mile distant from it.

Mrs. Slipslop desired the coachman to overtake him, which he attempted, but in vain; for the faster he drove the faster ran the parson, often crying out, 'Aye, aye catch me if you can'; till at length the coachman swore he would as soon attempt to drive after a greyhound, and, giving the parson two or three hearty curses, he cry'd, 'Softly, softly, boys,' to his horses, which the civil beasts immediately obeyed.

But we will be more courteous to our reader than he was to Mrs. Slipslop; and, leaving the coach and its company to pursue their journey, we will carry our reader on after parson Adams, who stretched forwards without once looking behind him, till, having left the coach full three miles in his rear, he came to a place where, by keeping the extremest track to the right, it was just barely possible for a human creature to miss his way. This track, however, did he keep, as indeed he had a wonderful capacity at these kinds of bare possibilities, and, travelling in it about three miles over the plain, he arrived at the summit of a hill, whence looking a great way backwards, and perceiving no coach in sight, he sat himself down on the turf, and pulling out his Aeschylus, determined to wait here for its arrival.

Henry Fielding, *Joseph Andrews*, 1742

IT HAS BECOME FASHIONABLE

Pray walk when the frost comes, young ladies, go a frost-biting. It comes into my head, that from the very time you first went to Ireland I have been always plying you to walk and read.

The young fellows have begun a kind of fashion to walk, and many of them have got swinging strong shoes on purpose; it has got as far as several young lords; if it hold, it would be a very good thing.

Jonathan Swift, *Journal to Stella*, 1710–13

A SHOW OF INDEPENDENCE

By this time the walk in the rain had reached Mrs. Elton, and her remonstrances now opened upon Jane.

'My dear Jane, what is this I hear? – Going to the post-office in the rain! – This must not be, I assure you – You sad girl, how could you do such a thing? – It is a sign I was not there to take care of you.'

Jane very patiently assured her that she had not caught any cold.

'Oh do not tell *me*. You really are a very sad girl, and do not know how to take care of yourself. – To the post-office indeed! Mrs. Weston, did you ever hear the like? You and I must positively exert our authority.'

'My advice,' said Mrs. Weston kindly and persuasively, 'I certainly do feel tempted to give. Miss Fairfax, you must not run such risks. – Liable as you have been to severe colds, indeed you ought to be particularly careful, especially at this time of year. The spring I always think requires more than common care. Better wait an hour or two, or even half a day for your letters, than run the risk of bringing on your cough again. Now do not you feel that you had? Yes, I am sure you are much too reasonable. You look as though you would not do such a thing again.'

'Oh! she *shall* not do such a thing again,' eagerly rejoined Mrs. Elton. 'We will not allow her to do such a thing again: – and nodding significantly – 'there must be some arrangement made, there must indeed. I shall speak to Mr. E. The man who fetches our letters every morning (one of our men, I forget his name) shall inquire for yours too and bring them to you. This will obviate all difficulties, you know; and from *us* I really think, my dear Jane, you can have no scruple to accept such an accommodation.'

'You are extremely kind,' said Jane; 'but I cannot give up my early walk. I am advised to be out of doors as much as I can, I must walk somewhere and the post-office is an object ...'

Jane Austen, *Emma*, 1815

TO BE WITH NATURE

A walk is always filled with significant phenomena, which are valuable to see and feel. A pleasant walk most often teems with imageries and living poems, with enchantments and natural beauties, be they ever so small. The lore of nature and the love of the country are revealed, charming and graceful, to the sense and eyes of the observant walker, who must of course walk not with downcast eyes but open and unclouded eyes, if the lovely significance and the gay, noble idea of the walk are to dawn on him.

Robert Walser, *The Walk*, 1917
(trans. Christopher Middleton, 1957)

TO SEE THE CITY

Walking is the best way to explore and exploit the city; the changes, shifts, breaks in the cloud helmet, movement of light on water. Drifting purposefully is the recommended mode, tramping asphalted earth in alert reverie, allowing the fiction of an underlying pattern to reveal itself. To the no-bullshit materialist this sounds suspiciously like *fin-de-siècle* decadence, a poetic of entropy – but the born-again *flâneur* is a stubborn creature, less interested in texture and fabric, eavesdropping on philosophical conversation pieces, than in noticing *everything*. Alignments of telephone kiosks, maps made from moss on the slopes of Victorian sepulchres, collections of prostitutes' cards, torn and defaced promotional bills for cancelled events at York Hall, visits to the homes of dead writers, bronze casts on war memorials, plaster dogs, beer mats, concentrations of used condoms, the crystalline patterns of glass shards surrounding an imploded BMW quarter-light window, meditations on the relationship between the brain damage suffered by the super-middleweight boxer Gerald McClellan (lights out in the Royal London Hospital, Whitechapel) and the simultaneous collapse of Barings, bankers to the Queen. Walking, moving across a retreating townscape, stitches it all together: the illicit cocktail of bodily exhaustion and a raging carbon monoxide high.

Iain Sinclair, *Lights Out for the Territory*, 1997

A SENSE OF PHYSICAL WELL-BEING

Dear Jette,

Above all, do not lose your desire to walk: every day I walk myself into a state of well-being and walk away from every illness. I have walked myself into my best thoughts, and I know of no thought so burdensome that one cannot walk away from it. Even if one were to walk for one's health and it were constantly one section ahead – *I would still say walk!* Besides, it is also apparent that in walking one constantly gets as close to well-being as possible, even if one does not quite reach it – *but by sitting still, and the more one sits still, the closer one comes to feeling ill.* Health and salvation can only be found in motion. If anyone denies that motion exists, I do as Diogenes did, I walk. If anyone denies that health resides in motion, then I walk away from all morbid objections. *Thus if one keeps on walking, everything will be all right.* And out in the country you have all the advantages; you do not risk being stopped before you are safe and happy outside your gate, nor do you run the risk of being intercepted on your way home. I remember exactly what happened to me a while ago and what has happened frequently since then. I had been walking for an hour and a half and had done a great deal of thinking, and with the help of motion had really become a very agreeable person to myself. What bliss, and, as you may imagine, what care did I not take to bring my bliss home as safely as possible. Thus, I hurry along, with downcast eyes I steal through the streets, so to speak; confident that I am entitled to the sidewalk, I do not consider it necessary to look about at all (for thereby one is so easily intercepted, just as one is looking about – in order to avoid) and thus hasten along the sidewalk with my bliss (for the ordinance forbidding one to carry anything on the sidewalk does not extend to bliss, which makes a person lighter) – and run directly into a man who is suffering from illness and who therefore with downcast eyes, defiant because of his illness, does not even think he must look about when he is not entitled to the sidewalk. I was stopped. It was quite an exalted gentleman who now honoured me with his conversation. Thus, all was lost. After the conversation ended, there was only one thing left for me to do; instead of going home, *to go walking again.*

Yours, S. Kierkegaard

Søren Aaby Kierkegaard, Letter to Henrietta Lund, 1847
(trans. Henrik Rosenmeier, 1978)

ANOTHER'S WELL-BEING

At the end of November 1974, a friend from Paris called and told me that Lotte Eisner was seriously ill and would probably die. I said that this must not be, not at this time, German cinema could not do without her now, we would not permit her death. I took a jacket, a compass and a duffel bag with the necessities. My boots were so solid and new that I had confidence in them. I set off on the most direct route to Paris, in full faith, believing that she would stay alive if I came on foot.

Werner Herzog, *Of Walking in Ice*, 1978
(trans. Alan Greenberg and Martje Herzog, 1980)

GOOD FOR THE SOUL

Calm was the day, and through the trembling air
Sweet breathing Zephyrs did softly play –
A gentle spirit, that lightly did delay
Hot Titan's beams, which then did glisten fair;
When I (whom sullen care,
Through discontent of my long fruitless stay
In princes court, and expectation vain
Of idle hopes, which still did afflict my brain)
Walked forth to ease my pain
Along the shore of silver streaming Thames.

Edmund Spenser, *Prothalamion*, 1596

A WALKING PHILOSOPHY TESTED

Next day I rose early, cut myself a stick, and went off beyond the town gate. Perhaps a walk would dissipate my sorrows. It was a beautiful day, bright and not too hot, a gay, fresh wind was gently wandering over the earth; playing and softly murmuring, it touched everything lightly, disturbing nothing.

For a long time I wandered over the hills and in the woods. I did not feel happy – I had started with the set purpose of giving myself up to gloomy reflections. But youth, the beauty of the day, the freshness of the air, the pleasure which comes from rapid walking, the delicious sensation of lying on thick grass far away from everyone, alone – all these proved too strong. The memory of those unforgettable words, of those kisses, once more pierced into my soul. I thought with a certain pleasure that Zinaida could not, after all, fail to recognize my resolution, my heroism … Others please her better than I, I thought; let them! But then others only speak of what they will do – whereas I have done it … And that's nothing to what I can still do for her!

I saw a vision of myself saving her from the hands of her enemies; I imagined how, covered with blood, I tore her from the very jaws of some dark dungeon and then died at her feet. I remembered the picture which used to hang in our drawing-room. Malek-Adel carrying off Matilda … and then my attention was absorbed by the appearance of a large, brightly coloured woodpecker, busily climbing up the slender stem of a birch tree, and peering nervously from behind it, alternately to the right and to the left, like a double bass player from behind the neck of his instrument.

After this I sang *Not white the snows* which presently turned into the song well known at that time *For thee I wait when zephyrs wanton*; then I began to declaim Yermak's apostrophe to the stars from Khomyakov's tragedy; tried to compose something myself in the sentimental style – even getting so far as to think of the concluding line of the entire poem: '… Oh Zinaida! Zinaida!' but in the end made nothing of it.

In the meanwhile dinner-time was approaching, and I

wandered down into the valley; a narrow sandy path wound its way through it towards the town. I walked along this path … The dull thud of horses' hooves sounded behind me. I looked round, stopped almost automatically, and took off my cap. I saw my father and Zinaida. They were riding side by side. My father was saying something to her; he was bending across towards her from the waist, with his hand propped on the neck of his horse; he was smiling. Zinaida listened to him in silence, her eyes firmly lowered, her lips pursed tightly. At first I saw only them; a few seconds later Byelovzorov came into view, in a hussar's uniform with a pelisse, on a foaming black horse. The noble animal tossed its head, pranced, snorted, while the rider at the same time held it back and spurred it on. I moved to one side, out of their way. My father gathered up the reins, and leant back away from Zinaida; she slowly lifted her eyes towards him, and they galloped off.

Byelovzorov raced after them, his sabre rattling. He is red as a lobster, I thought, she – why is she so pale? Out riding the whole morning – and yet so pale?

I walked twice as fast and got home just before dinner. My father was already sitting beside my mother's chair, washed and fresh and dressed for dinner, and was reading aloud to her, in his even, musical voice, the feuilleton from the *Journal des Débats*. But my mother listened to him without attention, and when she saw me asked what I had been doing with myself all day long, adding that she didn't like it when people went off God knows where and with God knows whom. 'But I was out for a walk, quite alone,' I was about to say, but glanced at my father, and for some reason remained silent.

Ivan Turgenev, *First Love*, 1860 (trans. Isaiah Berlin, 1950)

IT ENCOURAGES BOLDER THOUGHT

In thinking over the details of my life, which are lost to memory, what I most regret is that I did not keep diaries of my travels. Never did I think so much, exist so vividly, and experience so much myself – if I may use that expression – as in the journeys I have taken alone and on foot. There is something about walking which stimulates and enlivens my thoughts. When I stay in one place I can hardly think at all; my body has to be on the move to set my mind going. The sight of the countryside, the succession of pleasant views, the open air, a sound appetite, and the good health I gain by walking, the easy atmosphere of the inn, the absence of everything that makes me feel my dependence, of everything that recalls me to my situation – all these serve to free my spirit, to lend a greater boldness to my thinking, to throw me, so to speak, into the vastness of things, so that I can combine them, select them, and make them mine at will, without fear or restraint.

Jean-Jacques Rousseau, *Confessions*, 1781
(trans. J. M. Cohen, 1953)

AND IN THE COURSE OF THE WALK WAS PLANNED THE POEM

In reference to this Poem, I will here mention one of the most remarkable facts in my own poetic history and that of Mr Coleridge. In the Spring of the year 1798, he, my Sister, and myself started from Alfoxden, pretty late in the afternoon, with a view to visit Linton and the Valley of Stones near it, and as our united funds were very small we agreed to defray the expense of our tour by writing a Poem to be sent to the New Monthly Magazine set up by Phillips The Bookseller and edited by Dr Aiken. Accordingly we set off and proceeded along the Quantock Hills, towards Watchet, and in the course of this walk was planned the Poem of The Ancient Mariner, founded on a dream, as Mr Coleridge said, of his friend Mr Cruikshank.

We began the composition together on that memorable evening. I furnished two or three lines, in particular:

> And listened like a three years' child;
> The Mariner had his will.

These trifling contributions all but one (which Mr C. has with unnecessary scrupulosity recorded) slipt out of his mind as they well might. As we endeavoured to proceed conjointly (I speak of the same evening) our respective manners proved so wildly different that it would have been quite presumptuous in me to do anything but separate from an undertaking upon which I could only have been a clog. We returned after a few days from a delightful tour of which I have many pleasant and some of them droll enough recollections. We returned by Dulverton to Alfoxden. The Ancient Mariner grew and grew till it became too important for our first object which was limited to our expectation of five pounds, and we began to talk of a Volume, which was to consist as Mr Coleridge has told the world, of Poems chiefly on supernatural subjects taken from common life but looked at as much as might be, through an imaginative medium. Accordingly, I wrote the Idiot Boy, Her Eyes Are Wild, We Are Seven, The Thorn and some others. To return to We Are Seven, the piece that called forth this note, I composed it while walking in the grove at Alfoxden. My friends will not deem it too trifling to relate that while walking to and fro I composed the last stanza first, having begun with the last line. When it was all but finished, I came in and recited it to Mr Coleridge and my Sister, and said, 'A prefatory stanza must be added, and I should sit down to our little tea-meal with greater pleasure if my task were finished.'

William Wordsworth, 'Commentary' to the *Lyrical Ballads*, 1798

THOSE METRICAL FEET IN MOTION

Coleridge's manner is more full, animated and varied; Wordsworth's more equable, sustained, and internal. The one might be termed more dramatic, the other more lyrical. Coleridge has told me that he himself liked to compose in walking over uneven ground; or breaking through the straggling branches of a copse-wood; whereas Wordsworth always wrote (if he could) walking up and down a straight gravel walk ...

William Hazlitt, 'On My First Acquaintance with Poets', 1823

MORE WALKING, MORE WRITING

Froulish did not often leave the loft; a week or more might see him go no further than the impromptu wash-house in the yard below. But sometimes he went out for long solitary walks, and on this Saturday afternoon, Charles, settling down in the warmest corner for an after-lunch nap, was not surprised to see the novelist struggling into his tattered overcoat.

'I suppose you go out for these walks of yours to get ideas,' he said.

'Ideas nothing,' sneered Froulish. 'All you people ever think about is ideas. I suppose it has never struck you that in a work that has a certain chromatic range – that is, chromatic, somatic, vatic, any of the catch words you prefer – different physical states are necessary in the artist at different times.'

'You mean there are some passages you can only write when you are tired, or hungry, or have a cold in the head?'

'More or less,' said Froulish seriously. 'I have to write six pages expressive of intense weariness just now. So I'm going out to get physically tired. Not nervously, because the passage is supposed to have a certain response: muscular fatigue is what I need. I shall walk at least ten miles and then write this evening.'

John Wain, *Hurry on Down*, 1953

A COMPOSER WALKS THE BEAT

Like Wordsworth, Rimbaud, Mayakovsky and others, Satie was a great walker, and this was his main means of keeping fit. On most mornings after he moved to Arcueil, he would return to Paris on foot, a distance of about ten kilometres, stopping frequently at his favourite cafés *en route*. According to Templier, 'he walked slowly, taking small steps, his umbrella held tight under his arm. When talking he would stop, bend one knee a little, adjust his pince-nez and place his fist on his hip. Then he would take off once more, with small, deliberate steps.'

When he eventually reached Paris, he visited friends or arranged to meet them in other cafés by sending *pneumatiques* (the postal service then being fast and efficient). Often, the walking from place to place continued, focussing on Montmartre before the war, and subsequently on Montparnasse. From here, Satie would catch the last train back to Arcueil at about 1 a.m. or, if he was still engaged in serious drinking, he would miss it and begin the long walk home during the early hours of the morning. Then the daily round would begin again, although Satie rarely reached his first stop (Chez Tulard in Arcueil) before 11 a.m.

Roger Shattuck, in conversation with John Cage in 1982, put forward the interesting theory that 'the source of Satie's sense of musical beat – the possibility of variation within repetition, the effect of boredom on the organism – may be this endless walking back and forth across the same landscape day after day ... the total observation of a very limited and narrow environment'. This becomes the more relevant when we consider that most of Satie's pre-Arcueil music has a very slow pulse, while the faster, more mechanical regularity all belongs to the latter half of his career. *Parade*, with its constant pulse of 76 beats per minute, may thus reflect his slow walking speed as much as the human heart-beat. During his walks, Satie was also observed stopping to jot down ideas by the light of the street-lamps he passed. During the war, when these lights were often extinguished, a wicked myth circulated that Satie's productivity had dropped as a result. So although he invariably walked alone, he must have been a most familiar figure.

Robert Orledge, *Satie Remembered*, 1995
(trans. Robert Nicholls)

A WALK TO RECLAIM THE PAST (1)

There is charm in footing slow across a silent plain
Where Patriot Battle has been fought when K⁻osaka had the gain; There is a pleasure on the heath where Druids old have been, Where Mantles grey have rustled by and swept the nettles green; There is a joy in every spot, made known by times of old,
New to the feet, although the tale a hundred times be told:
There is a deeper joy than all, more solemn in the heart,
More parching to the tongue than all, of more divine a smart
When weary feet forget themselves upon a pleasant turf,
Upon hot sand, or flinty road, or Sea shore iron scurf,
Toward the Castle or the Cot where long ago was born
One who was great through mortal days and died of fame
Unshorn.

John Keats, 'Lines Written in the Highlands After a Visit to
Burns's Country', 1818

A WALK TO RECLAIM THE PAST (2)

His wandering step
Obedient to high thoughts, has visited
The awful ruins of the days of old:
Athens, and Tyre, and Balbec and the waste
Where stood Jerusalem, the fallen towers
Of Babylon, the eternal pyramids,
Memphis and Thebes, and whatso'er of strange
Sculptured on alabaster obelisk,
Or jasper tomb, or mutilated sphynx,
Dark Aethiopia in her desert hills
Conceals. Among the ruined temples there,
Stupendous columns, and wild images
Of more than man, where marble daemons watch
The Zodiac's brazen mystery, and dead men
Hang their mute thoughts on the mute walls around,
He lingered, poring on memorials
Of the world's youth, through the long burning day
Gazed on those speechless shapes, nor, when the moon
Filled the mysterious halls with floating shades
Suspended he that task, but ever gazed
And gazed, till meaning on his vacant mind
Flashed like strong inspiration, and he saw
The thrilling secrets of the birth of time.

Percy Bysshe Shelley, *Alastor; or the Spirit of Solitude*, 1816

IN THE ANCESTOR'S TRACKS,
AND BACK TO CREATION

In Islam, and especially among the Sufi Orders, *siyahat* or
'errance' – the action or rhythm of walking – was used as a
technique for dissolving the attachments of the world and

allowing men to lose themselves in God.

The aim of a dervish was to become a 'dead man walking': one whose body stays alive on the earth yet whose soul is already in Heaven. A Sufi manual, the *Kashf-al-Mahjub*, says that, towards the end of his journey, the dervish becomes the Way not the wayfarer, i.e. a place over which something is passing, not a traveller following his own free will.

Arkady, to whom I mentioned this, said it was quite similar to an Aboriginal concept, 'Many men afterwards become country, in that place, Ancestors.'

By spending his whole life walking and singing his Ancestor's Songline, a man eventually became the track, the Ancestor and the song ...

He went on to explain how each totemic ancestor, while travelling through the country, was thought to have scattered a trail of words and musical notes along the line of his foot-prints, and how these Dreaming-tracks lay over the land as 'ways' of communication between the most far-flung tribes.

'A song,' he said, 'was both map and direction-finder. Providing you knew the song, you could always find your way across country.'

'And would a man on "Walkabout" always be travelling down one of the Songlines?'

'In the old days, yes,' he agreed. 'Nowadays, they go by train or car.'

'Suppose the man strayed from his Songline?'

'He was trespassing. He might get speared for it.'

'But as long as he stuck to the track, he'd always find people who shared his Dreaming? Who were, in fact, his brothers?'

'Yes.'

'From whom he could expect hospitality?'

'And vice versa.'

'So a song is a kind of passport and meal-ticket?'

'Again, it's more complicated.'

In theory, at least, the whole of Australia could be read as a musical score. There was hardly a rock or creek in the country that could not be or had not been sung. One should perhaps visualize the Songlines as a spaghetti of Iliads and Odysseys, writhing this way and that, in which every episode was readable in terms of geology.

'By episode,' I asked, 'you mean – "sacred site"?'

'I do.'

'The kind of site you're surveying for the railway?'

'Put it this way,' he said. 'Anywhere in the bush you can point to some feature of the landscape and ask the Aboriginal with you, "What's the story there?" or "Who's that?" The chances are he'll answer "Kangaroo" or "Budgerigar" or "Jew Lizard", depending on which Ancestor walked that way.'

'And the distance between two such sites can be measured as a stretch of song?'

'That,' said Arkady, 'is the cause of all my troubles with the railway people.'

It was one thing to persuade a surveyor that a heap of boulders were the eggs of the Rainbow Snake, or a lump of reddish sandstone was the liver of a speared kangaroo. It was something else to convince him that a featureless stretch of gravel was the musical equivalent of Beethoven's Opus 111.

By singing the world into existence, he said, the Ancestors had been poets in the original sense of *poesis*, meaning 'creation'. No Aboriginal could conceive that the world was in any way perfect. His religious life had a single aim: to keep the land the way it was and should be. The man who went 'Walkabout' was making a ritual journey. He trod in the footprints of his Ancestor. He sang the Ancestor's stanza without changing a word or note – and so recreated the Creation.

Bruce Chatwin, *The Songlines*, 1987

A ROUTE TO GOD

I got up every morning before sunrise and climbed through a nearby orchard on to a road above the vineyard – which ran along the hill as far as Chambéry. As I walked up there I said my prayers, which did not consist merely of a vain motion of the lips, but of a sincere raising of the heart towards the Creator of that beauteous Nature whose charms lay beneath my eyes. I have never liked to pray in a room; walls and all the little works of man come between myself and God. I love to contemplate Him in His works, while my heart uplifts to him. I venture to say that my prayers were pure, and for that reason deserved to be heard.

Jean-Jacques Rousseau, *Confessions*, 1781 (trans. J. M. Cohen, 1953)

PETER'S FUNNY WAY OF MOURNING HIS DAD

Soon after my father's death, I found I needed to walk away from home. The disappointment I felt when this new compulsion was frustrated by rain or snow or fog was the keenest I had yet experienced. I cursed the weather for denying me the pleasure I most craved – that of escape.

My serious wandering began one Sunday when I told my mother that I was going for a walk. 'Don't leave the neighbourhood,' she cautioned. 'The dark's still coming down early.' I hadn't thought of leaving the neighbourhood before, but now the prospect of walking beyond Battersea, beyond the familiar, was irresistible. The whole of London awaited me. Even as I planned my first journey of exploration, I promised my mother that I would not go far.

I went as far that February afternoon as my legs would take me, to Hyde Park Corner. It was evening, almost bedtime, when I returned.

'Where on earth have you been?' asked my mother. 'I've been worried sick.'

'Walking.'

'Walking where?'

'Around and about.'

Where I walked on those early fatherless Sundays was my secret, not to be revealed. As the year progressed, and the weather brightened, and the dark came down later and later, I ventured farther – into the deserted City, bereft of its dealers, bankers and clerks; its huge monuments to wealth eerily silent, its ancient churches bolted and barred. In Threadneedle Street, the tall blackened buildings seemed to close in on me, and I knew an absurd fear. How and why I decided that the banks were my enemies and had plans to crush me I cannot remember, but the sight of them induced in me a feeling close to terror. I shrank back from their menacing presence. In St Paul's Cathedral, minutes later, I regained the calmness and common sense that had left me so suddenly and inexplicably. I rested there before the long journey homewards.

'You're wearing out good leather and costing me a fortune,' said my mother as she polished my boots, while I soaked my aching feet in a bowl of hot water. 'I don't suppose you're going to tell me where you've been today.'

'Around and about.'

'I supposed aright. It's the same tune every Sunday. I think I'll have you followed, and then I'll know where's around and where's about. That will put an end to the mystery.'

But the mystery was not to be put to an end, thanks to my stealth and cunning. Whenever I set off on one of my mysterious walks, I always assumed that I was being followed by an amateur detective my mother had hired with the promise of an apple pie or a rice pudding. It was not difficult to lose this shadow (if he or she existed), for my knowledge of London's streets was already thorough. I knew exactly when and how to give the pursuer the slip, by darting down an alley or rushing through a crowded museum, oblivious to its exhibits. My loneliness once secure, I walked on until I came to an unexplored part of the sprawling city, which I could now lay claim to, secretly.

I wandered north, south, west and east. My journeys had no plan, no design, and I had no map to guide me. I relied on instinct alone.

'If a stranger wants a word with you, don't stop and chat,' my mother advised. 'I know I've brought you up to be polite, but not with people who talk to children in the open air.'

During that year or so of compulsive walking, I was never approached by strangers, perhaps because I wore the mad look of a determined solitary. My features did not charm or beguile. It was only when my obsession was over, when I walked again at a steady, natural pace, that adults talked to me.

'It's a Sunday,' said my mother.

I didn't look up from the book I was reading. 'I know it is,' I muttered into the page.

'The weather's nice, too,' she went on.

'I know it is.'

'You usually go out for a walk of a Sunday. Around and about.'

'Not today. I want to finish this story.'

There was a silence, and then she said, strangely, 'That's a relief,' and left me in peace.

I did not ask myself why I needed to walk. I doubt if I had an answer, anyway. That was in my body, in its need, buried somewhere beneath intelligence.

My sister supplied the answer recently. She was talking of our father's death, and its consequences. 'Everyone cried except you. But Mother understood. "Wandering off is Peter's funny way of mourning his Dad," she said. She was right, wasn't she?'

'Yes,' I replied. 'I think she was.'

Paul Bailey, *An Immaculate Mistake*, 1990

IT IS A SOLITARY JOY

Oh, I do love to force a way
Through woods where lone the woodman goes,
Through all the matted shades to stray,
The brambles tearing at my clothes;
And it may tear, I love the noise
And hug the solitary joys.

John Clare, 'Walks in the Woods', 1821

JUST LEAVE ME IN PEACE!

Within two minutes it was all over. From one instant to the next, the hail had stopped and the wind abated. Now there was only a fine drizzle coming down. The cornfield by the side of the road where the gusts had come down earlier was completely flattened. There was nothing left of the maizefield behind it but a few stalks. The road looked as though it had been strewn with broken glass – as far as the eye could see, smashed hailstones, leaves, snapped twigs and ears of corn. Right at the end of the road I could see, dimmed by the drizzle, the form of a man walking away from us. I pointed him out to my father, and together we looked at the small, distant form, and it seemed like a miracle to us that somebody should be out of doors, walking, yes, even the fact that someone was still upright when all around had been flattened and demolished. We drove off, crunching over the hailstones.

As we approached the figure, I recognised the shorts, the long, knobbly-kneed, glistening legs, the black cape pushed out at the back by the outline of a rucksack, and Mr Sommer's furious walk.

We caught up with him, my father told me to wind down the window – the air outside was ice-cold. 'Mr Sommer!' he called out. 'Climb in! We'll give you a lift!' and I scrambled into the back to make room for him on the passenger seat. Mr Sommer made no reply. He didn't even stop. He barely gave us a glance. With hasty strides, propelled by the hazel staff, he went on walking down the hailstrewn road. My father drove after him. 'Mr Sommer!' he called through the open window. 'Please get in! In this weather! We'll run you home!'

But Mr Sommer didn't respond. Undaunted, he walked on. It seemed to me I saw his lips moving, making one of his inaudible replies. But I heard nothing, so perhaps it was just that his lips were trembling with the cold. Then my father leaned right across the front seat and – all the time he was driving along beside Mr Sommer – held open the passenger door and shouted, 'Now, for God's sake, get in! You're soaked to the skin! You'll catch your death of cold!'

Now, the expression 'You'll catch your death of cold!' was actually very uncharacteristic of my father. I had never heard him seriously say to anyone, 'You'll catch your death of cold!' 'That expression is a cliché,' he would say, if he happened to hear or read it somewhere, 'and a cliché – I'm telling you once and for all – is an expression that has been used so often aloud and in print, by every Tom, Dick and Harry, that it's become completely devoid of meaning. It's just as' – he continued, by now firmly on one of his hobbyhorses – 'it's just as bland and idiotic as the sentence "Have a nice cup of tea, my dear, and that'll set you to rights!" or, "How's our patient doing then, doctor? Do you think he'll pull through?" Sentences like that don't come from life, but from bad novels and silly films, and that's why – I'm telling you once and for all – I never want to hear that sort of thing pass your lips!'

That was what my father thought of sentences like 'You'll catch your death of cold!' But now, driving on the hailstrewn country road, in a thin drizzle, alongside Mr Sommer, there was my father shouting one of these very clichés through the open passenger door: 'You'll catch your death of cold!' And then Mr Sommer stopped. I think he stopped just when he heard the words 'death of cold', he froze, so suddenly that my father hurriedly had to put the brakes on so as not to drive past him. And then, Mr Sommer transferred his hazel stick from his right hand to his left, turned towards us, and, ramming the stick repeatedly into the ground with an air of stubbornness and exasperation, he blurted out, loud and clear, the following sentence: 'Why don't you just leave me in peace!' That was all. Just that one sentence. Then he slammed the passenger door shut, transferred his stick back into his right hand, and marched off, without a single look back.

'The fellow's completely mad,' said my father.

When we passed him, I could look into his face through the rear window. He was keeping his eyes to the ground, but lifting them with every few steps in order to check his bearings – wide-open, terrified eyes. The water flowed down his cheeks and dripped from his nose and chin. His mouth was slightly open. Once again, it seemed to me his lips were moving. Perhaps he was talking to himself as he walked.

Patrick Suskind, *The Story of Mr Sommer*, 1991
(trans. Michael Hoffman, 1992)

WARDING OFF MADNESS

I am told that when confronted by a lunatic or one who under the influence of some great grief or shock contemplates suicide, you should take the man out-of-doors and walk him about: Nature will do the rest.

Apsley Cherry-Garrard, *The Worst Journey in the World*, 1922

WALK AND TELL TALES

Come up the grove, where softly blow
The winds o'er the dust, and not with snow,
A-sighing through the leafless thorn,
But not o'er flow'rs or eary corn,
Though still the walk is in the lew
Beside the gapless hedge of yew,
And wind-proof ivy, hanging thick
On oaks beside the tawny rick;
And let us talk an hour away
While softly sinks the dying day.

Now few at evening are the sounds
Of life, on roads or moon-paled grounds;
So low be here our friendly words
While still'd around are men and birds,
Nor startle we the night that dims
The world to men of weary limbs;
But let us tell in voices low
Our little tales, lest wind may blow
Their flying sounds too far away,
To ears yet out as ends the day.

William Barnes, 'Walk and Talk', 1836

SOCIABILITY

Both the process of walking and its environment tend to sociability. The process is a good activity, shared by two or more concrete beings who are doing their best and are at their best; it lays a foundation of mutual respect more quickly and more surely than any specialised activity of the half or quarter man. The environment of a walk is exactly right; it is familiar enough to create a sense of ease, and yet strange enough to throw the walkers back on themselves with the instinct of human solidarity – that instinct which unites a rowing crew on a long journey and makes English visitors civil to each other in Swiss pensions. The scenery changes fast enough to be interesting, and not too fast to give a feeling of continuity and permanency. Finally, sun and wind and rain and lunch, and the consultation of maps and divination of the way, all combine to surround the walkers with an atmosphere of sociability.

A. H. Sidgwick, *Walking Essays*, 1912

TO WALK AND WOO

Now in 1868, his regiment, the 102nd Hussars, was posted to the garrison at Rouen.

He was soon well known in the town. Every evening above five, he appeared on the Cours Boïeldieu on his way to drink a glass of absinth at the Café de la Comédie, though before entering this establishment he made a point of taking a turn along the promenade to show off his legs, his waist, and his moustache.

The town's men of business, who also walked there with their hands behind their backs and their minds full of their business, talking of markets rising and falling, nevertheless gave a glance in his direction and murmured: 'By Jove! Now there's a fine figure of a man!' And when they knew who he was: 'Look, it's Captain Epivent. Say what you like, he's a hell of a fellow!'

When women passed him, they gave a slight movement of the head which was very droll, a sort of maidenly quiver, as though they had come over all weak or felt undressed before him. They lowered their eyes with just the shadow of a smile on their lips, wishing to be thought charming and to receive a glance from him. When he walked with a comrade, the comrade never failed to mutter enviously every time he witnessed the usual goings on: 'Old Epivent's got the luck of the devil!'

Among the town's whores there was a struggle, a race, to see who would get him first. They all turned up at the Cours Boïeldieu at five, the officers' regular time, and in twos they trailed their skirts from one end of the promenade to the other while lieutenants, captains, and commanders, also in twos, trailed their sabres over the pavement before entering the café.

One evening, the beautiful Irma – who was rumoured to be the mistress of Monsieur Templier-Papon, a rich manufacturer – ordered her driver to halt opposite the Café de la Comédie. As she stepped down, she gave every impression that she was about to buy some writing-paper or order some visiting cards from Monsieur Paulard, the engraver, though the whole thing was of course engineered to allow her to pass in front of the officers' table and to give Captain Epivent a look signifying: 'Ready when you are!' which was so transparent that Colonel Prune, who was drinking a glass of green absinth with his Lieutenant-Colonel, was unable to prevent himself muttering: 'That swine's got the luck of the devil!'

What the colonel said was repeated; and the next day Captain Epivent, in full dress uniform, delighted at having such high-level approval, strolled by (and did so again several times) under the windows of the beautiful Irma.

She saw him. She appeared at her window. She smiled. The same evening he became her lover.

Guy de Maupassant, 'Bed 29', 1884 (trans. David Coward, 1990)

A FAMILY OCCASION

The next day being Sunday, with no need to be up and stirring before high mass, if it was a moonlight night and warm, then, instead of taking us home at once, my father, in his thirst for personal distinction, would lead us on a long walk round by the Calvary, which my mother's utter incapacity for taking her bearings, or even for knowing which road she might be on, made her regard as a triumph of his strategic genius. Sometimes we would go as far as the viaduct, which began to stride on its long legs of stone at the railway station, and to me typified all the wretchedness of exile beyond the last outposts of civilisation, because every year, as we came down from Paris, we would be warned to take special care, when we got to Combray, not to miss the station, to be ready before the train stopped, since it would start again in two minutes and proceed across the viaduct, out of the lands of Christendom, of which Combray, to me, represented the farthest limit. We would return by the Boulevard de la Gare, which contained the most attractive villas in the town. In each of their gardens the moonlight, copying the art of Hubert Robert, had scattered its broken staircases of white marble, its fountains of water and gates temptingly ajar. Its beams had swept away the telegraph office. All that was left of it was a column, half shattered, but preserving the beauty of a ruin which endures for all time. I would by now be dragging my weary limbs, and ready to drop with sleep; the balmy scent of the lime-trees seemed a consolation which I could obtain only at the price of great suffering and exhaustion, and not worthy of the effort. From gates far apart the watchdogs, awakened by our steps in the silence, would set up an antiphonal barking, as I still hear them bark, at times, in the evenings, and it is in their custody (when the public gardens of Combray were constructed on its site) that the Boulevard de la Gare must have taken refuge, for wherever I may be, as soon as they begin their alternate challenge and acceptance, I can see it again with all its lime-trees, and its pavement glistening beneath the moon.

Suddenly my father would bring us to a standstill and ask my mother – 'Where are we?' Utterly worn out by the walk but still proud of her husband, she would lovingly confess that she had not the least idea. He would shrug his shoulders and laugh. And then, as though it had slipped, with his latchkey, from his waistcoat pocket, he would point out to us, where it stood before our eyes, the back-gate of our own garden, which had come, hand-in-hand with the familiar corner of the Rue du Saint-Esprit, to await us, to greet us at the end of our wanderings over paths unknown. My mother would murmur admiringly, 'You really are wonderful!' And from that instant I had not to take another step; the ground moved forward under my feet in that garden where, for so long, my actions had ceased to require any control, or even attention, from my will. Custom came to take me in her arms, carried me all the way up to my bed, and laid me down there like a little child.

Marcel Proust, *Swann's Way*, 1913
(trans. C. K. Scott Moncrieff, 1922)

CAPTAIN BARCLAY MAKES A SPORT OF IT

The climax of Barclay's career came with his famous and successful attempt to walk 1,000 miles in 1,000 successive hours. Many pedestrians had tried this previously, but all had had to give up suffering from loss of weight, swollen legs, and other ills arising not merely from the exertion but from lack of continuous sleep, long before they completed the course. The best of them did not last longer than thirty days. When Barclay announced his intention of taking up the challenge, there was great excitement among the sporting fraternity, and huge sums of money, amounting in all, it is said, to £100,000, were wagered on the result. Apart from paying a visit to Brighton, Barclay did not go into any special training this time, but he and his backers were certainly taking it very seriously. The match began, again at Newmarket, at midnight on 1st June 1809, and lasted for forty-two days. Arrangements were made for observers to be on duty the whole time keeping a record hour by hour of the captain's time and speed, together with notes as to his physical condition, and such meteorological observations as 'Cool and pleasant,' 'Hot, windy, and dusty,' 'Dark, with rain,' or 'Clear moonlight.' This log-book must afterwards have been of the greatest interest to connoisseurs, and was printed in full by Thom. Barclay himself worked to a regular routine each day. At five o'clock in the morning he breakfasted on a roasted fowl, a pint of strong ale, and two cups of tea with bread and butter. Thus fortified, he was able to keep going for seven hours till lunch at twelve, when, we are told, he consumed beef steaks and mutton chops on alternate days in considerable quantities. Dinner came at six, with more beef and mutton, some porter, and two or three glasses of wine; and supper of cold fowl (was it perhaps left over from breakfast?) at eleven. This richly protein diet was supported from day to day by such vegetables as were available. It seems to have suited Barclay. Throughout the contest his appetite remained good, and though he suffered from time to time from 'spasmodic affections' of the legs and eventually lost more than two stone in weight, and though progress became much slower towards the end (according to the log his average time for one mile during the last week was 21 minutes 4 seconds, whereas during the first week it had been 14 minutes 54 seconds), he was never in any danger of collapsing. His effortless style no doubt had something to do with this: he was said to have a plunging gait, and took very short steps, with the weight thrown forward on the knees, scarcely raising his feet from the ground, so that there was no energy wasted. As time went on the odds began to rise in his favour: there were no takers at 100 to 1 before the match was ended. People had crowded into the district, many of them very distinguished people. Every horse and vehicle was taken, and there was not a bed to be had. As Barclay completed the course, at 3 p.m. on 12th July, to the sound of church bells, he was greeted by one of the biggest crowds which have ever welcomed a triumphant pedestrian.

Such was his toughness, however, that in spite of his exhaustion it only required a hot bath, a bowl of gruel, and a few hours' sleep to bring him back to normal again; and five days later he rejoined his regiment at Ramsgate *en route* for Walcheren as aide-de-camp to Lieutenant-General the Marquis of Huntley.

It does not seem to be on record whether this achievement of 1,000 miles in 1,000 hours marked the end, as it was the climax, of Barclay's pedestrian career. But for the rest of his long life – he died in 1854 at the age of about seventy-five as a result of a kick from a horse – the name of Barclay carried a magic power in pedestrian and sporting circles, and his advice was much sought after.

Maurice Marples, *Shanks' Pony*, 1959

DON'T FORGET FITNESS

Walking is generally recommended. A woman with three cars in her garage will walk for miles, purely for fitness, wearing high-tech sneakers which require great erudition in the choosing, and many in conspicuous dollars to buy. She might even purchase a calibrated treadmill so that she can perform the same feat in her own home, protected from the pollution of the street.

Margaret Visser, *The Way We Are*, 1994

AND THOSE FOUR POUNDS . . .

We who walk for pleasure alone must never allow ourselves to think teleologically; our pleasure is in the walking, and in that alone, and we have no need to seek outside the walking for any justification of it. The rhythm of our stride (I take some 30,000 paces on the bridges walk); the gradual tempering of the lungs and muscles to the effort; the thoughts that fill our minds; the peace that descends on us as the miles go by; the sights and sounds that accompany us and divert us, whether we are in town or country or – as on the Hammersmith Embankment – *rus in urbe*; these are the happinesses of walking, and they are their own justification. As I lie in the bath and count the bridges, conjuring them up one by one, I am filled with the pleasure that they have given me, that any long walk gives me. I think I can allow myself one forbidden taste of smugness, one wisp of identification with those who walk because it does them good rather than because it does them pleasure, and I have succumbed to the lapse before stepping into the bath: the scales tell me that I have lost four pounds.

Bernard Levin, *Enthusiasms*, 1985

WE FANCY OURSELVES HEROIC

To come down to my own experience, my companion and I, for I sometimes have a companion, take pleasure in fancying ourselves as Knights of a new, or rather old, order – not

Equestrians or Chevaliers, not Ritters or riders, but Walkers, a still more ancient and honorable class, I trust. The chivalric and the holy spirit which once belonged to the Rider seems now to reside in, or perchance, to have subsided into, the Walker – not the Knight, but Walker Errant. He is a sort of fourth estate, outside of Church and State and People. We have felt that we almost hereabouts practiced alone this noble art; though to tell the truth, at least if their own assertions are to be received, most of my townsmen would fain walk sometimes, as I do, but they cannot. No wealth can buy capital in this profession. It comes only by the grace of God. It requires a direct dispensation from Heaven to become a walker. You must be born into the family of walkers.

Henry David Thoreau, 'Walking', *Excursions*, 1843

TWO

How to Walk

Very few men know how to take a walk.

Samuel Johnson

THE GAIT

(i)

Apes have flat feet, we have sprung arches. According to Professor Napier, the human gait is a long, lilting stride – 1 … 2 …1 … 2 – with a fourfold rhythm built into the action of our feet as they come into contact with the ground – 1, 2, 3, 4 … 1, 2, 3, 4 … heel strike; weight along the outside of the foot; weight transferred to the ball of the foot; push-off with big toe.

Bruce Chatwin, *The Songlines*, 1987

(ii)

Keep a regular stride, rising on the balls of the toes and not turning the toes out too much: Rodin's Statue of St. John, in the Luxemburg, shows the correct way to have the feet. How few people walk well. The secret is to let the shoulder *opposite* to the advancing foot swing well forward at each step.

Frank Tatchell, *The Happy Traveller*, 1925

(iii)

He had the strong and sinewy look of the determined and patient walker, who is always going off, his long legs moving quietly and very regularly, his head straight, his beautiful eyes fixed on the distance, and his face filled with a look of steady defiance, an air of expectation – ready for everything, without anger, without fear.

Ernest Delahaye on Arthur Rimbaud, 1925

DON'T LEAP AND RUN

I do not approve of that leaping and running. Both of these hurry the respiration; they both shake up the brain out of its glorious open-air confusion; and they both break the pace.

Uneven walking is not so agreeable to the body, and it distracts and irritates the mind. Whereas, when once you have fallen into an equable stride, it requires no conscious thought from you to keep it up, and yet it prevents you from thinking earnestly of anything else.

Robert Louis Stevenson, 'Walking Tours', 1881

THE WALKER'S TEMPO – ONE, TWO, ONE, TWO?

What it is may be disputed. At one time or another I have heard nearly every kind of tune sounding to the steps of a walker. Wagner and Purcell, Sullivan and Anon, symphony and opera, tone-poem and folk-song – nothing (with one exception) seems to come amiss to a walking company. And from this very large and variegated body of music one most remarkable fact emerges – namely, that nearly every kind of rhythm can, at some time or other, be accommodated to the walking stride. Regarding man as a biped, naturally inclined to 'lead' with one foot rather than the other (generally the left), you would say that even rhythms with two or four beats to the bar would suit him best; and perhaps (in the lowest sense of 'nature' as the starting point and not the finishing post) the natural rhythm of walking is the 'one, two, one, two.' But man is more than a biped; and if he likes a tune with three or five beats to the bar (or seven or eleven for that matter), he is quite capable of stepping accordingly, and of either 'leading' with each foot alternately, or of overlooking altogether the difference between the natural stresses of his feet. Further, as regards the three-time rhythms, many of them go quick, so that only one foot-beat is needed in each bar; and there is the incomparable six-eight, of which more will be said in the sequel.

At this point the scandalised mathematician inquiries, What becomes of the tempo? Is not the effect of walking on music purely Procrustean? A walker (let us say) takes two strides to a second; in order to suit his steps, a tune in even time must go at a particular rate, selected from the following schedule, to wit, (a) two bars to a second, with one foot-beat in each bar; (b) one bar to a second, with two beats in each bar; (c) one bar to two seconds, with four beats to each bar; for practical purposes we need not go beyond this point. For the three-times, there is an even more sharply divided scale, viz. (a) two bars to a second, one beat to each bar; (b) one bar to a second and a half, three beats to each bar; (c) one bar to three seconds, six beats to each bar. What, asks the mathematician, happens to the tunes whose proper pace falls, let us say, between (a) and (b): must they either be drawn out languorously to fit (b), or feverishly accelerated to fit (a)?

The answer to the mathematician's question is that in practice no difficulty arises. In the first place, a walker's rate of stride varies to some extent according as he is going uphill or downhill, on grass, rock, or road. Secondly, a little licence may surely be claimed by a walker in varying the orthodox tempo. After all, even conductors do this sometimes; and if one tune has to go a little quicker than an orchestra takes it, another will have to go a little slower, which is (I understand) only a slight extension of what the musicians call 'rubato.' Thirdly, and as a minor point, we may set against any possible disadvantages the peculiarly fine effects which the walker obtains in augmentation, when he whistles a tune with one step to a bar and repeats it with two steps to a bar. Finally, it is only in the three-times, between (a) and (b), that the matter becomes at all serious, (b) being one-third of the rate of (a). Now, it is a curious fact, that all the good three-time tunes (to speak broadly) fall quite easily under either (a) or (b). Cheerful songs and jigs and scherzos and most six-eight tunes go naturally with one step to each group of three notes, the swing of the body marking the weak stresses; more solemn themes, funereal folk-songs, the Unfinished Symphony, the last movement of the 'Pathétique,' and the Tristan prelude go naturally with three steps to a group of three notes; the Pilgrims' March takes six, with complicated cross-accents when the 'pulse of life' begins. The intermediate class of three-times, between (*a*) and (*b*), taking about one second or two strides to a bar, and therefore cutting across the walking rhythm, are generally waltz tunes, which no one in his senses wants to sing on a walk.

A. H. Sidgwick, *Walking Essays*, 1912

STAY ALERT

So, step for step, like oxen in the yoke,
Beside that burdened soul I held my way
So long as my kind schoolmaster would brook;

But when he said: 'Now leave him; come I say,
Press on; for here must each with sail and oar
Urge the ship forward strongly as he may,'

I raised me, as good walkers should, and bore
My body upright, though the thoughts in me
Remained bowed down and shrunken as before.

I'd put on speed and was most willingly
Following my master's footsteps, he and I
Showing how fleet of foot we both could be,

When he addressed me: 'Downward cast thine eye;
For solace of the way, 'twere good thou fall
To scanning what beneath thy feet may lie.'

Dante Alighieri, *The Divine Comedy: Purgatory*, 1310–20
(trans. Dorothy L. Sayers, 1949–62)

MR HACKMAN?

I encountered Mr. Hackman, an Englishman, who has been walking the length and breadth of Europe for several years. I enquired of him what were his chief observations. He replied gruffly, 'I never look up', and went on his way.

N. Brooke, MD, 1796

REGARDING MY LEGS

Take these knees of mine: manifest,
functional, private, like knots,
dividing the halves of my legs, in their crisp conformation:
two kingdoms distinct in themselves, two differing sexes,
are no less unlike than the halves of my legs.

Down from the knee to the foot – a tangible integer,
mineral, coolly available, appears
in a creaturely image of bones and persistence:
the ankles like pure resolution,
precise and essential, pursuing its will to the close.

And those legs, there, my masculine legs,
unsensual, bluff, and resilient; endowed
with their clustering muscles, complementary animals –
they, too, are a life, a substantial and delicate world,
alert and unfaltering, living watchful and strenuous there.

Pablo Neruda, 'The Ritual of My Legs', 1931
(trans. Ben Belitt)

LOVE YOUR FEET

(i)

You dread, perhaps, blisters on your feet – sponge your feet with cold vinegar, change your socks every ten miles and show me blisters after that if you can.

Wilkie Collins, *Rambles and Railways*, 1850

(ii)

Give your feet tender loving care both before you begin and along the Way. The soles, the heels, and front pads don't need to be hard. Paradoxically as it may seem, hard feet on a long tramp are a hazard – the skin tends to crack and bleed. What one needs is an underpinning of skin that is soft and supple, that can bend with the rocks and absorb their impact. The best way to achieve it is with lavish application of a good lanolin cream ... The pilgrim should have a careful pedicure before setting out; we are back on the subject of feet again but it is vital. The condition of one's toe nails, mundane as it may seem, is a key to contentment on the journey. Treat them like Bahranian pearls. Polish them, oil them, balance them, get them right, and the pilgrim is saved endless misery.

Nicholas Luard, *The Field of the Star*, 1998

AN EXPERT ON FOOTSTEPS

The footsteps outside at any given moment were such as one might hear in any hotel; and yet, taken as a whole, there was something very strange about them. There were no other footsteps. It was always a very silent house, for the few familiar guests went at once to their own apartments, and the well-trained waiters were told to be almost invisible until they were wanted. One could not conceive any place where there was less reason to apprehend anything irregular. But these footsteps were so odd that one could not decide to call them regular or irregular. Father Brown followed them with his finger on the edge of the table, like a man trying to learn a tune on the piano.

First, there came a long rush of rapid little steps, such as a light man might make in winning a walking race. At a certain point they stopped and changed to a sort of slow-swinging stamp, numbering not a quarter of the steps, but occupying about the same time. The moment the last echoing stamp had died away would come again the run or ripple of light, hurrying feet, and then again the thud of the heavier walking. It was certainly the same pair of boots, partly because (as has been said) there were no other boots about, and partly because they had a small but unmistakable creak in them. Father Brown had the kind of head that cannot help asking questions; and on this apparently trivial question his head almost split. He had seen men run in order to jump. He had seen men run in order to slide. But why on earth should a man run in order to walk? Or, again, why should he walk in order to run? Yet no other description would cover the antics of this invisible pair of legs. The man was either walking very fast down one half of the corridor in order to walk very slow down the other half; or he was walking very slow at one end to have the rapture of walking fast at the other. Neither suggestion seemed to make much sense. His brain was growing darker and darker, like his room.

Yet, as he began to think steadily, the very blackness of his cell seemed to make his thoughts more vivid; he began to see as in a kind of vision the fantastic feet capering along the corridor in unnatural or symbolic attitudes. Was it a heathen religious dance? Or some entirely new kind of scientific exercise? Father Brown began to ask himself with more exactness what the steps suggested. Taking the slow step first; it certainly was not the step of the proprietor. Men of his type walk with a rapid waddle, or they sit still. It could not be any servant or messenger waiting for directions. It did not sound like it. The poorer orders (in an oligarchy) sometimes lurch about when they are slightly drunk, but generally, and especially in such gorgeous scenes, they stand or sit in constrained attitudes. No; that heavy yet springy step, with a kind of careless emphasis, not specially noisy, yet not caring what noise it made, belong to only one of the animals of this earth. It was a gentleman of western Europe, and probably one who had never worked for his living.

G. K. Chesterton, *The Queer Feet*, 1910

TAKE EVERYTHING WITH YOU

For the information of future travellers on foot, it is my pleasure here to give details of my complete equipment.

A powder bag made out of a woman's glove.
A razor.
Thread.
Needles.
Scissors.
A comb, carried in one pair of dress shoes.
A pair of silk stockings.
Breeches, fine enough, when folded, not bigger than a fist.
Two very fine shirts.
Three cravats.
Three handkerchiefs.
The clothes in which I travelled.

The sundries I divided into three, two lots going into the silk stockings which served as bags, the third packet containing my shoes. I had six pockets: in three of them were stowed the packets, as described, when I was about to enter a house of convenience; but as this packing would be very inconvenient while walking, I was accustomed, on the road, to tie my three packets in a handkerchief and carry the loads over my shoulder at the end of my sword stick, on which I had grafted an umbrella which excited, everywhere, curiosity, and made the girls laugh – I can't tell why. The remaining pockets were reserved for letters, my pocket book, and ordinary uses.

Chevalier de la Tocnaye, *A Frenchman's Walk Through Ireland 1796–7* (trans. John Stevenson, 1917)

ONE SOCK OR TWO?

My one sartorial extravagance was a second pair of socks. In London, an expert traveller had pointed out that weight could be saved by carrying only *one* spare sock. Thus equipped with a total of three socks, the professional circulates them on the principle of crop rotation. Each morning, yesterday's right sock is moved to the left foot; yesterday's left sock is taken out of circulation for washing and mending; and yesterday's fallow sock, now clean and dry, is put on to the right foot. It is an ingenious system, but I anticipated two disadvantages: first, the diurnal rotation could become very muddling, and second, the system had the more serious drawback that the left foot would always be encased in a two-day-old sock. Reversing the direction of rotation would not be an option, since it would merely subject the right foot to the same low standard of comfort and hygiene. On balance, I decided that the extra calories I could burn by having to carry two spare ankle socks rather than one would be more than compensated for by the pleasure derived from starting each day with both feet cushioned in laundered cotton.

Nicholas Crane, *Clear Waters Rising*, 1996

THE BOOT AND SHOE DEBATE

There is little doubt that boots are better for rough ground and bog, and shoes for roads and level tracks; nails are necessary for rocks and steep grass-slopes, but are a burden on the hard highway. Again, shoes probably leave the feet freer, while boots add mechanically an extra inch or two to the stride. The question may be pursued through all its ramifications; and no doubt those who like quantitative thinking could ultimately produce some sort of determination of the foot-gear most likely to be suitable to the average man in the average country. Where comfort and utility only are concerned, the vulgar processes of comparing, adding and subtracting are quite sufficient to lead to a conclusion.

But quantitative reasoning, though invaluable in politics, is very poor fun. Life would have little flavour without occasional qualitative excursions into the *a priori*. The very bitterness of feeling aroused by discussions on walking equipment shows, I think, that something more is involved in them than the calculable considerations of comfort and utility. After all, it is mainly a man's own affair whether his feet are comfortable and whether he slips on a grass slope: and were these the only issues, we should have no more concern with his boots than with his breakfast or banking-account. And the same holds true for most of the doubtful points of walking equipment.

A. H. Sidgwick, *Walking Essays*, 1912

MORE ABOUT BOOTS

Boots and the Man I sing! For you cannot tramp without boots. The commonest distress of hoboes is thinness of sole.

Two friends set out last Spring from Bavaria to Venice, luggage in advance, knapsack on shoulder. But they had not the right sort of boots, and they lingered in the mountain inns quaffing steins of brown beer to take their thoughts away from their toes. They are in those mountains yet.

You should have leather lined boots with most substantial soles.

Stephen Graham, *The Gentle Art of Tramping*, 1926

MORE ABOUT SHOES

ASTON. Try these.

DAVIES *takes the shoes, takes off his sandals and tries them on.*

DAVIES. Not a bad pair of shoes. (*He trudges round the room.*) They're strong, all right. Yes. Not a bad shape of shoe. This leather's hardy, en't? Very hardy. Some bloke tried to flog me some suede the other day. I wouldn't wear them. Can't beat leather, for wear. Suede goes off, it creases, it stains for life in five minutes. You can't beat leather. Yes. Good shoe this.

ASTON. Good.

DAVIES *waggles his feet.*

DAVIES. Don't fit though.

ASTON. Oh?

DAVIES. No. I got a very broad foot.

ASTON. Mmnn.

DAVIES. These are too pointed, you see.

ASTON. Ah.

DAVIES. They'd cripple me in a week. I mean these ones I got on, they're no good but at least they're comfortable. Not much cop, but I mean they don't hurt. (*He takes them off and gives them back.*) Thanks anyway, mister.

ASTON. I'll see what I can look out for you.

DAVIES. Good luck. I can't go on like this. Can't get from one place to another. And I'll have to be moving about, you see, try to get fixed up.

ASTON. Where you going to go?

DAVIES. Oh, I got one or two things in mind. I'm waiting for the weather to break.

Harold Pinter, The Caretaker, Act I, 1960

BARE THE SOLE

Footwear is tricky. I treat my feet like premature twins. The moment I feel even a slight twinge of discomfort I stop and put it right. Most people advocate stout boots and thick socks. I know of nothing more uncomfortable. They give you a leaden, non-springy stride. You can't trot along in boots. I bought two pairs, broke them in and eventually threw them aside. On a trip across the desert some years ago, I wore tennis shoes, but these, I found, are useless in Britain, for they become sodden. After trying various kinds of shoes, I settled for an expensive Italian pair with light commando-type soles. They weighed about fifteen ounces each and, when oiled, fitted me like gloves. I had no trouble with shoes. Certainly not from blisters, although in the last stages of the journey some of my toe-nails dropped off. In places I went barefoot through bogs, and on warm days in deserted country I sometimes wore only a pair of shorts.

John Hillaby, Journey Through Britain, 1968

WHEN IT RAINS

It is a good plan to carry an umbrella and a light cycling cape; if you are caught when out in the country and away from shelter, crouch down in the road until the shower is over, and if the rain falls in 'buckets', half lower your umbrella, so that the rain shoots off instead of coming through. After the shower, stand your umbrella in the road and stroll about with your cape still on; both will be dried by the sun before you have had time to smoke a cigarette.

Frank Tatchell, *The Happy Traveller*, 1923

MAPS

When the inspiration for walking and tramping has come we realise what a boon maps are, we come to love them, as inseparable companions. You put local maps of countries and towns and countrysides in your pockets, and large folded maps of the Continent in your knapsacks. You unfold them in the desert; you lie on them, you crawl about with a magnifying glass examining their small print and the lost names of villages in smudged mountain-ranges. You learn by the scale what the length of your thumb or little finger means in kilometres and miles. You survey with a curious joy the dotted line of your peregrinations up to that point.

Have you seen enough of the world? Are you sure you will rest content at Kensal Rise or Père Lachaise when the time comes? Take a map to the world and a blue pencil, go back in memory over the whole of your life, start the pencil at your birthplace and begin to draw the line of your goings to and fro in this world. How you will rejoice in yourself if you can conduct that blue pencil chart across a great ocean, across Atlantic or Pacific! The longer and more bulging and more loopy the line the more you will feel you have lived. In the later years of your life you will be able to say: 'I was born into the world and I have seen something of it.'

Of course maps have another function besides that of firing the imagination. They are for helping you to find your way. When tramping across forest and mountain it is as well to carry with you sections of the Government survey, by the aid of which you can often locate yourself when otherwise hopelessly lost. You know also where you must make for for provisions, and whether you are approaching a marshy region which cannot be traversed on foot, where the fordings and ferries and bridges of a river and stream are to be found, where a forest ends, where open country is resumed.

This sort of map ought to be stoutly mounted as it comes in for much use and is entirely in a different category from the large composite maps suitable for home or for folding within the large inner pocket of the knapsack. You thumb them so much because almost inevitably you come upon error, even in the best survey. It is highly difficult to digest square miles and square inches. Every map has an element of artistic impressionism, and has to be studied somewhat intuitively. What you would mark, it omits, because the map-maker was of a different temperament. For that you have to allow, and not lose your patience and tear up your guide.

At home it is well to have a map-cupboard and preserve and put in it every little map which has ever served you on the road or in foreign cities. You may help others with your old maps upon occasion, and you may help yourself when thinking of returning at some time upon an old track.

Stephen Graham, *The Gentle Art of Tramping*, 1926

DOES EQUIPMENT MATTER?

Boots have grown limp; clothes have settled natural skin-like rumples: the stick is warm and smooth to our touch: the map slips easily in and out of our pockets, lucubrated by dog's ears: every article in the knapsack has found its natural place, and the whole has settled onto our shoulders. The equipment is no longer an armour of which we are conscious. At the start this coat was a glorious thing to face the world in: now it is merely an outer skin. At the start this stick was mine: now it is myself.

When it is all over the coat will go back to the cupboard and the curved suspensor and the shirts and stockings will go to the wash, to resume conventional form and texture, and take their place in the humdrum world. But in the darkest hours of urban depression I will sometimes take out the dog's-eared map and dream awhile of more spacious days; and perhaps a dried blade of grass will fall out of it to remind me that once I was a free man on the hills, and sang the Seventh Symphony to the sheep on Wetherlam ...

A. H. Sidgwick, *Walking Essays*, 1912

IF YOU HAD TO CHOOSE ONE STIMULANT ...

The best all round stimulant is tea. I say it advisedly, knowing full well that to Dr Alexander Haig and the anti-uric acid dietists tea is Anathema Maranatha. But every mining prospector, every rail-road constructor, every lumber man, every out in the wilds worker throughout America and Australia drinks tea – proof, surely, that it is efficacious, even if it be in a sense deleterious. In huge quantities, and constantly taken, I dare say deleterious. But personally I know of no other pick-me-up preferable to tea, when cold, hungry, land-tired at the end of a long day's tramp, you find yourself 'done-on' and unable to eat.

I recall an instance of the extraordinary efficacy of tea – quite weak, but hot. It was at the end of a forty-mile walk through a monotonous country in cold, wind, and rain. We arrived tired out; and although we knew we were hungry (for we had had precious little to eat all day), the thought of food was repulsive, though the restaurant we had reached displayed a variety of viands. I ordered hot tea in the biggest teapot procurable. It was brought. We sipped indeed; and after supper one of the party proposed to walk the forty miles back.

Perhaps Dr Haig will say that plain hot water would have done just as well. Humph! Give me weak – but good – TEA.

Arnold Haultain, *The Tramp's Dietary*, 1914

WHICH BOOKS IN THE BAG?

I suppose some may prefer to read a book on the country through which they are tramping, and in that case a librarian's aid may be sought. There are now scores of volumes on almost every country in the world. It is as well to look over several of them before making a choice – many prove to be slap-dash, ill-informed compositions.

Does one take accounts of travel in lands other than that one is tramping in? I imagine not. *Unknown Arabia* is out of place in a tramp through California. But a tramp's account of his own life is interesting reading anywhere, and one naturally thinks of W. H. Davies' autobiography in this connection. There are few tramp writers. But probably the best short story of Maxim Gorky's tells of his tramping life, and is called *The Fellow Traveller*. Jack London's *Valley of the Moon* contains some tramping episodes. Jack London, Rudyard Kipling, Cunninghame Graham, Belloc, Chesterton, Carl Sandburg, Vachel Lindsay, are all delightful writers in the tramping mood and ask a place in the knapsack. Then there are Harry Franck's untiring pedestrian tours in Patagonia, China, and elsewhere, perhaps in too ponderous a form as yet for field use.

I once met a tramping publisher, *rara avis*, a very black swan; he began his life as a colporteur of the British and Foreign Bible Society and spent twenty years on the road, going from Bibles to leaflets, which he printed himself, and thence to booklets, thence to books and an office and a vast organisation. He had a simple way of business. I handed him a manuscript; he opened a drawer and handed out a wad of notes, and the transaction was concluded without a word in writing. But I suppose that was unusual even in his business. There was a savour of tramp meeting tramp in the affair.

The Bible colporteur ought, at least, to know one book the better for his calling. When all is said, there is one book more worth taking than all the rest; poetry, philosophy, history, fantasy, treatise, novel, and drama, you have all in one in the Bible, the inexhaustible book of books. You need not take it all, take the prophecies, the psalms, the Gospels. It means much to tramp with one Gospel in the inner pocket of the coat.

Stephen Graham, *The Gentle Art of Tramping*, 1926

GO IT ALONE

One of the pleasantest things in the world is going on a journey; but I like to go by myself. I can enjoy society in a room; but out of doors, nature is company enough for me. I am never less alone when alone.

'The fields his study, nature was his book.'

I cannot see the wit of walking and talking at the same time. When I am in the country, I wish to vegetate like the country. I am not for criticising hedge-rows and black cattle. I go out of town in order to forget the town and all that is in it. There are those who for this purpose go to watering places, and carry the metropolis with them. I like more elbow room, and fewer incumbrances. I like solitude, when I give myself up to it, for the sake of solitude; nor do I ask for

'*a friend in my retreat*
Whom I may whisper solitude is sweet.'

The soul of a journey is liberty, perfect liberty, to think, feel, do just as one pleases. We do a journey chiefly to be free of all impediments and of all inconveniences; to leave ourselves behind, much more to be rid of others. It is because I want a little breathing space to muse on indifferent matters, where Contemplation

'*May plume her feathers and let grow her wings*
That in the various bustle of resort
Were all too ruffled, and sometimes impair'd,'

that I absent myself from town for a while, without feeling at a loss the moment left by myself. Instead of a friend in a post-chaise or in a Tilbury, to exchange good things with, and vary the same stale topics over again, for once let me have a truce with impertinence. Give me the blue sky over my head, and the green turf beneath my feet, a winding road before me, and a three hours' march to dinner – and then to thinking.

It is hard if I cannot start some game on those lone heaths. I laugh, I run, I leap, I sing for joy. From the point of yonder rolling cloud, I plunge into my past being, and revel there, as the sun-burnt Indian plunges headlong into the wave that wafts him to his nature shore. Then long-forgotten things, like 'sunken wrack and sumless treasures' burst upon my eager sight, and I begin to feel, think, and be myself again. Instead of an awkward silence, broken by attempts at wit or dull common-sense, mine is that undisturbed silence of the heart which alone is perfect eloquence.

No one likes puns, alliterations, antithesis, argument, and analysis better than I do; but I sometimes had rather be without them. 'Leave, oh, leave me to my repose!' I have just now other business in hand, which would seem idle to you, but is with me 'very stuff of the conscience'. Is not this wild rose sweet without a comment? Does not this daisy leap to my heart set in its coat of emerald? Yet if I were to explain to you the circumstance that has so endeared it to me, you would only smile. Had I not better then keep it to myself, and let it serve me to brood over, from here to yonder craggy point and from thence onward to the far-distant horizon? I should be but bad company all that way – and therefore prefer being alone.

William Hazlitt, 'On Going a Journey', 1822

I'M AS HAZLITT

Now, to be properly enjoyed, a walking tour should be gone upon alone. If you go in company, or even in pairs, it is no longer a walking tour in anything but name; it is something else and more in the nature of a picnic. A walking tour should be gone upon alone, because freedom is of the essence; because you should be able to stop and go on, and follow this way or that, as the freak takes you; and because you must have your own pace, and neither trot alongside a champion walker, nor mince time with a girl. And then you must be open to all impressions and let your thoughts take colour from what you see. You should be as a pipe for any wind to play on. 'I cannot see the wit,' says Hazlitt, 'of walking and talking at the same time. When I am in the country I wish to vegetate like the country' – which is the gist of all that can be said upon the matter. There should be no cackle of voices at your elbow, to jar on the meditative silence of the morning. And so long as a man is reasoning he cannot surrender himself to that fine intoxication that comes of much motion in the open air, that begins in a sort of dazzle and sluggishness of the brain, and ends in peace that passes comprehension.

Robert Louis Stevenson, 'Walking Tours', 1876

CHOOSE COMPANY CAREFULLY

I have had the expedition in mind for many years; for, as you know, I have lived in this region from infancy, having been cast here by that fate which determines the affairs of men. Consequently the mountain, which is visible from a great distance, was ever before my eyes, and I have conceived the plan of some time doing what I have at last accomplished today. The idea took hold upon me with especial force when, in re-reading Livy's *History of Rome*, yesterday, I happened upon the place where Philip of Macedon, the same who waged war against the Romans, ascended Mount Haemus in Thessaly, from whose summit he was able to see, it was said, two seas, the Adriatic and the Euxine. Whether this be true or false I have not been able to determine, for the mountain is too far away, and writers disagree. Pomponius Mela, the cosmographer – not to mention others who have spoken of this occurrence – admits its truth without hesitation; Titus Livius, on the other hand, considers it false. I, assuredly, should not have left the question long in doubt, had that mountain been as easy to explore as this one. Let us leave this matter aside, however, and return to my mountain here, – it seems to me that a young man in private life may well be excused for attempting what an aged king could undertake without arousing criticism.

When I came to look for a companion I found, strangely enough, that hardly one among my friends seemed suitable, so rarely do we meet with just the right combination of personal tastes and characteristics, even among those who are dearest to us. This one was too apathetic, that one over anxious; this one too slow, that one too hasty; one was too sad, another over-cheerful; one more simple; another more sagacious, than I desired. I feared this one's taciturnity and that one's loquacity. The heavy deliberation of some repelled me as much as the lean incapacity of others. I rejected those who were likely to irritate me through cold want of interest, as well as those who might weary me by their excessive enthusiasm ...

Such defects, however grave, could be borne with at home, for charity suffereth all things, and friendship accepts such burden; *but it is quite otherwise on a journey, where very weakness becomes much more serious.* So, as I was bent upon pleasure and anxious that my enjoyment should be unalloyed, I looked about me with unusual care, balanced against one another the various characteristics of my friends and without committing any breach of friendship I silently condemned every trait which might prove disagreeable on the way. And – *would you believe it!* – I finally turned homeward for aid, and proposed the ascent to my only brother, who is younger than I, and with whom you are well acquainted. He was delighted and gratified beyond measure by the thought of holding the place of friend as well as brother.

Petrarch, *The Ascent of Mount Ventoux*, 1336

WALK AND THE RIGHT TALK

If, then, we are to talk, the talker should be eliminated before starting. But this does not mean that our walk will be a silent one. There are many forms of utterance besides talking, strictly so called; and nearly all of these are possible and even desirable concomitants of walking.

Thus, there is the simple and natural babble of the first few miles, while the body is settling down to work: the intellect, so to say, is blowing off steam preparatory to a period of quiescence. Then there is monologue of the purely spontaneous kind, which asks for no listener and desired no reply – the mere happy wagging of a tongue connected with anything that could be called a meaning. There may even be relatively continuous and intelligible statements or discussions, provided that these arise naturally out of the walk and the surrounding circumstances – for example, discussions on the weather, the way, the place for lunch, the utility of hard-boiled eggs, the peculiar pungency of wedding-cake in the wind. All these fit in easily with the walking frame of mind.

A. H. Sidgwick, *Walking Essays*, 1912

COMPANY ABROAD

I should not feel confident in venturing on a journey in a foreign country without a companion. I should want at intervals to hear the sound of my own language. There is an involuntary antipathy in the mind of an Englishman to foreign manners and notions that requires the assistance of social sympathy to carry it off. As the distance from home increases, this relief, which was at first a luxury, becomes a passion and an appetite. A person would almost feel stifled to find himself in the deserts of Arabia without friends and countrymen: there must be allowed to be something in the view of Athens or old Rome that claims the utterance of speech; and I own that the Pyramids are too mighty for any single contemplation. In such situations, so opposite to one's ordinary train of ideas, one seems a species by one's-self, a limb torn off from society, unless one can meet with instant fellowship and support.

William Hazlitt, 'On Going a Journey', 1822

HOW TO SLEEP OUT (1)

It was already hard upon October before I was ready to set forth, and at the high altitudes over which my road lay there was no Indian summer to be looked for. I was determined, if not to camp out, at least to have the means of camping out in my possession; for there is nothing more harassing to an easy mind than the necessity of reaching shelter by dusk, and the hospitality of a village inn is not always to be reckoned sure by those who trudge on foot. A tent, above all for a solitary traveller, is troublesome to pitch, and troublesome to strike again; and even on the march it forms a conspicuous feature in your baggage. A sleeping-sack, on the other hand, is always ready – you have only to get into it; it serves a double purpose – a bed by night, a portmanteau by day; and it does not advertise your intention of camping out to every curious passer-by. This is a huge point. If the camp is not secret, it is but a troubled resting-place; you become a public character; the convivial rustic visits your bedside after an early supper; and you must sleep with one eye open, and be up before the day. I decided on a sleeping-sack; and after repeated visits to Le Puy, and a deal of high living for myself and my advisers, a sleeping-sack was designed, constructed, and triumphantly brought home.

This child of my invention was nearly six feet square, exclusive of two triangular flaps to serve as a pillow by night and as the top and bottom of the sack by day. I call it 'the sack,' but it was never a sack by more than courtesy: only a sort of long roll or sausage, green waterproof cart cloth without and blue sheep's fur within. It was commodious as a valise, warm and dry for a bed. There was luxurious turning room for one; and at a pinch the thing might serve for two. I could bury myself in it up to the neck; for my head I trusted to a fur cap, with a hood to fold down over my ears and a band to pass under my nose like a respirator; and in case of heavy rain I proposed to make myself a little tent, or tentlet, with my waterproof coat, three stones, and a bent branch.

Robert Louis Stevenson, *Travels with a Donkey*, 1879

HOW TO SLEEP OUT (2)

I slept out that night under an outcrop of pines, facing east on a slight incline, with the lights of Costaros far away to my left. The turf was springy, and the pine needles seemed to discourage insects. As I lay in my bag, a number of late rooks came winging in out of the gloaming, and settled in the pine branches, chuckling to each other. They gave me a sense of companionship, even security: nothing could move up through the trees below me without disturbing them. Once or twice I croaked up at them (it was the wine) and they croaked back: '*Tais-toi, tais-toi.*' This night I fell asleep quickly. Only once, waking, I drank two ice-cold mouthfuls of water from my can and, leaning back, saw the Milky Way astonishingly bright through the pine tops, and felt something indescribable – like falling upwards into someone's arms.

Richard Holmes, *Footsteps*, 1985

HUSTLING A BED

I stood under a lamp and looked round at the uninviting rows of cottages and ill-lit dingy shops without much hope. I should get accommodation somewhere; I had never failed yet. But it was such an effort to get my tired legs in motion again and start my search. There were groups of people everywhere; young fellows and girls laughing and joking on the pavements; elderly parties loaded with parcels, gossiping in a language I could not understand; shouting, excited children. Not one of these, I told myself as I pushed between them, had a concern for the night's shelter: I was friendless and alone.

As events turned out, I could have spared myself these miserable forebodings. There is a Good Samaritan in Alston, and destiny directed my faltering steps to her front door. I made my wants known to her, and reluctantly she had to deny me, for friends of her daughter were staying there for the weekend. I thanked her, and went slowly away; slowly, because I could see she was hesitant and was watching me as I moved away along the street. She called me back, as I hoped she would; the house was plain and unprepossessing, but the next might be worse. But again I was disappointed. She thought hard how she could oblige me, and I waited silently for her decision. No, she said at length, she was sorry, very sorry, but she was afraid it was out of the question. Ah well, I replied, and slung my rucksack over my shoulder with a gesture of despair.

I was artful now, and cunning: I could see the woman was in some distress at having to turn me away, and the thought of having to go through all the overtures again at another front door made me all the more determined to get in here somehow. Ah well, I said again, with a sigh which must just have been perceptible to her; I supposed I would get shelter somewhere in the town. I gave her a brave grin, which I hoped she would perceive as forced, and limped away more slowly than ever. She called me back again, told me to come in; she would arrange for the girls to sleep together.

Once inside, and seated by the big fire in the kitchen with my shoes off, I would not have budged even if it meant the whole family sleeping in a row on the rug. My despondency vanished, snatched from me by the roaring flames and whirled up the chimney and out into the inhospitable darkness of the night. It was half-past eight when I entered, feeling ready for bed, but it was long after midnight before I went upstairs. There never was a busier hive of activity than this warm kitchen on this particular evening. I was not left to brood quietly by myself; instead, I sat and witnessed a succession of events, a parade of faces, which bewildered me and made me forget my own troubles.

Arthur Wainwright, *A Pennine Journey*, 1986

CERTAIN RESPONSIBILITIES

And the walker has his social duties. He must be careful not to leave gates open, not to break fences, not to walk through hay or crops, and not to be rude to farmers. In the interview, always try to turn away from wrath, and in most cases you will succeed. A second duty is to burn or bury the fragments that remain from lunch. To find the neighbourhood of a stream-head, on some well known walking route like Scarfell, littered with soaked paper and the relics of the feast is disgusting to the next party. And this brief act of reverence should never be neglected, even in the most retired nooks of the world. For all nature is sacred, and in England there is none too much of it.

George Trevelyan, *Clio: A Muse and Other Essays*, 1913

BUT FREE TO ROAM

Trespassers will be prosecuted –
   How? By whom? Who has the right? –
Hush, go your way; let lip be muted
   With finger; trees will screen from sight –

Then who has placed this notice-board? –
   No one; myself; what matter who?
The one who claims to be landlord
   Of this hill coppice and path through,

Each cracking stick, loose flint and all
   Wild flowers, untenanted snail shell,
White butterflies that rise and fall,
   Round holes of rabbits and all else.

But why dispute? Thick crowd the leaves;

Deeper sleeps moss across the trunk;
Wayfarer notes on thorn-stabbed sleeves
Green caterpillar's arching back.

Ten years from now, at most a score,
This tangled pathway will be lost,
And where its owner walked before
Moonlight will stumble like a ghost.

Andrew Young, 'Private', 1917

AND KNOW YOUR DESTINATION

Every one knows what a difference there is between walking with an object and without one, so I always choose a goal like Rome, the Paris Exhibition, Stonehenge, etc., worth walking to. Of course, the goal must depend on the amount of time at your disposal. In this case I had five weeks for walking and reckoning 150 miles a week, I looked for some spot 700 miles away worth the making for. My eyes lighted on Venice. 'One sun, one Venice,' says an old proverb, and I who have seen the sun will see Venice too. That matter settled, the route comes next.

'How do you find your way?' I am often asked, and so I will explain matters. I draw a straight line from the place I start from to the place I am going – in this instance, from Antwerp to Venice, and I mark down all the principal places on the line and make for them. Anyone doing this will see that I shall go through Liège, Carlsruhe, Constance, Verona and so on to Venice.

It was on the 1st October I set out. I like to be particular with dates.

The Reverend A. N. Cooper, MA, Vicar of Filey, Yorks.,
Tramps of the 'Walking Parson', 1902

THREE

Setting Off

There was only one way to start that day. Get up, get ready, get going.

A through-trailer, Oregon

EARLY START

You don't have to do anything to teach your child to walk. When his muscles, his nerves and his spirit are ready, you won't be able to stop him. I remember a mother who got herself into a jam by walking her baby around a great deal before he was able to do it by himself. He was so delighted with this suspended walking that he demanded it all day long. Her back was almost broken.

Dr Benjamin Spock, *Baby and Child Care*, 1945

CLASSIC START

The stooping figure of my mother, waist-deep in the grass and caught there like a piece of sheep's wool, was the last I saw of my country home as I left to discover the world. She stood old and bent at the top of the bank, silently watching me go, one gnarled red hand raised in farewell and blessing, not questioning why I went. At the bend of the road I looked back again and saw the gold light die behind her; then I turned the corner, passed the village school, and closed that part of my life forever.

It was a bright Sunday morning in early June, the right time to be leaving home. My three sisters and a brother had already gone before me; the two other brothers had yet to make up their minds. They were still sleeping that morning, but my mother had got up early and cooked me a heavy breakfast, had stood wordlessly while I ate it, her hand on my chair, and then had helped me pack up my few belongings. There had been no fuss, no appeals, no attempts at advice or persuasion, only a long and searching look. Then, with my bags on my back, I'd gone into the early sunshine and climbed through the long wet grass to the road.

It was 1934. I was nineteen years old, still soft at the edges, but with a confident belief in good fortune. I carried a small rolled-up tent, a violin in a blanket, a change of clothes, a tin of treacle biscuits, and some cheese. I was excited, vainglorious, knowing I had far to go; but not as yet, how far. As I left home that morning and walked away from the sleeping village, it never occurred to me that others had done this before.

I was propelled, of course, by the traditional forces that had sent many generations along this road – by the small tight valley closing in around one, stifling the breath with its mossy mouth, the cottage walls narrowing like the arms of an iron maiden, the local girls whispering, 'Marry and settle down.' Months of restless unease, leading to this inevitable moment, had been spent wandering about the hills, mournfully whistling, and watching the high open fields stepping away eastwards under gigantic clouds.

And now I was on my journey, in a pair of thick boots and with a hazel stick in my hand.

Laurie Lee, *As I Walked Out One Midsummer Morning*, 1969

INCOMPLETE START

Perhaps it's only when we set the greatest store by a seemingly trivial adventure that the metaphysical content of a certain variety of yearning becomes apparent. Yet why was I so upset that we could not start our walk from home? It would add an extra day, Fritz said. He could not get an extra day off work. Then the children were not eager to set out from home. They know the paths round there too well. Children can only be persuaded to walk if there is excitement involved. Hardship must be accompanied by glory. My wife drove us towards the peaks visible in the distance.

San Giorgio Veronese to Folgaria through fifty miles of mountains in three days. Myself, my friend Fritz, Michele aged eleven, Stefi eight. Italy's coldest summer on record. One Indian tradition puts down many of our anxieties to the fact that all the universe is nothing other than the dispersed and broken body of the first progenitor god. We benefit from this dissolution – we could not exist as individuals without it – and yet yearn for a lost wholeness. Could this be, I put it to Fritz as we faced the first bracing slope, why I was so sad about not starting from home? I had wanted the feeling of having covered the whole distance, of having put something back together, extended myself the whole way from home to Folgaria. It was more likely, he suggested, that I was merely an obsessive. I attached my happiness to small and mindless achievements. Stefi said she was exhausted. We had been walking the best part of fifteen minutes.

Tim Parks, *Glory*, 1998

LAST START

Slowly, the sun had climbed up the hard white downs, till it broke with little of the mysterious ritual of dawn upon a sparkling world of snow. There had been a hard frost during the night, and the birds, who hopped about here and there with scant tolerance of life, left no trace of their passage on the silver pavements. Once upon the skyline, the sun seemed to climb more quickly, and as it rose higher it began to give out a heat that blended with the keenness of the wind.

It may have been this strange alternation of heat and cold that disturbed the old tramp in his dreams, for he struggled for a moment with the snow that covered him, like a man who finds himself twisted uncomfortably in the bed-clothes, and then sat up with staring, questioning eyes. 'Lord! I thought I was in bed,' he said to himself as he took in the vacant landscape, 'and all the while I was out here.' He stretched his limbs, and, rising carefully to his feet, shook the snow off his body. As he did so the wind set him shivering, and he knew that his bed had been warm.

'Come, I feel pretty fit,' he thought. 'I suppose I am lucky to wake at all in this. Or unlucky – it isn't much of a business to come back to.' He looked up and saw the downs shining against the blue like the Alps on a picture post-card. 'That means another forty miles or so, I suppose,' he continued grimly. 'Lord knows what I did yesterday. Walked till I was done, and now I'm only about twelve miles from Brighton. Damn the snow, damn Brighton, damn everything!' The sun crept up higher and higher, and he started walking patiently along the road with his back turned to the hills.

'Am I glad or sorry that it was only sleep that took me, glad or sorry, glad or sorry?' His thoughts seemed to arrange themselves in a metrical accompaniment to the steady thud of his footsteps and he hardly sought an answer to his question. It was good enough to walk to.

Richard Middleton, *On the Brighton Road*, 1912

FOUR

With Nature

Walking is primitive and simple; it brings us into contact with mother earth and unsophisticated nature.

Leslie Stephen

IN THE GARDEN

After I came into the garden I turned on the right hand, and descended into a very pleasant and delicious walke, at the entrance whereof I read the second inscription made in stone over a faire gate.

Si te imprudentum graviores
Forte
Huc usque insequutae sunt
Curae
Eas velint nolint procul
Nunc ut abeant facito.
Hilaritati namque & Genio
Pars haec potiss. Dicata est.

Againe, having passed through the gate and walke which was but short, I entered into a third walke of a notable length (for it was at the least two hundred paces long) beset with most delightful trees on both sides. At the entrance of this walke there standeth another stately gate, over which I read this third inscription, which indeede is most witty and elegant.

Cedros hosce qui dempserit,
Floresve carpserit,
Is sacrilegus esto;
Vertumnoque & Pomonae,
Queis sunt sacri,
Poenas luito.

In both sides of this walke I saw Cedar trees, Orange, Lemmon, Pome-Citron trees, and fruits of all these kindes ripe. Amongst the rest I observed passing faire Citrons, which made my mouth even water upon them, and caused me almost to transgresse his law. One side of the walke is invironed with a goodly wall, by which the fruits doe grow. About the middle of the walke ther is built a prety convenient house, wherein tame connies and divers sorts of fine birds are kept, as Turtles etc. In the middle of the garden is built a faire round roofe, supported with eight pillars of fine stone, it is said that it shall all be covered with lead, but it was not when I was there. Also I saw fine Labyrinth made of boxe, but the dore was locked that I could not get in. And many lofty Pine trees, but some of them were so nipped with the cold frost and snow that fell the winter before, as those were in the king of Frances garden at the Tuilleries, that they were even starved. Also for the more addition of pleasure to the place, there is a sweet river full of fine fish running by that fruitful walke, wherehence is ministred store of water to moisten the garden in time of drougth. Finally, to conclude, such is the affluence of all delights and pleasures in the garden, that it is the most peerlesse and comparable plot for the quantity that ever I saw.

Thomas Coryate, *Coryats Crudities*, 1611

INTO THE FIELDS . . .

And now into the fields I go,
Where thousand flaming flowers grow;
And ev'ry neighb'ring hedge I greet,
With honeysuckles smelling sweet.
Now o'er the daisy meads I stray,
And meet with, as I pace my way,
Sweetly shining on the eye,
A riv'let, gliding smoothly by;
Which shows with what an easy tide
The moments of the happy glide.

John Dyer, 'The Country Walk', *c.*1727

NEW VIEW, NEW KINGDOM

When we walk, we naturally go to the fields and the woods. But even some sects of philosophers have felt the necessity of importing the woods to themselves, since they did not go to the woods. 'They planted groves and walks of Platanes,' where they took *subdiales ambulationes* in porticoes open to the air. Of course it is no use to direct our steps to the woods if they do not carry us thither. I am alarmed when it happens that I have walked a mile into the woods bodily without getting there in spirit. In my afternoon I would forget all my morning occupations and my obligations to society.

My vicinity affords many good walks; and though for many years I have walked every day, and sometimes for several days together, I have not yet exhausted them. An absolutely new prospect is a great happiness, and I can still get this any afternoon. Two or three hours walking will carry me to as strange a country as I expect ever to see. A single farmhouse which I had not seen before is sometimes as good as the dominions of the King of Dahomey. There is in fact a sort of harmony discoverable between the capabilities of the landscape within a circle of ten miles' radius, or the limits of an afternoon walk, and the threescore years and ten of human life. It will never become quite familiar to you.

Henry David Thoreau, 'Walking', *Excursions*, 1863

JOG ON

Jog on, jog on, the footpath way
And merrily hent the stile-a:
A merry heart goes all the day,
Your sad tires in a mile-a.

William Shakespeare, *The Winter's Tale*, 1611

NATURE CAN MAKE THE WALKER SMALL

We had a pleasant walk the next morning along the side of the lake under the grey cliffs, the green hills and azure sky; now passing under the open gateway of some dilapidated watch-tower that had in former times connected the rocky barrier with the water, now watching the sails of a boat slowly making its way among the trees on the banks of the Rhone, like butterflies expanding their wings in the breeze, or the snowy ridges that seemed close to us at Vevey receding farther into a kind of lofty back-ground as we advanced. The speculation of Bishop Berkeley, or some other philosopher, that distance is measured by motion and not by the sight, is verified here at every step. After going on for hours, and perceiving no alteration in the form or appearance of the object before you, you begin to be convinced that it is out of ordinary calculation, or, in the language of the *Fancy*, an 'ugly customer;' and our curiosity once excited, is ready to magnify every circumstance relating to it to an indefinite extent. The literal impression being discarded as insufficient, the imagination takes out an unlimited letter of credit for all that is possible or wonderful, and what the eye sees is considered thenceforward merely as an imperfect hint, to be amplified and filled up on a colossal scale by the understanding and rules of proportion. To say the truth, you also suffer a change, feel like Lilliputians, and can fancy yourselves transported to a different world, where the dimensions and relations of things are regulated by some unknown law. The inn where we stopped at Vionnax is bad. Beyond this place, the hills at the eastern end of the lake form into an irregular and stupendous amphitheatre; and you pass through long and apparently endless vistas of tall flourishing trees, without being conscious of making much progress. There is a glass-manufactory at Vionnax, which I did not go to see; others who have more curiosity may. It will be there (I dare say) next year for those who choose to visit it: I liked neither its glare nor its heat. The cold icy crags that hang suspended over it have been there a thousand years, and will be there a thousand years to come. Shortlived as we are, let us attach ourselves to the immortal, and scale (assisted by earth's giant brood) the empyrean of pure thought! But the English abroad turn out of their way to see every pettifogging, huckstering object that they could see better at home, and are as *fussy* and fidgetty, with their smoke-jacks and mechanical inventions among the Alps, as if they had brought Manchester and Sheffield in their pockets! The finest effect along this road is the view of the bridge as you come near St. Maurice. The mountains on either side here descend nearly to a point, boldly and abruptly; the river flows rapidly through the tall arch of the bridge, on one side of which you see an old fantastic turret, and beyond it the hill called the Sugar-loaf, rising up in the centre of immense ranges of mountains, and with fertile and variously-marked plains stretching out in the intervening space. The landscape painter has only to go there, and make a picture of it. It is already framed by nature to his hand! I mention this the more, because that kind of *grouping* of objects which is essential to the picturesque, is not always to be found in the most sublime or even beautiful scenes. Nature (so to speak) uses a larger canvass than man, and where she is greatest and most prodigal of her wealth, often neglects that principle of concentration and contrast which is an indispensable preliminary before she can be translated with effect into the circumscribed language of art. We supped at Martigny, at the Hotel de la Poste (formerly a convent), and the next morning proceeded by the Valley of Trie and the Col de Peaume to Chamouni.

William Hazlitt, *Notes of a Journey Through France and Italy*, 1826

A DIFFERENT PERSPECTIVE

It is most wonderful when I walk alone in the twilight on the beach – flat dunes behind me, the tossing immeasurable sea before me, the heavens like a great crystal dome above me – and I seem to see myself as small as an ant, and yet there is such breadth in my soul – miles wide. The great simplicity of nature all around me curbs and exalts me at once, and the influence is more powerful than it has ever been in any other sublime environment. A cathedral has never been large enough for me; my soul with its old Titanic prayer strove to soar higher than the Gothic pillars, and wished always to burst out through the roof. On the summit of Rosstrappe the colossal rocks in their bold grouping made an impression on me at the first moment; but not for long, for my soul was only surprised, not overwhelmed, and those monstrous heaps of stone grew gradually smaller in my eyes, and in the end they appeared to be no more than the paltry ruins of the razed palace of a giant cathedral, in which my soul would not have been comfortable.

Heinrich Heine *Memoir*, 1825
(trans. Gilbert Cannan, 1910)

THE SIMPLON PASS

Brook and road
Were fellow-travellers in this gloomy Pass,
And with them did we journey several hours
At a slow step. The immeasurable height
Of woods decaying, never to be decayed,
The stationary blasts of waterfalls,
And in the narrow rent, at every turn,
Winds thwarting winds bewildered and forlorn,

The torrents shooting from the clear blue sky,
The rocks that muttered close upon our ears,
Black drizzling crags that spake by the wayside
As if a voice were in them, the sick sight
And giddy prospect of the raving stream,
The unfettered clouds and region of the heavens,
Tumult and peace, the darkness and the light –
Were all like workings of one mind, the features
Of the same face, blossoms upon one tree,
Characters of the great Apocalypse,
The types and symbols of Eternity,
Of first, and last, and midst, and without end.

William Wordsworth, *The Prelude*, Book VI, 1850

SCENES FROM A WINTER WALK

We Unlatch the Door

Silently we unlatch the door, letting the drift fall in, and step abroad to face the cutting air. Already the stars have lost some of their sparkle, and a dull, leaden mist skirts the horizon. A lurid, brazen light in the east proclaims the approach of day, while the western landscape is dim and spectral still, and clothed in a sombre Tartarian light, like the shadowy realms. They are Infernal sounds only that you hear, – the crowing of cocks, the barking of dogs, the chopping of wood, the lowing of kine, all seem to come from Pluto's barn-yard and beyond the Styx; – not for any melancholy they suggest, but their twilight bustle is too solemn and mysterious for earth. The recent tracks of the fox or otter in the yard remind us that each hour of the night is crowded with events, and the primeval nature is still working and making tracks in the snow. Opening the gate, we tread briskly along the lone country road, crunching the dry and crisped snow under our feet, or aroused by the sharp, clear creak of the wood-sled, just starting for the distant market, from the early farmer's door, where it has lain the summer long, dreaming amid the chips and stubble; while far through the drifts and powdered windows we see the farmer's early candle, like a paled star, emitting a lonely beam, as if some severe virtue were at its matins there. And one by one the smokes begin to ascend from the chimneys amidst the trees and snows.

Sun-up

The sun at length rises through the distant woods, as if with the faint clashing, swinging sound of cymbals, melting the air with his beams, and with such rapid steps the morning travels, that already his rays are gilding the distant western mountains. Meanwhile we step hastily along through the powdery snow, warmed by an inward heat, enjoying an Indian summer still, in the increased glow of thought and feeling. Probably if our lives were more conformed to nature, we should not need to defend ourselves against her heats and colds, but find her our constant nurse and friend, as do plants and quadrupeds. If our bodies were fed with pure and simple elements, and not with a stimulating and heating diet, they would afford no more pasture for cold than a leafless twig, but thrive like the trees, which find even winter genial to their expansion.

A Puritan Toughness

The wonderful purity of nature at this season is a most pleasing fact. Every decayed stump and moss-grown stone and rail, and the dead leaves of autumn, are concealed by a clean napkin of snow. In the bare fields and tinkling woods, see what virtue survives. In the coldest and bleakest places, the warmest charities still maintain a foothold. A cold and searching wind drives away all contagion, and nothing can withstand it but what has a virtue in it; and accordingly, whatever we meet with in cold and bleak places, as the tops of mountains, we respect for a sort of sturdy innocence, a Puritan toughness. All things beside seem to be called in for shelter, and what stays out must be part of the original frame of the universe, and of such valour as God himself. It is invigorating to breathe the cleansed air. Its greater fineness and purity are visible to the eye, and we would fain stay out long and late, that the gales may sigh through us too, as through the leafless trees, and fit us for the winter: – as if we hoped so to borrow some pure and steadfast virtue, which will stead us in all seasons.

Signs in the Snow

Still, in the midst of the arctic day, we may trace the summer to its retreats, and sympathise with some contemporary life. Stretched over the brooks, in the midst of the frost-bound meadows, we may observe the submarine cottages of the caddice-worms, the larvae of the Plicipennes. Their small cylindrical cases built around themselves, composed of flags, sticks, grass, and withered leaves, shells, and pebbles, in form and colour like the wrecks which strew the bottom, – now drifting along over the pebbly bottom, now whirling in tiny eddies and dashing down steep falls, or sweeping rapidly along with the current, or else swaying to and fro at the end of some grass-blade or root. Anon they will leave their sunken habitations, and, crawling up the stems of plants, or to the surface, like gnats, as perfect insects henceforth, flutter over the surface of the water, or sacrifice their short lives in the flame of our candles at evening. Down yonder little glen the shrubs are drooping under their burden, and the red alder-berries contrast with the white ground. Here are the marks of a myriad feet which have already been abroad. The sun rises as proudly over such a glen as over the valley of the Seine or the Tiber, and it seems the residence of a pure and self-subsistent valour, such as they never witnessed; which never knew defeat nor fear. Here reign the simplicity and purity of a primitive age, and a health and hope far remote from towns and cities. Standing quite alone, far in the forest, while the wind is shaking down snow from the trees, and leaving the only human tracks behind us, we find our reflections of a richer variety than the life of cities. The chicadee and nut-hatch are more inspiring society than statesmen and philosophers, and we shall return to these last, as to more vulgar companions. In this lonely glen, with its brook draining the slopes, its creased ice and crystals of all hues, where the spruces and hemlocks stand up on either side, and the rush and sere wild oats in the rivulet itself, our lives are more serene and worthy to contemplate.

Yonder, the Broad Country

Now our path begins to ascend gradually to the top of this high hill, from whose precipitous south side we can look over the broad country, of forest and field and river, to the distant snowy mountains. See yonder thin column of smoke curling up through the woods from some invisible farmhouse; the standard raised over some rural homestead. There must be a warmer and more genial spot there below, as where we detect the vapour from a spring forming a cloud above the trees. What fine relations are established between the traveller who discovers this airy column from some eminence in the forest and him who sits below! Up goes the smoke as silently and naturally as the vapour exhales from the leaves, and as busy disposing itself in wreaths as the housewife on the hearth below. It is a hieroglyphic of man's life, and suggests more intimate and important things than the boiling of a pot. Where its fine column rises above the forest, like an ensign, some human life has planted itself; and such is the beginning of Rome, the establishment of the arts, and the foundation of empires, whether on the prairies of America, or the steppes of Asia.

Henry David Thoreau, 'A Winter Walk', 1843

JANUARY SUN

On Monday, Jan 8th, I rose as usual. The metropolitan carriage called for me at eight o'clock. I was habited, and ready to start. But there was something so genial in the atmosphere ... (whilst opening the garden gate to make my exit,) that I felt impelled to shake my head at the coachman. This signified that he was to go on without me. 'Out of sight, out of mind,' thought I, as I retraced my steps, determined to do something out of the common way.

Now the voices of the common bird were every moment becoming more musical. It was too much for me. 'A walk,' shouted I, mentally, – 'and a long one!' The air freshened, and sun peeped out, as my mind became decided. An over-coat, weighing some eight ounces, was thrown on my shoulders; a trusty stick was my companion, and, away, at once, I bounded.

William Kidd, *Progress of the Seasons*, 1855

MARCH DOUBTS

All day the winter seemed to have gone. The horses' hoofs on the moist, firm road made a clear 'cuck-oo' as they rose and fell; and far off, for the first time in the year, a ploughboy, who remembered spring and knew that it would come again, shouted 'Cuckoo! cuckoo!'

A warm wind swept over the humid pastures and red sand-pits on the hills and they gleamed in a lightly muffled sun. Once more in the valleys the ruddy farmhouses and farm-buildings seemed new and fair again, and the oast-house cones stood up as prophets of spring, since the south wind had turned all their white vanes towards the north, and they felt the sea that lay – an easy journey on such a day – beyond the third or fourth wooded ridge in the south. The leaves of goose-grass, mustard, vetch, dog's mercury, were high above the dead leaves on hedge banks. Primrose and periwinkle were blossoming. Like flowers were the low ash-tree boles where the axe had but lately cut off the tall rods; flower-like and sweet also the scent from the pits where labourers dipped the freshly peeled ash poles in tar. In the elms, sitting crosswise on a bough, sang thrush and missel thrush; in the young corn, the larks; the robins in the thorns; and in all the meadows the guttural notes of the rooks were mellowed by love and the sun.

Making deep brown ruts across the empty green fields came the long wagons piled high with faggots; the wheels rumbled; the harness jingled and shone; the horses panted and the carters cracked their whips.

Soon would the first chiff-chaff sing in the young larches; at evening the calm, white, majestic young clouds should lie along the horizon in a clear and holy air; and climbing a steep hill at that hour, the walker should see a window, as it were, thrown open in the sky and hear a music that should silence thought and even regret – as when, on the stage, a window is opened and someone invisible is heard to sing a heavy-laden song below it.

But as I walked and the wind fell for the sunset, the path led me under high, stony beeches. The air was cool and still and moist and waterish dark, and no bird sang. A wood-pigeon spread out his barry tail as he ascended perpendicularly to a hidden place among the branches, and then there was no sound.

The waterish half-light seemed to have lasted for ever and to have an eternity ahead. Through the trees a grassy, deeply-rutted road wound downwards, and at the edge the ruts were broad and full of dark water. Still retaining some corruption of the light of the sky upon its surface, that shadowed water gave an immense melancholy to the wood. The reflections of the beeches across it were as the bars of a cage that imprisoned some child of light. It was but a few inches deep of rain, and yet, had it been a legendary pool, or had a drowned woman's hair been stamped into the mud at its edge and left a green forehead exposed, it could not have stained and filled the air more tragically. The cold, the silence, the leaflessness found an expression in that clouded shining surface among the ruts. Life and death seemed to contend there, and I recalled a dream which I had lately dreamed.

I dreamed that someone had cut the cables that anchored me to such tranquillity as had been mine, and that I was drifted out upon an immensity of desolation and solitude. I was without hope, without even the energy of despair that might in time have given birth to hope. But in that desolation I found one business: to search for a poison that should kill slowly, painlessly, and unexpectedly. In that search I lost sight of what had persuaded me to it; yet when at last I succeeded, I took a draught and went out into the road and began to walk. A calm fell upon me such as I had sometimes found in June thunderstorms on lonely hills, or in midnights when I stepped for a moment after long foolish labours to my door, and heard the nightingales singing out from the Pleiades that overhung the wood, and saw the flower-faced owl sitting on the gate. I walked on, not hastening with a too great desire nor lingering with a too careful quietude. It was as yet early morning, and the wheat sheaves stood on the gentle hills like yellow-haired women kneeling to the sun that was about to rise. Now and then I passed the corners of villages, and sometimes at windows and through doorways I saw the faces of men and women I had known and seemed to forget, and they smiled and were glad, but not more glad than I. Labouring in the fields also were men whose faces I was happy to recognize and see smiling with recognition. And very sweet it was to go on thus, at ease, knowing neither trouble nor fatigue. I could have gone on, it seemed, for ever, and I wished to live so for ever, when suddenly I remembered the poison. Then of each one I met I begged a remedy. Some reminded me that formerly I had made a poor thing of life, and said that it was too late. Others supposed that I jested. A few asked me to stay with them and rest. The sky and the earth, and the men and women drank of the poison that I had drunken, so that I could not endure the use of my eyes, and I entered a shop to buy some desperate remedy that should end all at once, when, seeing behind the counter a long-dead friend in wedding attire, I awoke.

Even so in the long wet ruts did the false hope of spring contend with the shadows: even so at last did it end, when the dead leaves upon the trees began to stir madly in the night wind, with the sudden, ghastly motion of burnt paper on a still fire when a draught stirs it in a silent room at night; and even the nearest trees seemed to be but fantastic hollows in the misty air.

Edward Thomas, *The Heart of England*, 1906

A DAILY CONSTITUTION

5th April 1798. Coleridge came to dinner. William and I walked in the wood in the morning. I fetched eggs from Coombe.
6th. Went a part of the way home with Coleridge. A pleasant warm morning, but a showery day. Walked a short distance up the lesser Coombe, with an intention of going to the source

of the brook, but the evening closing in, cold prevented us.

7th. Walked before dinner up the Coombe, to the source of the brook, and came home by the tops of the hills; a showery morning, at the hilltops; the view opened upon us very grand.

8th. Easter Sunday. Walked in the morning in the wood, and half way to Stowey; found the air at first oppressively warm, afterwards very pleasant.

9th. Walked to Stowey, a fine air in going, but very hot in returning. The sloe in blossom, the hawthorns green, the larches in the park changed from black to green in two or three days. Met Coleridge in returning.

10th. I was hanging out linen in the evening. We walked to Holford. I turned off to the bakers and walked beyond Woodlands, expecting to meet William, met him on the hill; a close warm evening.

11th. In the wood in the morning, walked to the top of the hill, then I went into the wood. A pleasant evening, a fine air, the grass in the park becoming green, many trees green in the dell.

12th. Walked in the wood in the morning. In the evening up the Coombe, fine walk. The Spring advances rapidly, multitudes of primroses, dog-violets, periwinkles, stichwort.

13th. Walked in the wood in the morning. In the evening went to Stowey. I staid with Mrs Coleridge. William went to Poole's. Supped with Mrs Coleridge.

14th. Walked in the wood in the morning. The evening very stormy, so we staid within doors. Mary Wollstonecraft's Life etc came.

15th. Set forward after breakfast to Crookham, and returned to dinner at three o'clock. A fine cloudy morning. Walked about the squire's grounds. Quaint waterfalls about, about which Nature was very successfully striving to make beautiful what art had deformed – ruins, hermitages etc, etc. In spite of all these things, the dell romantic and beautiful, though everywhere painted with unnaturalised trees. Happily we cannot shape the huge hills, or carve out the valleys according to our fancy.

Dorothy Wordsworth, *Alfoxden Journal*, 1798

THE GIRLS ARE WALKING ABOUT BAREFOOTED

I intended to have written to you from Kirkudbright, the town I shall be in tomorrow – but I will write now because my Knapsack has worn my coat in the seams, my coat has gone to the Taylors [*sic*] and I have but one coat to my back in these parts. I must tell you how I went to Liverpool with George and our new sister and the Gentleman my fellow traveller through the Summer and Autumn – We had a tolerable journey to Liverpool – which I left the morning before George was up for Lancaster – Then we set off from Lancaster on foot with our Knapsacks on, and have walked a little Zig Zag through the mountains and Lakes of Cumberland and Westmorland – We came from Carlisle yesterday to this place – We are employed in going up Mountains, looking at strange towns, prying into old ruins and eating very hearty breakfasts. Here we are full in the Midst of broad Scotch 'How is it a' wi yousel' the Girls are walking about bare footed and in the worst cottages the smoke finds its way out of the door. I shall come home full of news for you and for fear I could choke you by too great a dose at once I must make you used to it by a letter or two. We have taken for travelling Jewellers, Razor sellers and Spectacle vendors because friend Brown wears a pair – The first place we stopped at with our Knapsacks contained one Richard Bradshaw, a notorious tippler. He stood in the shape of a 3 and balanced himself as well as he could saying with his nose right in Mr. Brown's face 'Do – yo-u sell spec-ta-cles?' Mr. Abbey says we are Don Quixotes – tell him we are more generally taken for Pedlars. All I hope is that we may not be taken for excisemen in this whiskey country. We are generally up about 5 walking before breakfast and we complete our 20 miles before dinner. – Yesterday we visited Burns's Tomb and this morning the fine Ruins of Lincluden. – I had done thus far when my coat came back fortified at all points – so as we lose no time we set forth again through Galloway – all very pleasant and pretty with no fatigue when one is used to it. We are in the midst of Meg Merrilies' country of whom I suppose you have heard.

John Keats, Letter to Fanny Keats, 1818

THE GIRLS ARE PLAYING KISS-IN-THE-RING

I went out, still alone, for a walk and without a guide, found my way to the public park and the public gardens. I cannot say that they are perfect in horticultural beauty and in surroundings, but they are spacious with ample room for improvement, well arranged as far as they are arranged, and with a promise of being very superior to anything of the kind at Capetown. The air was as sweet, I think, as any that I ever breathed. Through them I went on, leaving the town between me and the sea, on to a grassy illimitable heath on which, I told myself, that with perseverance I might walk on till I came to Grand Cairo. I had my stick in my hand and was prepared for any lion that I might meet. But on this occasion I met no lion. After a while I found myself descending into a valley, – a pretty little green valley altogether out of sight of the town, and which as I was wending along seemed at first to be an interruption in my way to the centre of the continent. But as I approached the verge from which I could look down into its bosom, I heard the sound of voices, and when I had reached a rock which hung over it, I saw beneath me a ring, as it might be of fairy folk, in full glee – of folk, fairy or human, running hither and thither with extreme merriment and joy. After standing awhile and gazing I perceived that the young people of Fort Elizabeth were playing kiss-in-the-ring. Oh, – how long ago it was since I played kiss-in-the-ring, and how nice I used to think it! It was many many years since I had even seen the game. And these young people played it with an energy and an ecstasy which I had never seen equalled. I walked down, almost amongst them, but no one noticed me. I felt among them like Rip Van Winkle. I was as a ghost, for they seemed not even to see me. How the girls ran, and could always have escaped from the lads had they listed, but always were caught round some corner out of the circle! And how awkward the lads were in kissing, and how clever the girls in taking care that it should always come off at last, without undue violence! But it seemed to me that had I been a lad I should have felt that when all the girls had been once kissed, or say twice, – and when every girl had been kissed twice round by every lad, the thing would have become tame, and the lips unhallowed. But this was merely the cynicism of an old man, and no such feeling interrupted the sport. There I left them still hard at work, and returned sadly to my dinner at the club.

Anthony Trollope, *South Africa*, 1879

SUNDAY WALKS

A six days' prisoner, life's support to earn
From dusty cobwebs and the murky barn,
The weary thresher meets the rest that's given,
And thankful soothes him in the boon of heaven;
But happier still in Sabbath-walks he feels,
With love's sweet pledges poddling at his heels,
That oft divert him with their childish glee

In fruitless chases after bird and bee;
And, eager gathering every flower they pass
Of yellow lambtoe and totter glass,
Oft wimper round him disappointment's sigh
At sight of blossom that's in bloom too high,
And twitch his sleeve with all their coaxing powers
To urge his hand to reach the tempting flower:
Then as he climbs, their eager hopes to crown,
On gate or stile to pull the blossoms down
Of pale hedge-rows straggling wild and tall,
And scrambling woodbines that outgrow them all,
He turns to days when he himself would tease,
And smiles with rapture, as he plucks the flowers,
To meet the feelings of these lovely hours,
And blesses Sunday's rest, whose peace at will
Retains a portion of those pleasures still.

John Clare, 'Sunday Walks', 1818

A BRILLIANT SUNDAY

I was now about to leave Llangollen, for a short time, and to set out on an expedition to Bangor, Snowdon, and one or two places in Anglesea. I had determined to make the journey on foot, in order that I might have perfect liberty of action, and enjoy the best opportunities of seeing the country. My wife and daughter were to meet me at Bangor, to which place they would repair by the railroad, and from which, after seeing some of the mountain districts, they would return to Llangollen by the way they came, where I proposed to rejoin them, returning, however, by a different way from the one I went, that I might traverse new districts. About eleven o'clock of a brilliant Sunday morning I left Llangollen, after reading the morning-service of the Church to my family. I set out on a Sunday because I was anxious to observe the general demeanour of the people, in the interior of the country, on the Sabbath.

I directed my course towards the west, to the head of the valley. My wife and daughter after walking with me about a mile bade me farewell, and returned. Quickening my pace I soon left the Llangollen valley behind me and entered another vale, along which the road which I was following, and which led to Corwen and other places, might be seen extending for miles. Lumpy hills were close upon my left, the Dee running noisily between steep banks, fringed with trees, was on my right; beyond it rose hills which form part of the wall of the vale of Clwyd; their tops bare, but their sides pleasantly coloured with yellow corn-fields and woods of dark verdure. About an hour's walking, from the time when I entered the valley, brought me to a bridge over a gorge, down which water ran to the Dee. I stopped and looked over the side of the bridge nearest to the hill. A huge rock about forty feet long, by twenty broad, occupied the entire bed of the gorge, just above the bridge, with the exception of a little gullet to the right, down which between the rock and a high bank, on which stood a cottage, a run of water purled and brawled. The rock looked exactly like a huge whale lying on its side, with its back turned towards the runnel. Above it was a glen with trees. After I had been gazing a little time a man making his appearance at the door of the cottage just beyond the bridge I passed on, and drawing nigh to him, after a slight salutation, asked him in English the name of the bridge.

'The name of the bridge, sir,' said the man, in very good English, 'is Pont y Pandy.'

'Does not that mean the bridge of the fulling mill?'

'I believe it does, sir,' said the man.

'Is there a fulling mill near?'

'No sir, there was one some time ago, but it is now a sawing mill.'

Here a woman, coming out, looked at me steadfastly.

'Is that gentlewoman your wife?'

'She is no gentlewoman, sir, but she is my wife.'

'Of what religion are you?'

'We are Calvinistic-Methodists, sir.'

'Have you been to chapel?'

'We are just returned, sir.'

Here the woman said something to her husband, which I did not hear, but the purport of which I guessed from the following question which he immediately put.

'Have you been to chapel, sir?'

'I do not go to chapel; I belong to the Church.'

'Have you been to church, sir?'

'I have not – I said my prayers at home, and then walked out.'

'It is not right to walk out on the Sabbath day, except to go to church or chapel.'

'Who told you so?'

'The law of God, which says you shall keep holy the Sabbath day.'

'I am not keeping it unholy.'

'You are walking about, and in Wales when we see a person walking idly about, on the Sabbath day, we are in the habit of saying Sabbath breaker, where are you going?'

'The Son of Man walked through the fields on the Sabbath day, why should I not walk along the roads?'

'He who called Himself the Son of Man was God, and could do what He pleased, but you are not God.'

'But He came in the shape of a man to set an example. Had there been anything wrong in walking about on the Sabbath day, He would not have done it.'

Here the wife exclaimed, 'How worldly-wise these English are!'

'You do not like the English,' said I.

'We do not dislike them,' said the woman; 'at present they do us no harm, what ever they did of old.'

'But you still consider them,' said I, 'the seed of Y Sarfes cadwynog, the coiling serpent.'

'I should be loth to call any people the seed of the serpent,' said the woman.

'But one of your great bards did,' said I.

'He must have belonged to the Church, and not to the chapel then,' said the woman. 'No person who went to chapel would have used such bad words.'

'He lived,' said I, 'before people were separated into those of the Church, and the chapel; did you ever hear of Taliesin Ben Beirdd?'

'I never did,' said the woman.

'But I have,' said the man; 'and of Owain Glendower too.'

'Do people talk much of Owen Glendower in these parts?' said I.

'Plenty,' said the man, 'and no wonder, for when he was alive he was much about here – some way farther on there is a mount, on the bank of the Dee, called the mount of Owen Glendower, where it is said he used to stand and look out after his enemies.'

'Is it easy to find?' said I.

'Very easy,' said the man, 'it stands right upon the Dee and is covered with trees; there is no mistaking it.'

I bade the man and his wife farewell, and proceeded on my way. After walking about a mile, I perceived a kind of elevation which answered to the description of Glendower's mount, which the man by the bridge had given me. It stood on the right hand, at some distance from the road, across a field. As I was standing looking at it a man came up from the direction in which I myself had come. He was a middle-aged man plainly but decently dressed, and had something of the appearance of a farmer.

'What hill may that be?' said I in English, pointing to the elevation.

'Dim Saesneg, sir,' said the man, looking rather sheepish, 'Dim gair o Saesneg.'

Rather surprised that a person of his appearance should not have a word of English I repeated my questions in Welsh.

'Ah, you speak Cumraeg, sir;' said the man evidently surprised that a person of my English appearance should speak Welsh. 'I am glad of it! What hill is that you ask – Dyna Mont Owain Glyndwr, sir.'

'Is it easy to get to?' said I.

'Quite easy, sir,' said the man. 'If you please I will go with you.'

I thanked him, and opening a gate he conducted me across the field to the mount of the Welsh hero.

The mount of Owen Glendower stands close upon the southern bank of the Dee, and is nearly covered with trees of various kinds. It is about thirty feet high from the plain, and about the same diameter at the top. A deep black pool of the river which here runs far beneath the surface of the field, purls and twists under the northern side, which is very steep, though several large oaks spring out of it. The hill is evidently the work of art, and appeared to me to be some burying-place of old.

'And this is the hill of Owain Glyndwr?' said I.

'Dyma Mont Owain Glyndwr, sir, lle yr oedd yn seffyll i edrych am ei elynion yn dyfod o Caer Lleon. This is the hill of Owen Glendower, sir, where he was in the habit of standing to look out for his enemies coming from Chester.'

'I suppose it was not covered with trees then?' said I.

'No sir; it has not been long planted with trees. They say, however, that the oaks which hang over the river are very old.'

'Do they say who raised this hill?'

'Some say that God raised it, sir; others that Owain Glendower raised it. Who do you think raised it?'

'I believe that it was raised by man, but not by Owen Glendower. He may have stood upon it, to watch for the coming of his enemies, but I believe it was here long before his time and that it was raised over some old dead king by the people whom he had governed.'

'Do they bury kings by the side of rivers, sir?'

'In the old time they did, and on the tops of mountains; they burnt their bodies to ashes, placed them in pots and raised heaps of earth or stones over them. Heaps like this have frequently been opened, and found to contain pots with ashes and bones.'

'I wish all English could speak Welsh, sir.'

'Why?'

'Because then we poor Welsh who can speak no English could learn much which we do not know.'

Descending the monticle we walked along the road together. After a little time I asked my companion of what occupation he was and where he lived.

'I am a small farmer, sir,' said he, 'and live at Llansanfraid Glyn Dyfrdwy across the river.'

'How comes it,' said I, 'that you do not know English?'

'When I was young,' said he, 'and could have easily learnt it, I cared nothing about it, and now that I am old and see its use, it is too late to acquire it.'

'Of what religion are you?' said I.

'I am of the Church,' he replied.

I was about to ask him if there were many people of his persuasion in these parts; before, however, I could do so he turned down a road to the right which led towards a small bridge, and saying that was his way home, bade me farewell and departed.

I arrived at Corwen which is just ten miles from Llangollen and which stands beneath a vast range of rocks at the head of the valley up which I had been coming, and which is called

Glyndyfrdwy, or the valley of the Dee water. It was now about two o'clock, and feeling rather thirsty I went to an inn very appropriately called the Owen Glendower, being the principal inn in the principal town of what was once the domain of the great Owen. Here I stopped for about an hour refreshing myself and occasionally looking into a newspaper in which was an excellent article on the case of poor Lieutenant P. I then started for Cerrig y Drudion, distant about ten miles, where I proposed to pass the night. Directing my course to the north-west, I crossed a bridge over the Dee water and then proceeded rapidly along the road, which for some way lay between corn-fields, in many of which sheaves were piled up, showing that the Welsh harvest was begun. I soon passed over a little stream the name of which I was told was Alowan. 'O, what a blessing it is to be able to speak Welsh!' said I, finding that not a person to whom I addressed myself had a word of English to bestow upon me. After walking for about five miles I came to a beau-tiful but wild country of mountain and wood with here and there a few cottages. The road at length making an abrupt turn to the north I found myself with a low stone wall on my left on the verge of a profound ravine, and a high bank covered with trees on my right. Projecting out over the ravine was a kind of looking place, protected by a wall, forming a half-circle, doubtless made by the proprietor of the domain for the use of the admirers of scenery. There I stationed myself, and for some time enjoyed one of the wildest and most beautiful scenes imaginable. Below me was the deep narrow glen or ravine down which a mountain torrent roared and foamed. Beyond it was a mountain rising steeply, its nearer side, which was in deep shade, the sun having long sunk below its top, hirsute with all kinds of trees, from the highest pinnacle down to the torrent's brink. Cut on the top surface of the wall, which was of slate and therefore easily impressible by the knife, were several names, doubtless those of tourists, who had gazed from the

look-out on the prospect, amongst which I observed in remarkably bold letters that of T . . .

'Eager for immortality Mr. T.,' said I; 'but you are no H. M.,
no Huw Morris.'

Leaving the looking place I proceeded, and, after one or two
turnings, came to another, which afforded a view if possible
yet more grand, beautiful and wild, the most prominent objects
of which were a kind of devil's bridge flung over the deep glen
and its foaming water, and a strange-looking hill beyond it,
below which with a wood on either side stood a white farmhouse – sending from a tall chimney a thin misty reek up to
the sky. I crossed the bridge, which however diabolically fantastical it looked at a distance, seemed when one was upon it,
capable of bearing any weight, and soon found myself by the
farm-house past which the way led. An aged woman sat on a
stool by the door.

'A fine evening,' said I in English.

'Dim Saesneg;' said the aged woman.

'O, the blessing of being able to speak Welsh,' said I; and
then repeated in that language what I had said to her in the
other tongue.

'I dare say,' said the aged woman, 'to those who can see.'

'Can you not see?'

'Very little. I am almost blind.'

'Can you not see me?'

'I can see something tall and dark before me; that is all.'

'Can you tell me the name of the bridge?'

'Pont y Glyn blin – the bridge of the glen of trouble.'

'And what is the name of this place?'

'Pen y bont – the head of the bridge.'

'What is your own name?'

'Catherine Hughes.'

'How old are you?'

'Fifteen after three twenties.'

'I have a mother three after four twenties; that is eight years older than yourself.'

'Can she see?'

'Better than I – she can read the smallest letters.'

'May she long be a comfort to you!'

'Thank you – are you the mistress of the house?'

'I am the grandmother.'

'Are the people in the house?'

'They are not – they are at the chapel.'

'And they left you alone?'

'They left me with my God.'

'Is the chapel far from here?'

'About a mile.'

'On the road to Cerrig y Drudion?'

'On the road to Cerrig y Drudion.'

I bade her farewell, and pushed on – the road was good, with high rocky banks on each side. After walking about the distance indicated by the old lady I reached a building, which stood on the right-hand side of the road, and which I had no doubt was the chapel from a half-groaning, half-singing noise which proceeded from it. The door being open I entered, and stood just within it, bare-headed. A rather singular scene presented itself. Within a large dimly-lighted room a number of people were assembled, partly seated in rude pews, and partly on benches. Beneath a kind of altar, a few yards from the door, stood three men – the middlemost was praying in Welsh in a singular kind of chant, with his arms stretched out. I could distinguish the words, 'Jesus descend among us! sweet Jesus descend among us – quickly.' He spoke very slowly, and towards the end of every sentence dropped his voice, so that what he said was anything but distinct. As I stood within the door a man dressed in coarse garments came up to me from the interior of the building, and courteously and in excellent Welsh, asked me to come with him and take a seat. With equal courtesy but far inferior Welsh, I assured him that I meant no harm, but wished to be permitted to remain near the door, whereupon with a low bow he left me. When the man had concluded his prayer the whole of the congregation began singing a hymn, many of the voices were gruff and discordant, two or three, however, were of great power, and some of the female ones of surprising sweetness – at the conclusion of the hymn another of the three men by the altar began to pray, just in the same manner as his comrade had done, and seemingly using much the same words. When he had done there was another hymn, after which seeing that the congregation was about to break up I bowed my head towards the interior of the building, and departed.

George Borrow, *Wild Wales*, 1862

There will be many footpaths in Utopia.

H. G. Wells, *Modern Utopia*, 1905

THE WORKERS TAKE A DAY OFF

There are some fields near Manchester, well known to the inhabitants as 'Green Heys Fields', through which runs a public footpath to a little village about two miles distant. In spite of these fields being flat, and low, nay, in spite of the want of wood (the great and usual recommendation of level tracts of land), there is a charm about them which strikes even the inhabitant of a mountainous district, who sees and feels the effect of contrast in these commonplace but thoroughly rural fields, with the busy, bustling manufacturing town he left but half-an-hour ago. Here and there an old black farmhouse, with its rambling outbuildings, speaks of other times and other occupations than those which now absorb the neighbourhood. You cannot wonder, then, that these fields are popular places of resort at every holiday time; and you would not wonder, if you could see, or I properly describe, the charm of one particular style, that it should be, on such occasions a crowded halting place. Close by it is a deep, clear pond, reflecting in its dark green depths the shadowy trees that bend over it to exclude the sun. The only place where its banks are shelving is on the side next to a rambling farmyard, belonging to one of those Old World, gabled, black and white houses I named above, overlooking the field through which the public footpath leads.

I do not know whether it was on a holiday granted by the masters, or a holiday seized in right of Nature and her beautiful springtime by the workmen, but one afternoon (now ten or a dozen years ago) these fields were much thronged. It was an early May evening – the April of the poets; for heavy showers had fallen all the morning, and the round, soft, white clouds which were blown by a west wind over the dark blue sky, were sometimes varied by one blacker and more threatening. The softness of the day tempted forth the young green leaves, which almost visibly fluttered into life; and the willows, which that morning had only a brown reflection in the water below, were now of that tender grey-green which blends so delicately with the spring harmony of colours.

Groups of merry and somewhat loud talking girls, whose ages might range from twelve to twenty, came by with a buoyant step. They were most of them factory girls, and wore the usual out-of-doors dress of that particular class of maidens; namely, a shawl which at midday or in fine weather was allowed to be merely a shawl, but towards evening, if the day was chilly, became a sort of Spanish mantilla or Scotch plaid, and was brought over the head and hung loosely down, or was pinned under the chin in no un-picturesque fashion.

Their faces were not remarkable for beauty; indeed, they were below the average, with one or two exceptions; they had dark hair, neatly and classically arranged, dark eyes but sallow complexions and irregular features. The only thing to strike a passer-by was an acuteness and intelligence of countenance, which has often been noticed in a manufacturing population.

There were also numbers of boys, or rather young men, rambling among these fields, ready to bandy jokes with anyone, and particularly ready to enter into conversations with the girls, who, however, held themselves aloof, not in a shy, but rather in an independent way, assuming an indifferent manner to the noisy wit or obstreperous compliments of the lads. Here and there came a sober, quiet couple, either whispering lovers, or husband and wife, as the case may be; and if the latter, they were seldom unencumbered by an infant, carried for the most part by the father, while occasionally, even three or four little toddlers had been carried or dragged thus far, in order that the whole family might enjoy the delicious May afternoon together.

Elizabeth Gaskell, *Mary Barton*, 1848

OUR FEET ABSORB THE EARTH'S GOODNESS

All the parts of the earth's surface on which we tread will fulfil a particular service of life for the health of the body. This if we walk on the young and living grass we shall receive its fresh and living – yet soothing – virtue. If we walk on the mountain turf, *not* in the sun's rays, we shall receive the very strength of the mountain.

If we walk in a pine-wood, an oak wood, a birch or larch wood we shall surely receive of the peculiar virtues of these fragrant creatures of Life. If we walk on the sands of the sea we shall taste the various qualities of the salts therein. If we walk on dry clay or mud we shall at once recognise that the nutrition thus imparted to our nerval body is finer or more comforting than that conveyed through rough sand or fine shingle.

If you walk on the red-land you will absorb of the blood of Demeter and if you walk on the mountains' rocky sides you will absorb of her various elementary virtues, and they will nourish your finer body. If you walk in a hill-burn you will taste the trout of the hill-burn. It is only to be compared to that of the mountain lamb, whose joy you will taste by walking among the bonnie wee beasties over the grassy braes.

And if you wish to know even for once the fine intoxication of the radiant energy of the sun, you will soon get it by walking over the sun baked pavements of the city.

Wondrous it is the bounty of Nature!

James Leith Macbeth Bain, *The Barefoot League*, 1914

THE AUTHOR GOES ON AND ON

Irving was in a sort the Captain of our expedition; had been there before; could recommend everything – was made (unjustly by us) quasi-responsible for everything. The Trosachs I found really grand and impressive, Loch Katrine exquisitely so (my first taste of the beautiful in scenery); not so, any of us, the dirty smoky farm-hut at the entrance, with no provision in it, but bad oatcakes and unacceptable whisky, or the 'Mr. Stewart' who somewhat royally presided over it, and dispensed these dainties, expecting to be flattered like an independency, as well as paid like an innkeeper. Poor Irving could not help it: – but in fine the rains, the hardships, the ill diet were beginning to act on us all; and I could perceive we were in danger (what I have since found usual) of splitting into two parties; Brown (eight or ten years my senior) leader of the Opposition, myself considerably flattered by him; though *not* seduced by him into factious courses, only led to see how strong poor Pears was for the Government interest! This went to no length, never bigger than a summer cloud, or the incipiency of one; but Brown, in secret, would never quite let it die out (a jealous kind of man, I gradually found; had been much commended to us, by Irving, as of superior intellect and honesty, – which qualities I likewise found in him, though with the above abatement); and there were, or were like to be, divisions of vote in the walking Parliament, two against two; and had there not been at this point, by a kind of outward and legitimate reason, what proved very sanatory in the case, an actual division of routes, the folly might have lasted longer and become audible and visible, which it never did. Sailing up Loch Katrine, in the top or unpicturesque part, Irving and Pears settled with us (house fully heard) that only we two should go across Loch Lomond, round by Tarbet, Roseneath, Greenock; they meanwhile making direct for Paisley country (where they had business); and so on stepping out, and paying our boatman, they said adieu, and at once struck leftward, we going straight ahead; rendezvous to be at Glasgow again, on such and such a day. [What feeble trash is all this; ah me, no better than Irving's 'penny-wheep' with the gas *gone out* of it! Stop to-day, *4th October* 1866.]

The heath was bare, trackless, sun going almost down; Brown and I (our friends soon disappearing) had an interesting march, good part of it dark, and flavoured just to the right pitch with something of anxiety and sense of danger. The sinking sun threw his reflexes on a tame-looking House with many windows, some way to our right, – the '*Kharrison*' of *Infersnaidt*' (an ancient Anti-*Rob Roy* establishment), as two rough Highland wayfarers had lately informed us; other house or person we did not see; but made for the shoulder of Ben Lomond and the Boatman's Hut, partly, I think, by the Stars. Boatman and Huthold were in bed; but he, with a ragged little Sister or Wife cheerfully roused themselves; cheerfully, and for most part in silence, rowed us across (under the spangled vault of midnight, which with the Lake waters silent as if in deep dream, and several miles broad here, had their due impression on us) correctly to Tarbet, a most hospitable, clean, and welcome little country inn (now a huge 'Hotel' I hear, – worse luck to it, with its nasty 'Hotel Company, Limited!'). – On awakening next morning, I heard from below the sound of a churn; prophecy of new genuine butter, or even of ditto rustic butter-milk.

Brown and I did very well on our separate branch of pilgrimage; pleasant walk and talk down to the west margin of the Loch (incomparable among Lochs or Lakes yet known to me), past Smollett's Pillar, emerge pleasantly on Helensburgh, on the view of Greenock, and across the Roseneath Manse, where with a Rev. Mr. Story, not yet quite inducted, – whose *Life* has since been published – who was an acquaintance of Brown's, we were warmly welcomed and well entertained for a couple of days. Story I never saw again; – but he, acquainted in Haddington neighbourhood, saw some time after, incidentally, a certain Bright Figure, to whom I am obliged to him at this moment for speaking favourably of me! 'Talent Plenty; fine vein of satire in him!' something like that; – I suppose they had been talking of Irving, whom both of them knew and liked well; *Her*, probably, at that time I had still never seen; but she told me long afterwards. We have had Story's Son, *Biographer* and Successor, here once; who considerably resembles him, but is not so smart and clever.

At Greenock I first saw *Steamers* on the water; queer little dumpy things, with a red sail to each (and legible name, '*Defiance*' and such like), bobbing about there, and making continual passages to Glasgow as their business. Not till about two years later (1819, if I mistake not), did Forth see a Steamer; Forth's first was far bigger than the Greenock ones, and called itself '*The Tug*,' being intended for towing ships in those narrow waters, as I have often seen it doing.

Those old three days at Roseneath are all very vivid to me,

and marked in white: the great blue mountain masses, giant 'Cobler' overhanging, bright seas, bright skies; Roseneath new Mansion (still unfinished, and standing as it did, the present Duke of Argyll has told me), the grand old oaks, – and a certain handfast, middle-aged, practical and most polite 'Mr. Campbell' (the Argyll Factor there), with his two Sisters, excellent lean old ladies with their wild Highland accent, wiredrawn but genuine good-manners and good principles, – and not least their astonishment, and shrill interjections, at once of love and fear, over the talk they contrived to get out of me one evening and perhaps another, when we went across to tea: – all this is still pretty to me to remember. They are all dead, these good souls (Campbell himself, the Duke told me, died only lately, very old); but they were, to my rustic eyes, of a superior, richly furnished stratum of society; and the new thought that I too might perhaps be 'one-and-somewhat' (*Ein und Etwas*) among my fellow-creatures by and by, was secretly very welcome at their hands. We rejoined Irving and Pears at Glasgow (transit, place of meeting uterly forgotten); I remember our glad embarkation in a track-boat towards Paisley by canal; visit preappointed for us at Paisley by Irving, in a good old lady's house, whose son was Irving's boarder; the dusty, sunny Glasgow evening; and my friend's joy to see Brown and me (or *me* and Brown, I might perhaps put it, as *his* thought). Irving was very good and jocund-hearted: most blithe his good old lady, whom I had seen at Kirkcaldy before; and we had a pleasant day or two in those neighbourhoods; the picturesque, the comic, and the genially common all prettily combining, particulars now much forgotten. Pears went to eastward, Dunse, his native country; 'born i' Dunse,' equal in sound to *born a dunce* as Irving's laugh would sometimes remind him; 'opposition party' (except it were in the secret of Brown's jealous heart) there was now none. Irving, in truth, was the natural King [of walking] among us; and his qualities of captaincy in such a matter were indisputable.

Brown, he, and I went by the Falls of Clyde; I do not recollect the rest of our route.

Thomas Carlyle, Reminiscences, 1881

MARCH OF THE CLOUDS

A bank of low black clouds, which had appeared on the southern horizon after midday, began to draw nearer as I walked the last few miles into Appleby. A dark cloak was spread across the sky, and beneath its creeping shadow the face of the earth grew cold and sullen. Only the north, whence I had come, held warmth and brightness, and there too the change must soon come. I watched the slow advance of a mighty host, marching with inexorable purpose. I saw detachments sent on ahead, forerunners that drifted rapidly above in ragged array and became wisps of smoke where the sun glinted on them. But the main mass was resolute; nothing could stay its approach. Cloud piled upon cloud; their heavens before me were a tumult of writhing shapes, as though the earth were smouldering and sending up great coils of heavy smoke. A powerful force was working within this vast assembly, urging them ever onwards, but creating discord and strife so that they came not in harmony but in seething discontent, an angry quarrelsome, agitated mob. There was an evil portent in their convulsive movements, in their weighty ponderous appearance, in their colour. They were black where they overhung the countryside, an ominous grey above, where the wind kept them constantly mobile. Only aloft were the white banners displayed.

I raced the rain into Appleby.

Arthur Wainwright, A Pennine Journey, 1986

RAIN IS A LIVELY COMPANION

Rain was universal; a thick robe of it swept from hill to hill; thunder rumbled remote, and between the ruffled roars the downpour pressed on the land with a great noise of eager gobbling, much like that of the swine's trough fresh filled, as though a vast assembly of the hungered had seated themselves clamorously and fallen to on meats and drinks in a silence, save of the chaps. A rapid walker poetically and humourously minded gathers multitudes of images on his way. And rain, the heaviest you can meet, is a lively companion when the resolute pacer scorns discomfort of wet clothes and squealing boots. South-western rain-clouds, too, are never long sullen: they enfold and will have the earth in a good strong glut of the kissing overflow; then, as a hawk with feathers on his beak of the bird in his claw lifts head, they rise and take veiled feature in long climbing watery lines: at any moment they may break the veil and show soft upper cloud, show sun on it, show sky, green near the verge they spring from, of the green of grass in early dew; or, along a travelling sweep that rolls asunder overhead, heaven's laughter of purest blue among titanic white shoulders: it may mean fair smiling for awhile, or be the lightest interlude; but the water lines, and the drifting, the chasing, the upsoaring, all in a shadowy fingering of form, and the animation of the leaves of the trees pointing them on, the bending of the tree-tops, the snapping of branches, and the hurrahings of the stubborn hedge at wrestle with the flaws, yielding but a leaf at most, and that on a fling, make a glory of contest and wildness without aid of colour to inflame the man who is at home in them from old association on road, heath, and mountain. Let him be drenched, his heart will sing. And thou, trim cockney, that jeerest, consider thyself, to whom it may occur to be out in such a scene, and with what steps of a nervous dancing-master it would be thine to play the hunted rat of the elements, for the preservation of the one imagined dry spot about thee, somewhere on thy luckless person! The taking of rain and sun alike befits men of our climate, and he who would have the secret of a strengthening intoxication must court the clouds of the South-west with a lover's blood.

Vernon's happy recklessness was dashed by fears for Miss Middleton. Apart from those fears, he had the pleasure of a gull wheeling among foam-streaks of the wave. He supposed the Swiss and Tyrol Alps to have hidden their heads from him for many a day to come, and the springing and chiming South-west was the next best thing. A milder rain descended; the country expanded darkly defined underneath the moving curtain; the clouds were as he liked to see them, scaling; but their skirts dragged. Torrents were in store, for they coursed streamingly still and had not the higher life, or eagle ascent, – which he knew for one of the signs of fairness, nor had the hills any belt of mist-like vapour.

On a step of the stile leading to the short-cut to Rendon young Crossjay was espied. A man-tramp sat on the top-bar:

'There you are; what are you doing there? Where's Miss Middleton?' said Vernon. 'Now, take care before you open your mouth.'

Crossjay shut the mouth he had opened.

'The lady has gone away over to a station, sir,' said the tramp.

'You fool!' roared Crossjay, ready to fly at him.

'But ain't it now, young gentleman? Can you say it ain't?'

'I gave you a shilling, you ass!'

'You give me that sum, young gentleman, to stop here and take care of you, and here I stopped.'

'Mr Whitford!' Crossjay appealed to his master, and broke off in disgust. 'Take care of me! As if anybody who knows me would think I wanted taking care of! Why, what a beast you must be, you fellow!'

'Just as you like, young gentleman. I chaunted you all I know, to keep up your downcast spirits. You did want comforting. You wanted it rarely. You cried like an infant.'

'I let you "chaunt", as you call it, to keep you from swearing.'

'And why did I swear, young gentleman? because I've got an itchy coat in the wet, and no shirt for a lining. And no breakfast to give me a stomach for this kind of weather. That's what I've come to in this world! I'm a walking moral. No wonder I swears, when I don't strike up a chaunt.'

'But why are you sitting here wet through, Crossjay! Be off home at once, and change, and get ready for me.'

'Mr Whitford, I promised, and I tossed this fellow a shilling not to go bothering Miss Middleton.'

'The lady wouldn't have none o' the young gentleman, sir, and I offered to go pioneer for her to the station, behind her, at a respectful distance.'

'As if! – you treacherous cur!' Crossjay ground his teeth at the betrayer. 'Well, Mr Whitford, and I didn't trust him, and I stuck to him, or he'd have been after her whining about his coat and stomach, and talking of his being a moral. He repeats that to everybody.'

'She has gone to the station?' said Vernon.

Not a word on that subject was to be won from Crossjay.

'How long since?' Vernon partly addressed Mr Tramp.

The latter became seized with shivers as he supplied the information that it might be a quarter of an hour or twenty minutes. 'But what's time to me, sir? If I had reg'lar meals, I should carry a clock in my inside. I got the rheumatics instead.'

'Way there!' Vernon cried, and took the stile at a vault.

'That's what gentlemen can do, who sleeps in their beds warm,' moaned the tramp. 'They've no joints.'

Vernon handed him a half-crown piece, for he had been of use for once.

'Mr Whitford, let me come. If you tell me to come I may.

Do let me come,' Crossjay begged with great entreaty. 'I sha'nt see her for ...'

'Be off, quick!' Vernon cut him short and pushed on.

The tramp and Crossjay were audible to him; Crossjay spurning the consolations of the professional sad man.

Vernon spun across the fields, timing himself by his watch to reach Rendon station ten minutes before eleven, though without clearly questioning the nature of the resolution which precipitated him. Dropping to the road, he had better foothold than on the slippery field-path, and he ran. His principal hope was that Clara would have missed her way. Another pelting of rain agitated him on her behalf. Might she not as well be suffered to go? – and sit three hours and more in a railway-carriage with wet feet!

George Meredith, *The Egoist*, 1879

THE STREAM INVITES US TO FOLLOW

The stream invites us to follow: the impulse is so common that it might be set down as instinct; and certainly there is no more fascinating pastime than to keep company with a river from its source to the sea. Unfortunately, this is not easy in a country where running waters have been enclosed, which should be free as the rain and sunshine to all, and were once free, when England was England still, before landowners annexed them, even as they annexed or stole the commons and shut up the footpaths and made it an offence for a man to go aside from the road to feel God's grass under his feet. Well, they have also got the road now, and cover and blind and choke us with its dust and insolently hoot-hoot at us. Out of the way, miserable crawlers, if you don't want to be smashed! They have got the roads and have a Parliament of motorists to maintain them in possession, but it yet remains to be seen whether or not they will be able to keep them.

Sometimes the way is cut off by huge thorny hedges and fences of barbed wire – man's devilish improvement on the bramble – brought down to the water's edge. The river-follower must force his way through these obstacles, in most cases greatly to the detriment of his clothes and temper – or, should they prove impassable, he must undress and go into the water.

W. H. Hudson, *Afoot in England*, 1903

MEETINGS WITH MANY FISH

My favourite before-breakfast walk in this 'up-state' home of mine was along the river by the edge of a spinney about half a mile from my house. To reach this I had to scramble along a little bank whose twisted tree-roots, emerging from the mud, reminded me of the higher bank at Sherborne above Lover's Lane where I used to climb with Littleton. It pleased me to think that the skill I had acquired at eleven, in clinging to tree roots on a sloping declivity, had remained with me to be used at sixty-one; but this was nothing to the pleasure I got when, walking along the river's edge, looking for trout or the little fishes called 'shiners', I suddenly thought of the Wissey and of the intense eagerness with which Littleton and I followed its windings looking for roach and dace.

John Cowper Powys, *Autobiography*, 1934

MEETINGS WITH STRANGE PLANTS

Florida is so watery and vine-tied that pathless wanderings are not easily possible in any direction. I started to cross the State by a gap hewn for the locomotive, walking sometimes between the rails, stepping from tie to tie, or walking on the strip of sand at the sides, gazing into the mysterious forest, Nature's own. It is impossible to write the dimmest picture of plant grandeur so redundant, unfathomable.

Short was the measure of my walk to-day. A new, canelike grass, or big lily, or gorgeous flower belonging to tree or vine, would catch my attention, and I would throw down my bag and press and splash through the coffee-brown water for specimens. Frequently I sank deeper and deeper until compelled to turn back and make the attempt in another and still another place. Oftentimes I was tangled in a labyrinth of armed vines like a fly in a spider-web. At all times, whether wading or climbing a tree for specimens of fruit, I was overwhelmed with the vastness and unapproachableness of the great guarded sea of sunny plants.

Magnolia grandiflora I had seen in Georgia; but its home, its better land, is here. Its large dark-green leaves, glossy bright above and rusty brown beneath, gleam and mirror the sunbeams most gloriously among countless flowerheaps of the climbing, smothering vines. It is bright also in fruit and more tropical in form and expression than the orange. It speaks itself a prince among its fellows.

Occasionally, I came to a little strip of open sand, planted with pine (*Pinus palustris* or *Cubensis*). Even these spots were mostly wet, though lighted with free sunshine, and adorned with purple liatris, and orange-coloured *Osmunda cinnamomea*. But the grandest discovery of this great wild day was the palmetto.

I was meeting so many strange plants that I was much excited, making many stops to get specimens. But I could not force my way far through the swampy forest, although so tempting and full of promise. Regardless of water snakes or insects, I endeavoured repeatedly to force a way through the tough vine-tangles, but seldom succeeded in getting farther than a few hundred yards.

It was while feeling sad to think that I was only walking on the edge of the vast wood, that I caught sight of the first palmetto in a grassy place, standing almost alone. A few magnolias were near it, and bald cypresses, but it was not shaded by them. They tell us that plants are perishable, soulless creatures, that only man is immortal, etc.; but this, I think, is something that we know very nearly nothing about. Anyway, this palm was indescribably impressive and told me grander things than I ever got from human priest.

This vegetable has a plain grey shaft, round as a broom-handle, and a crown of varnished channelled leaves. It is a plainer plant than the humblest of Wisconsin oaks; but, whether rocking and rustling in the wind or poised thoughtful and calm in the sunshine, it has a power of expression not excelled by any plant high or low that I have met in my whole walk thus far.

This, my first specimen, was not very tall, only about twenty-five feet high, with fifteen or twenty leaves, arching equally and evenly all around. Each leaf was about ten feet in length, the blade four feet, the stalk six. The leaves are channelled like half-open clams and are highly polished, so that they reflect the sunlight like glass. The undeveloped leaves on the top stand erect, closely folded, all together forming an oval crown over which the tropic light is poured and reflected from its slanting mirrors in sparks and splinters and long-rayed stars.

I am now in the hot gardens of the sun, where the palm meets the pine, longed and prayed for and often visited in dreams, and, though lonely tonight amid this multitude of strangers, strange plants, strange winds blowing gently, whispering, cooing, in a language I never learned, and strange birds also, everything solid or spiritual full of influences that I never before felt, yet I thank the Lord with all my heart for his goodness in granting me admission to this magnificent realm.

John Muir, *A Thousand Mile Walk to the Gulf*, 1916

BIRDSONG

Thus I went wide-where, walking alone,
In a wide wilderness, by a wood-side.
Bliss of the birds song made me abide there,
And on a lawn under a linden I leaned awhile
To listen to their lays, their lovely notes.

William Langland, *Piers Plowman*, 1367–86 (1550 edition)

SOME REMARKABLE TREES

Our autumn walks were delightful: the sun ceased to scorch; the want of flowers was no longer peculiar to Ohio; and the trees took a colouring, which in richness, brilliance and variety, exceed all description. I think it is the maple, or sugar tree, that first sprinkles the forest with rich crimson; the beech follows, with all its harmony of golden tints, from pale yellow up to brightest orange. The dogwood gives almost the purple colour of the mulberry; the chestnut softens all with its frequent mass of delicate brown, and the sturdy oak carries its deep green into the very lap of winter. These tints are too bright for the landscape painter; the attempt to follow nature in an American autumn scene must be abortive.

Frances Trollope, *Domestic Manners of the Americans*, 1832

SECLUSION

On a frosty morning with a little February sun, Clifford and Connie went for a walk across the park to the wood. That is, Clifford chuffed in his motor-chair, and Connie walked beside him.

The hard air was still sulphurous, but they were both used

to it. Round the near horizon went the haze, opalescent with frost and smoke, and on the top lay the small blue sky; so that it was like being inside an enclosure, always inside. Life always a dream or a frenzy, inside an enclosure.

The sheep coughed in the rough, sere grass of the park, where frost lay bluish in the sockets of the tufts. Across the park ran a path to the wood-gate, a fine ribbon of pink. Clifford had had it newly gravelled with sifted gravel from the pit-bank. When the rock and refuse of the underworld had burned and given off its sulphur, it turned bright pink, shrimp-coloured on dry days, darker, crab-coloured on wet. Now it was pale shrimp-colour, with a bluish-white hoar of frost. It always pleased Connie, this underfoot of sifted, bright pink. It's an ill wind that brings nobody good.

Clifford steered cautiously down the slope of the knoll from the hall, and Connie kept her hand on the chair. In front lay the wood, the hazel thicket nearest, the purplish density of oaks beyond. From the wood's edge rabbits bobbed and nibbled. Rooks suddenly rose in a black train, and went trailing off over the little sky.

Connie opened the wood-gate, and Clifford puffed slowly through into the broad riding that ran up an incline between the clean-whipped thickets of the hazel. The wood was a remnant of the great forest where Robin Hood hunted, and this riding was an old, old thoroughfare coming across country. But now, of course, it was only a riding through the private wood. The road from Mansfield swerved round to the north.

In the wood everything was motionless, the old leaves on the ground keeping the frost on their underside. A jay called harshly, many little birds fluttered. But there was no game; no pheasants. They had been killed off during the war, and the wood had been left unprotected, till now Clifford had got his game-keeper again.

Clifford loved the wood; he loved the old oak-trees. He felt they were his own through generations. He wanted to protect them. He wanted this place inviolate, shut off from the world.

The chair chuffed slowly up the incline, rocking and jolting on the frozen clods. And suddenly, on the left, came a clearing where there was nothing but a ravel of dead bracken, a thin and spindly sapling leaning here and there, big sawn stumps, showing their tops and their grasping roots, lifeless. And patches of blackness where the woodmen had burned the brushwood and rubbish.

This was one of the places that Sir Geoffrey had cut during the war for trench timber. The whole knoll, which rose softly on the right of the riding, was denuded and strangely forlorn. On the crown of the knoll where the oaks had stood, now was bareness; and from there you could look out over the trees to the colliery railway, and the new works at Stacks Gate. Connie had stood and looked, it was a breach in the pure seclusion of the wood. It let in the world. But she didn't tell Clifford.

This denuded place always made Clifford curiously angry. He had been through the war, had seen what it meant. But he didn't get really angry till he saw his bare hill. He was having it replanted. But it made him hate Sir Geoffrey.

Clifford sat with a fixed face as the chair slowly mounted. When they came to the top of the rise he stopped; he would not risk the long and very jolty down-slope. He sat looking at the greenish sweep of the riding downwards, a clear way through the bracken and oaks. It swerved at the bottom of the hill and disappeared; but it had such a lovely easy curve, of knights riding and ladies on palfreys.

'I consider this is really the heart of England,' said Clifford to Connie, as he sat there in the dim February sunshine.

'Do you?' she said, seating herself, in her blue knitted dress, on a stump by the path.

'I do! This is the old England, the heart of it; and I intend to keep it intact.'

'Oh yes!' said Connie. But as she said it she heard the eleven o'clock hooters at Stacks Gate colliery. Clifford was too used to the sound to notice.

'I want this wood perfect ... untouched. I want nobody to trespass in it,' said Clifford.

There was a certain pathos. The wood still had some of the mystery of wild, old England; but Sir Geoffrey's cuttings during the war had given it a blow. How still the trees were, with their crinkly, innumerable twigs against the sky, and their grey, obstinate trunks rising from the brown bracken! How safely the birds flitted among them! And once there had been deer, and archers, and monks padding on asses. The place remembered, still remembered.

D. H. Lawrence, *Lady Chatterley's Lover*, 1928

LOST IN A PUBLIC PARK

Following the spring in the other direction led me deeper and deeper into damp scrub. It seemed pointlessly timid to stay to the paths in such a place, so I began to scrabble through the dense bushes. In a while I came to the realisation that after four months' ferreting round labyrinthine gravel pits and over-grown wastelands hundreds of acres in extent, I had got myself lost in a public park.

Of course I was not really lost. If I had walked a straight quarter-of-a-mile in any direction I could not have failed to strike a road, or at least a well-used path. But the illusion was there. I could see and hear not a single human sound. I had no idea what lay in front of me, nor the direction I ought to take to get out of this swamp. It is chastening to have this experience once in a while. It reminds you of your place – which in the countryside, unlike the town, is usually as an ill-adapted, clumsy intruder. I was given a sharp and sudden lesson in how literally true this is when I suddenly went down to my knees in the mud. I really ought to have known better, I decided, eyeing the telltale rust-coloured films on the soil as I dragged my suèdes clear. It was no excuse to say that those few seconds of disorientation had made me quicken my pace. Yet I was a little proud of my caked jeans. I'd got my hands dirty – or at least my feet – some sort of evidence of a job done. Weeks of watching from comfortable Greenline seats and park benches had made me feel a little soft and guilty.

Feeling smug about my hard morning down t'park lasted just until I took my lunchtime pint, and the broiling July sun started to make me smell like a sewerworker. I retired to a dark corner of the pub in some embarrassment – which was just as well, since as anyone who has ever had their feet caked with hog mud will have predicted, itches started of such devastation that I had to rip my shoes and socks off and dry my feet with pages torn from my notebook. And burning a hole on my lap were those damned binoculars again. I began to feel like a thinly disguised bumpkin spy parachuted down in the wrong country.

But that spell of sobering drying-out was some way off yet. There were the woods to the north still to be explored, cool, spacious groves of oak, birch and chestnut. The paths into them were thickly grassed, good for wiping the mud off, and worn to just the openness they needed by the walkers who used them. There was not much ground vegetation left inside the woods themselves, and no sign of the bluebells and wood anemones that once grew here in profusion. But at least the ground was honest soil, not yet plastered over with asphalt or gravel paths. I found two new balsams here, the small yellow in a dark corner, and some young shoots of the Himalayan balsam (known as policeman's helmet from the shape of its bell-shaped flowers) at the edge of one of the wood bogs, which for the benefit of the foot-loose, are clearly marked in these open areas by red signs. And there were nuthatches, crisp blue and chestnut, trilling in the top branches.

I was allowed one more treat before departing to show off my ham-footedness, when I tracked down a grey squirrel by his querulous chatter. He was up in the top of an old hawthorn, only feet away from his drey – which could well have contained young at this time of year and accounted for the creature's peevish slanging. He was a wild and stringy fellow, not at all like his elegant cousins in Regent's Park, and he leaned forward on the branch to curse me more effectively.

Richard Mabey, *The Unofficial Countryside*, 1973

HONORARY PRESIDENT OF THE RAMBLERS' ASSOCIATION

Sir Jack enjoyed marching out across land belonging to others. He would raise his stick approvingly at the cut-out cows on the hillside, the shire horses in bell-bottoms, the rolls of hay like Shredded Wheat. But he never made the mistake of imagining that any of it was simple, or natural.

He entered a wood, nodding to a couple of young hikers coming the other way. Did he hear a snicker pass between them? Perhaps they were surprised by his tweed deerstalker, hunter's jacket, cavalry twills, gaiters, hand-crafted doe-skin boots and fell-walker's stave. All made in England, of course: Sir Jack was a patriot in his private moments too. The receding hikers were dressed in shell-suits of industrial colour, with rubber trainers below, baseball caps above and nylon day-packs behind; one wore earpieces and in all probability was not listening to the Mighty Pastoral. But again, Sir Jack was not a snob. There had been a motion before the Ramblers'

Association a few years ago proposing that walkers be obliged to wear colours which blended with the landscape. Sir Jack had fought that motion tooth and nail, root and branch. He had described the proposal as fantastical, élitist, unworkable and undemocratic. Besides, he was not without his interests in the leisurewear market.

The path through the wood, several generations of springy beech leaves, was quilted underfelt. Layered fungi on a rotting bog made a Corbusier maquette of workers' dwellings. Genius has the ability to transform: thus the nightingale, the quail and the cuckoo became the flute, the oboe and the clarinet. And yet was not genius also the ability to see things as with the eyes of an innocent child?

He left the wood and climbed a small hill: below him, an undulating field led down past a copse to a thin river. He leaned on his stick and brooded on his meeting with Jerry Batson. Not exactly a patriot, in Jack's view. Something a bit evasive about him. Didn't meet you man to man, didn't look you in the eye, out there in a trance like a haute-couture hippie. Still, if you crossed his palm with silver, Jerry would usually put his finger on it for you. Time. You are as old, and exactly as old, as you are. A statement so apparently obvious that it was almost mystical. So how old was Sir Jack? Older than it said on his passport, that was for sure. How much time did he have? There were moments when he felt strange misgivings. In his personal bathroom at Pitman House, athwart his porphyry toilet, a sense of frailty would sometimes come upon him. An ignoble end, to be caught with your trousers down.

No, no! This was not the way to think. Not little Jacky Pitman, not Jolly Jack, not Sir Jack, not the future Lord Pitman of wherever he chose. No, he must keep moving, he must act, he must not wait for time, he must seize time by the throat. On, on! He swiped at a thicket with his stave and disturbed a pheasant, which rose heavily into the air, its fairisle sweater aflap, whirring off like a model aeroplane with a wonky propeller.

The clean October breeze was sharpening as he followed the edge of an escarpment. A rusting wind-pump offered itself as a cheeky cockerel by Picasso. He could already see a few early lights in the distance: a village of commuters, a pub returned to authenticity by the brewers. His journey was ending too quickly. Not yet, thought Sir Jack, not yet! He felt at times such kinship with old Ludwig, and it was true that magazine profiles of Sir Jack frequently used the word genius. Not always embedded in flattering contexts, but then, as he said, there were only two kinds of journalist: those he employed, and those employed by envious rivals. And they could have chosen another word, after all. But where was his Ninth Symphony? Was this it, stirring within him at the moment? It was purely the case that if Beethoven had died after completing only eight, the world would still have recognized him as a mighty figure. But the Ninth, the Ninth!

A jay flew past, advertising the new season's car colours. A beech hedge flamed like anti-corrosion paint. If only we could dip ourselves in that ... *Muss es sein?* Any Beethovenian – and Sir Jack counted himself among their number – knew the reply to that one. *Es muss sein.* But only after the Ninth.

He cross-fastened his hunter's collar against the rising wind, and set course for a gap in a distant hedge. A double brandy at The Dog and Badger, whose mutton-chopped host would patriotically waive the bill – 'A pleasure and an honour as always, Sir Jack' – then the limo back to London. Normally, he would fill the car with the Pastoral, but not today, perhaps. The Third? The Fifth? Dare he risk the Ninth? As he reached the hedge, a crow took silk and wing.

Julian Barnes, *England England*, 1998

SIGNS THAT KEEP YOU GOING

Wednesday 4th December

An immaculately clear, cool morning. Everything is hazy on the plain, but one can hear life down there. The mountains, full and distinct in front of me, some elevated fog and, in between, a cool daytime moon, only half visible, opposite the sun. I walk straight between sun and moon. How exhilarating. Vineyards, sparrows, everything's so fresh. The night was pretty bad, no sleep from three o'clock on; in the morning making up for it, the boots have lost their painful places and the legs are in order. The cool smoke of a factory rises calmly and vertically. Do I hear ravens? Yes, and dogs as well.

Thursday 5th December

A rainbow before me all at once fills me with the greatest confidence. What a sign it is, over and in front of him who walks. Everyone should walk.

Werner Herzog, *Of Walking in Ice*, 1978
(trans. Alan Greenberg and Martje Herzog, 1980)

RECOLLECTIONS AFTER AN EVENING WALK

Just as the even-bell rang, we set out
To wander the fields and the meadow about;
And the first thing we mark'd that was lovely to view
Was the sun hung on nothing, just bidding adieu:
He seem'd like a ball of pure gold in the west,
In a cloud like a mountain blue, dropping to rest;
The skies all around him were ting'd with his rays,
And the trees at a distance seem'd all on a blaze,
Till, lower and lower, he sank from our sight,

And the blue mist came creeping with silence and night.
The woodman then ceas'd with his hatchet to hack,
And bent away home with his kid on his back;
The mower, too, lapt up his scythe from our sight,
And put on his jacket, and bid us good night;
The thresher once lumping, we heard him no more,
He left his barn-dust, and had shut up his door;
The shepherd had told all his sheep in his pen,
And humming his song, sought his cottage agen:
But the sweetest of all seeming music to me
Were the songs of the clumsy brown-beetle and bee;
The one was seen hast'ning away to his hive,
The other was just from his sleeping alive –
'Gainst our hats he kept knocking as if he'd no eyes,
And when batter'd down he was puzzled to rise.
The little gay moth, too, was lovely to view,
A-dancing with lily-white wings in the dew;
He whisk'd o'er the water-pudge flirting and airy,
And perch'd on the down-headed grass like a fairy.
And there came the snail from his shell peeping out,
As fearful and cautious as thieves on the rout;
The sly jumping frog, too, had ventur'd to tramp,
And the glow-worm had just 'gun to light up his lamp;
To sip of the dew the worm peep'd from his den,
But dreading our footsteps soon vanish'd agen:
And numbers of creatures appear'd in our sight,
That live in the silence and sweetness of night,
Climbing up the tall grasses or scaling the bough,
But these were all nameless, unnotic'd till now.
And then we wound round 'neath the brook's willow row,
And look'd at the clouds that kept passing below;
The moon's image too, in the brook we could see't,
As if 'twas the other world under our feet;
And we listen'd well pleas'd at the guggles and groans

The water made passing the pebbles and stones.
And then we turn'd up by the rut-rifted lane,
And sought for our cot and the village again;
For night gather'd round, and shut all from the eye,
And a black sultry cloud crept all over the sky;
The dew on the bush, soon as touch'd it would drop,
And the grass 'neath our feet was as wet as a mop:
And, as to the town we approach'd very fast,
The bat even popp'd in our face as he past;
And the crickets sang loud as we went by the house,
And by the barn-side we saw many a mouse
Quirking round for the kernels that, litter'd about,
Were shook from the straw which the thresher hurl'd out.
And then we came up to our cottage once more,
And shut out the night-dew, and lock'd up the door;
The dog bark'd a welcome, well-pleas'd at our sight,
And the owl o'er our cot flew, and whoop'd a 'good night.'

John Clare, 'Recollections After an Evening Walk', 1821

MIRAGE

On our evening walks, the boys go off in one direction, Balu in another, myself in a third, and the ladies in yet another. In the meantime the sun goes down, its golden glow fades from the sky, things become vague in the darkness, until gradually my own faint shadow tells me that the thin crescent moon is casting her light. Pale white moonlight on pale sand somehow tricks the eyes – which is sand? which the water? which the land? and which the sky? The confusing illusion makes the whole world seem like a mirage.

Rabindranath Tagore, *Glimpses of Bengal*, 1921
(trans. Andrew Robinson and Krishna Dutta, 1991)

FIVE

On the Road

I could follow those long, straight, flat monotonous roads for miles and miles, north, south, east and west.

John Cowper Powys

ALL BEFORE US

Afoot and light hearted I take to the open road,
Healthy, free, the world beforeme,
The long brown path before me leading wherever I choose.

Henceforth I ask not good-fortune, I myself am good-fortune,
Henceforth I whimper no more, postpone no more, need nothing,
Done with indoor complaints, libraries, querulous criticisms,
Strong and content I travel the open road.

Walt Whitman, 'Song of the Open Road', 1860

THREE THOUSAND MILES . . .

It was early on the morning of March the twenty-seventh that
I took to the road. There was darkness lingering in the sky,
and the moon was still visible, though gradually thinning away.
The faint shadow of Mount Fuji and the cherry blossoms of
Ueno and Yanaka were bidding me a last farewell. My friends
had got together the night before, and they all came with me
to the boat to keep me company for the first few miles. When
we got off the boat at Senju, however, the thought of the three
thousand miles before me suddenly filled my heart, and neither
the houses of the town nor the faces of my friends could be
seen by my tearful eyes except as a vision.

> The passing spring
> Birds mourn
> Fishes weep
> With tearful eyes.

With this poem to commemorate my departure, I walked
forth on my journey, but lingering thoughts made my steps

heavy. My friends stood in a line and waved good-bye as long as they could see my back.

I walked all through that day, ever wishing to return after seeing the strange sights of the far north, but not really believing in the possibility, for I knew that departing like this on a long journey in the second year of Genroku I should only accumulate more frosty hairs on my head as I approached the colder regions. When I reached the village of Soka in the evening, my bony shoulders were sore because of the load I had carried, which consisted of a paper coat to keep me warm at night, a light cotton gown to wear after the bath, scanty protection against the rain, writing equipment, and gifts from certain friends of mine. I wanted to travel light, of course, but there was always certain things I could not throw away for either practical or sentimental reasons.

Bashō (Matsuo Munefusa), *The Narrow Road to the Deep North*, 1702 (trans. Nobuyuki Yuasa, 1966)

I LOVE ROADS

I love a public road: few sights there are
That please me more; such object hath had power
O'er my imagination since the dawn
Of childhood, when its disappearing line,
Seen daily afar off, on one bare steep
Beyond the limits which my feet had trod
Was like a guide into eternity,
At least to things unknown and without bound.

William Wordsworth, *The Prelude*, Book XII, 1850

(iii)

There is an old proverb which says that the other side of the road always looks best, and I often test this by changing from one side of the road to the other.

Frank Tatchell, *The Happy Traveller*, 1923

TWO MEET ON THE 'DRY, EMPTY, AND WHITE'

Along the road walked an old man. He was white-headed as a mountain, bowed in the shoulders, and faded in general aspect. He wore a glazed hat, an ancient boat-cloak, and shoes; his brass buttons bearing an anchor upon their face. In his hand was a silver-headed walking-stick, which he used as a veritable third leg, perseveringly dotting the ground with its point at every few inches' interval. One would have said that he had been, in his day, a naval officer of some sort or other.

Before him stretched the long, laborious road, dry, empty, and white. It was quite open to the heath on each side, and bisected that vast dark surface like the parting-line on a head of black hair, diminishing and bending away on the furthest horizon.

The old man frequently stretched his eyes ahead to gaze over the tract that he had yet to traverse. At length he discerned, a long distance in front of him, a moving spot, which appeared to be a vehicle, and it proved to be going the same way as that in which he himself was journeying. It was the single atom of life that the scene contained, and it only served to render the general loneliness more evident. Its rate of advance was slow, and the old man gained upon it sensibly.

When he drew nearer he perceived it to be a spring van, ordinary in shape, but singular in colour, this being a lurid red. The driver walked beside it: and, like his van, he was completely red. One dye of that tincture covered his clothes, the cap upon his head, his boots, his face, and his hands. He was not temporarily overlaid with the colour: it permeated him.

The old man knew the meaning of this. The traveller with the cart was a reddleman – a person whose vocation it was to supply farmers with redding for their sheep. He was one of a class rapidly becoming extinct in Wessex, filling at present in the rural world the place which, during the last century, the dodo occupied in the world of animals. He is a curious, interesting and nearly perished link between obsolete forms of life and those which generally prevail.

The decayed officer, by degrees, came up alongside his fellow wayfarer, and wished him good evening. The reddleman turned his head, and replied in sad and occupied tones. He was young, and his face, if not exactly handsome, approached so near to handsome that nobody would have contradicted an assertion that it really was so in its natural colour. His eye, which glared so strangely through his stain, was in itself attractive – keen as that of a bird of prey, and blue as autumn mist. He had neither whisker nor moustache, which allowed the soft curves of the lower part of his face to be apparent. His lips were thin, and though, as it seemed, compressed by thought, there was a pleasant twitch at their corners now and then. He was clothed throughout in a tight-fitting suit of corduroy, excellent in quality, not much worn, and well-chosen for its purpose; but deprived of its original colour by his trade. It showed to advantage the good shape of his figure. A certain well-to-do air about the man suggested that he was not poor for his degree. The natural query of an observer would have been, Why should such a promising being as this have hidden his prepossessing exterior by adopting that singular occupation?

After replying to the old man's greeting he showed no inclination to continue in talk, although they still walked side by side, for the elder traveller seemed to desire company. There were no sounds but that of the booming wind upon the stretch of tawny herbage around them, the cracking wheels, the tread of men, and the footsteps of the two shaggy ponies which drew the van. They were small, hardy animals, of a breed between Galloway and Exmoor, and were known as 'heath-croppers' here.

Now, as they thus pursued their way, the reddleman occasionally left his companion's side, and, stepping behind the van, looked into its interior through a small window. The look was always anxious. He would then return to the old man, who made another remark about the state of the country and so on, to which the reddleman again abstractedly replied, and then again they would lapse into silence. The silence conveyed to neither any sense of awkwardness; in these lonely places wayfarers, after a first greeting, frequently plod on for miles without speech.

Thomas Hardy, *The Return of the Native*, 1878

THE THREE OF US

A conference betwix't an Angler, a Falconer, and a Hunter, each commending his recreation.

PISCATOR, VENATOR, AUCEPS.

PISCATOR: You are well overtaken, Gentlemen! A good morning to you both! I have stretched my legs up Tottenham Hill to overtake you, hoping your business may occasion you towards Ware whither I am going this fine fresh May morning.

VENATOR: Sir, I, for my part, shall almost answer your hopes; for my purpose is to drink my morning's draft at the Thatched House in Hoddesden; and I think not to rest till I come thither, where I have appointed a friend or two to meet me: but for this gentleman that you see with me, I know not how far he intends his journey; he came so lately into my company, that

I have scarce had time to ask him the question.

AUCEPS: Sir, I shall by your favour bear you company as far as Theobalds, and there leave you; for then I turn up to a friend's house, who mews a hawk for me, which I now long to see.

VENATOR: Sir, we are all so happy as to have a fine, fresh, cool morning; I hope we shall each be the happier in the others' company. And, Gentlemen, that I may not lose yours, I shall either abate or amend my pace to enjoy it, knowing that, as the Indians say, 'Good company in a journey makes the way seem shorter.'

Izaak Walton, *The Compleat Angler*, 1653

KINGS AND QUEENS OF THE ROAD

The chance use of the word 'Tramp' brought that numerous fraternity so vividly before my mind's eye, that I had no sooner laid down my pen than a compulsion was upon me to take it up again, and make notes of the Tramps whom I perceived on all the summer roads in all directions.

Mr and Mrs

Whenever a tramp sits down to rest by the wayside, he sits with his legs in a dry ditch; and whenever he goes to sleep (which is very often indeed), he goes to sleep on his back. Yonder, by the high road, glaring white in the bright sunshine, lies, on the dusty bit of turf under the bramble-bush that fences the coppice from the highway, the tramp of the order savage, fast asleep. He lies on the broad of his back, with his face turned up to the sky, and one of his ragged arms loosely thrown across his face. His bundle (what can be the contents of that mysterious bundle, to make it worth his while to carry it about?) is thrown down beside him, and the waking woman with him sits with her legs in the ditch, and her back to the road. She wears her bonnet rakishly perched on the front of her head, to shade her face from the sun in walking, and she ties her skirts round her in conventionally tight tramp-fashion with a sort of apron. You can seldom catch sight of her, resting thus, without seeing her in a despondently defiant manner doing something to her hair or her bonnet, and glancing at you between her fingers. She does not often go to sleep herself in the daytime, but will sit for any length of time beside the man. And his slumberous propensities would not seem to be referable to the fatigue of carrying the bundle, for she carries it much oftener and further than he. When they are afoot, you will mostly find him slouching on ahead, in a gruff temper, while she lags heavily behind with the burden. He is given to personally correcting her, too – which phase of his character develops itself oftenest, on benches outside alehouse doors – and she appears to become strongly attached to him for these reasons; it may usually be noticed that when the poor creature has a bruised face, she is the most affectionate. He has no occupation whatever, this order of tramp, and has no object whatever in going anywhere. He will sometimes call himself a brickmaker, or a sawyer, but only when he takes an imaginative flight. He generally represents himself, in a vague way, as looking out for a job of work; but he never did work, he never does, and he never will. It is a favourite fiction with him, however (as if he were the most industrious character on earth), that *you* never work; and as he goes past your garden and sees you looking at your flowers, you will overhear him growl with a strong sense of contrast, '*You* are a lucky hidle devil, *you* are!'

A Gentleman of the Road

There is another kind of tramp, whom you encounter this bright summer day – say, on a road with the sea-breeze making its dust lively, and sails of ships in the blue distance beyond

the slope of Down. As you walk enjoyingly on, you descry in
the perspective at the bottom of a steep hill up which your
way lies, a figure that appears to be sitting airily on a gate,
whistling in a cheerful and disengaged manner. As you approach
nearer to it, you observe the figure to slide down from the gate,
to desist from whistling, to uncock its hat, to become tender
of foot, to depress its head and elevate its shoulders, and to
present all the characteristics of profound despondency.
Arriving at the bottom of the hill and coming close to the
figure, you observe it to be the figure of a shabby young man.
He is moving painfully forward, in the direction in which you
are going, and his mind is so preoccupied with his misfortunes
that he is not aware of your approach until you are close upon
him at the hill-foot. When he is aware of you, you discover
him to be a remarkably well-behaved young man, and a remarkably well-spoken young man. You know him to be well-behaved,
by his respectful manner of touching his hat: you know him
to be well-spoken, by his smooth manner of expressing himself.
He says in a flowing confidential voice, and without punctua-
tion, 'I ask your pardon sir but if you would excuse the liberty
of being so addressed upon the public Iway by one who is
almost reduced to rags though it as not always been so and by
no fault of his own but through ill elth in his family and many
unmerited sufferings it would be a great obligation sir to know
the time.' You give the well-spoken young man the time. The
well-spoken young man, keeping well up with you, resumes: 'I
am aware sir that it is a liberty to intrude a further question
on a gentleman walking for his entertainment but might I make
so bold as to ask the favour of the way to Dover sir and about
the distance?' You inform the well-spoken young man that the
way to Dover is straight on, and the distance some eighteen
miles. The well-spoken young man becomes greatly agitated.
'In the condition to which I am reduced,' says he, 'I could not
ope to reach Dover before dark even if my shoes were in a

state to take me there or my feet were in a state to old out over the flinty road and were not on the bare ground of which any gentleman has the means to satisfy himself by looking Sir may I take the liberty of speaking to you?' As the well-spoken young man keeps so well up with you that you can't prevent his taking the liberty of speaking to you, he goes on, with fluency: 'Sir it is not begging that is my intention for I was brought up by the best of mothers and begging is not my trade I should not know sir how to follow it as a trade if such were my shameful wishes for the best of mothers long taught otherwise and in the best of omes though now reduced to take the present liberty on the Iway Sir my business was the law-stationering and I was favourably known to the Solicitor-General the Attorney-General the majority of the Judges and the ole of the legal profession but through ill elth in my family and the treachery of a friend for whom I became security and he no other than my own wife's brother the brother of my own wife I was cast forth with my tender partner and three young children not to beg for I will sooner die of deprivation but to make my way to the seaport town of Dover where I have a relative i in respect not only that will assist me but that would trust me with untold gold Sir in appier times and hare this calamity fell upon me I made for my amusement when I little thought that I should ever need it excepting for my air this' – here the well-spoken young man put his hand into his breast – 'this comb! Sir I emplore you in the name of charity to purchase a tortoiseshell comb which is a genuine article at any price that your humanity may put upon it and may the blessings of a ouseless family awaiting with beating arts the return of a husband and a father from Dover upon the cold stone seats of London-bridge ever attend you Sir may I take the liberty of speaking to you I implore you to buy this comb!' By this time, being a reasonably good walker, you will have been too much for the well-spoken young man, who will stop short and express his disgust and his want of breath, in a long expectoration, as you leave him behind.

Poor Fellow

Another class of tramp is a man, the most valuable part of whose stock-in-trade is a highly perplexed demeanour. He is got up like a countryman, and you will often come upon the poor fellow, while he is endeavouring to decipher the inscription on a milestone – quite a fruitless endeavour, for he cannot read. He asks your pardon, he truly does (he is very slow of speech, this tramp, and he looks in a bewildered way all round the prospect while he talks to you), but all of us shold do as we wold be done by, and he'll take it kind, if you'll put a power man in the right road fur to jine his eldest son as has broke his leg bad in the masoning, and is in this heere Orspit'l as is wrote down by Squire Pouncerby's own hand as wold not tell a lie fur no man. He then produces from under his dark frock (being always very slow and perplexed) a neat but worn old leathern purse, from which he takes a scrap of paper. On this scrap of paper is written, by Squire Pouncerby, of The Grove, 'Please to direct the Bearer, a poor but very worthy man, to the Sussex County Hospital, near Brighton' – a matter of some difficulty at the moment, seeing that the request comes suddenly upon you in the depths of Hertfordshire. The more you endeavour to indicate where Brighton is – when you have with the greatest difficulty remembered – the less the devoted father can be made to comprehend, and the more obtusely he stares at the prospect; whereby, being reduced to extremity, you recommend the faithful parent to begin by going to St. Albans, and present him with half-a-crown. It does him good, no doubt, but scarcely helps him forward, since you find him lying drunk that same evening in the wheelwright's sawpit under the shed where the felled trees are, opposite the sign of the Three Jolly Hedgers.

One to Avoid

But, the most vicious, by far, of all the idle tramps, is the tramp who pretends to have been a gentleman. 'Educated,' he writes, from the village beer-shop in pale ink of a ferruginous complexion; 'educated at Trin. Coll. Cam. – nursed in the lap of affluence – once in my small way the patron of the Muses,' &c. &c. – surely a sympathetic mind will not withhold a trifle, to help him on to the market-town where he thinks of giving a Lecture to the *fruges consumere nati*, on things in general? This shameful creature lolling about hedge tap-rooms in his ragged clothes, now so far from being black that they look as if they never can have been black, is more selfish and insolent than even the savage tramp. He would sponge on the poorest boy for a farthing, and spurn him when he had got it; he would interpose (if he could get anything by it) between the baby and the mother's breast. So much lower than the company he keeps, for his maudlin assumption of being higher, this pitiless rascal blights the summer road as he maunders on between the luxuriant hedges; where (to my thinking) even the wild convolvulus and rose and sweetbriar, are the worse for his going by, and need time to recover from the taint of him in the air.

The Lads

The young fellows who trudge along barefoot, five or six together, their boots slung over their shoulders, their shabby bundles under their arms, their sticks newly cut from some roadside wood, are not eminently prepossessing, but are much less objectionable. There is a tramp-fellowship among them. They pick one another up at resting stations, and go on in companies. They always go at a fast swing – though they generally limp too – and there is invariably one of the company who has much ado to keep up with the rest. They generally talk about horses, and any other means of locomotion than walking: or, one of the company relates some recent experiences of the road – which are always disputes and difficulties. As for example, 'So as I'm a standing at the pump in the market, blest if there don't come up a Beadle, and he ses, "Mustn't stand here," he ses. "Why not?" I ses. "No beggars allowed in this town," he ses. "Who's a beggar?" I ses. "You are," he ses. "Who ever see *me* beg? Did *you*?" I ses. "Then you're a tramp," he ses. "I'd rather be that than a Beadle," I ses.' (The company express great approval.) '"Would you?" he ses to me. "Yes, I would," I ses to him. "Well," he ses, "anyhow, get out of this town." "Why, blow your little town!" I ses, "who wants to be in it? Wot does your dirty little town mean by comin' and stickin' itself in the road to anywhere? Why don't you get a shovel and barrer, and clear your town out o' people's way?"' (The company expressing the highest approval and laughing aloud, they all go down the hill.)

Soldier Sailor

On the hot dusty roads near seaport towns and great rivers, behold the tramping Soldier. And if you should happen never to have asked yourself whether his uniform is suited to his work, perhaps the poor fellow's appearance as he comes distressfully towards you, with his absurdly tight jacket unbuttoned, his neck-gear in his hand, and his legs well chafed by his trousers of baize, may suggest the personal inquiry, how you think *you* would like it. Much better the tramping Sailor, although his cloth is somewhat too thick for land service. But, why the tramping merchant mate should put on a black velvet waistcoat, for a chalky country in the dog-days, is one of the great secrets of nature, that will never be discovered.

An Exodus

I have my eye upon a piece of Kentish road, bordered on either side by a wood, and having on one hand, between the road-dust and the trees, a skirting patch of grass. Wild flowers grow in abundance on this spot, and it lies high and airy, with a distant river stealing away to the ocean, like a man's life. To gain the milestone here, which the moss, primroses, violets, blue-bells, and wild roses, would soon render illegible but for peering travellers pushing them aside with their sticks, you must come up a steep hill, come which way you may. So, all the tramps with carts or caravans – the Gipsy-tramp, the Show-tramp, the Cheap Jack – find it impossible to resist the temptations of the place, and all turn the horse loose when they come to it, and boil the pot. Bless the place, I love the ashes of the vagabond fires that have scorched its grass! What tramp children do I see here, attired in a handful of rags, making a gymnasium of the shafts of the cart, making a feather-bed of the flints and brambles, making a toy of the hobbled old horse who is not much more like a horse than any cheap toy would be! Here, do I encounter the cart of mats and brooms and baskets – with all thoughts of business given to the evening wind – with the stew made and being served out – with Cheap Jack and Dear Jill striking soft music out of the plates that are rattled like warlike cymbals when put up for auction at fairs and markets – their minds so influenced (no doubt) by the melody of the nightingales as they begin to sing in the woods behind them, that if I were to propose to deal, they would sell me anything at cost price. On this hallowed ground has it been my happy privilege (let me whisper it) to behold the White-haired Lady with the pink eyes, eating meat-pie with the Giant: while, by the hedge-side, on the box of blankets which I knew contained the snakes, were set forth the cups and saucers and the teapot. It was on an evening in August, that I chanced upon this ravishing spectacle, and I noticed that, whereas the Giant reclined half concealed beneath the overhanging boughs and seemed indifferent to Nature, the white hair of the gracious Lady steamed free in the breath of evening, and her pink eyes found pleasure in the landscape. I heard only a single sentence of her uttering, yet it bespoke a talent for modest repartee. The ill-mannered Giant – accursed be his evil race! – had interrupted the Lady in some remark, and, as I passed that enchanted corner of the wood, she gently reproved him, with the words, 'Now, Cobby;' – Cobby! so short a name! – 'ain't one fool enough to talk at a time?'

Within appropriate distance of this magic ground, though not so near it as that the song trolled from tap or bench at door, can invade its woodland silence, is a little hostelry which no man possessed of a penny was ever known to pass in warm weather. Before its entrance are certain pleasant trimmed limes; likewise a cool well, with so musical a bucket-handle that its fall upon the bucket rim will make a horse prick up his ears and neigh, upon the droughty road half a mile off. This is a house of great resort for hay-making tramps and harvest tramps, insomuch that as they sit within, drinking their mugs of beer, their relinquished scythes and reaping-hooks glare out of the open windows, as if the whole establishment were a family war-coach of Ancient Britons. Later in the season, the whole countryside, for miles and miles, will swarm with hopping tramps. They come in families, men, women, and children, every family provided with a bundle of bedding, an iron pot, a number of babies, and too often with some poor sick creature quite unfit for the rough life, for whom they suppose the smell of the fresh hop to be a sovereign remedy. Many of these hoppers are Irish, but many come from London. They crowd all the roads, and camp under all the hedges and on all the scraps of common-land, and live among and upon the hops until they are all picked, and the hop-gardens, so beautiful through the summer, look as if they had been laid waste by an invading army. Then, there is a vast exodus of tramps out of the country; and if you ride or drive round any turn of any road, at more than a foot pace, you will be bewildered to find that you have charged into the bosom of fifty families, and that there are splashing up all around you, in the utmost prodigality of confusion, bundles of bedding, babies, iron pots, and a good-humoured multitude of both sexes and all ages, equally divided between perspiration and intoxication.

Charles Dickens, 'Tramps', 1860

THE SCHOOL RUN

School began at nine o'clock, but the hamlet children set out on their mile-and-a-half walk there as soon as possible after their seven o'clock breakfast, partly because they liked plenty of time to play on the road and partly because their mothers wanted them out of the way before house-cleaning began.

Up the long, straight road they straggled, in twos and threes and in gangs, their flat, rush dinner-baskets over their shoulders and their shabby little coats on their arms against rain. In cold weather some of them carried two hot potatoes which had been in the oven, or in the ashes, all night, to warm their hands on the way and to serve as a light lunch on arrival.

They were strong, lusty children, let loose from control, and there was plenty of shouting, quarrelling, and often fighting among them. In more peaceful moments they would squat in the dust of the road and play marbles, or sit on a stone heap and play dibs with pebbles, or climb into the hedges after birds' nests or blackberries, or to pull long trails of bryony to wreathe round their hats. In winter they would slide on the ice on the puddles, or make snowballs – soft ones for their friends, and hard ones with a stone inside for their enemies.

After the first mile or so the dinner-baskets would be raided; or they would creep through the bars of the padlocked field gates for turnips to pare with the teeth and munch, or for handfuls of green pea shucks, or ears of wheat, to rub out the sweet, milky grain between the hands and devour. In spring they ate this young green from the hawthorn hedges, which they called 'bread and cheese', and sorrel leaves from the wayside, which they called 'sour grass', and in autumn there was an abundance of haws and blackberries and sloes and crab-apples for them to feast upon. There was always something to eat, and they ate, not so much because they were hungry as from habit and relish of the wild food.

At the early hour there was little traffic upon the road. Sometimes, in winter, the children would hear the pounding of galloping hoofs and a string of hunters, blanketed up to the ears and ridden and led by grooms, would loom up out of the mist and thunder past on the grass verges. At other times the steady tramp and jingle of the teams going afield would approach, and, as they passed, fathers would pretend to flick their offspring with whips, saying: 'There! that's for that time you deserved it an' didn't get it'; while elder brothers, themselves at school only a few months before, would look patronizingly down from the horses' backs and call: 'Get out o' th' way, you kids!'

Going home in the afternoon there was more to be seen. A farmer's gig, on the way home from market, would stir up the dust; or the miller's van or the brewer's dray, drawn by four immense, hairy-legged, satin-backed carthorses. More exciting was the rare sight of Squire Harrison's four-in-hand, with ladies in bright, summer dresses, like a garden of flowers, on the top of the coach, and Squire himself, pink-cheeked and white-hatted, handling the four greys. When the four-in-hand passed, the children drew back and saluted, the Squire would gravely touch the brim of his hat with his whip, and the ladies would lean from their high seats to smile on the curtseying children.

A more familiar sight was the lady on a white horse who rode slowly on the same grass verge in the same direction every

Monday and Thursday. It was whispered among the children
that she was engaged to a farmer living at a distance, and that
they met half-way between their two homes. If so, it must have
been a long engagement, for she rode past at exactly the same
hour twice a week throughout Laura's schooldays, her face
getting whiter and her figure getting fuller and her old white
horse also putting on weight.

It has been said that every child is born a little savage and
has to be civilized. The process of civilization had not gone
very far with some of the hamlet children; although one civilization had them in hand at home and another at school, they
were able to throw off both on the road between the two places
and revert to a state of Nature. A favourite amusement with
these was to fall in a body upon some unoffending companion,
usually a small girl in a clean frock, and to 'run her', as they
called it. This meant chasing her until they caught her, then
dragging her down and sitting upon her, tearing her clothes,
smudging her face, and tousling her hair in the process. She
might scream and cry and say she would 'tell on' them; they
took no notice until, tiring of the sport, they would run
whooping off, leaving her sobbing and exhausted.

The persecuted one never 'told on' them, even when reproved
by the schoolmistress for her dishevelled condition, for she
knew that, if she had, there would have been a worse 'running'
to endure on the way home, and one that went to the tune of:

> Tell-tale tit!
> Cut her tongue a-slit,
> And every little puppy-dog shall have a little bit!

It was no good telling the mothers either, for it was the rule
of the hamlet never to interfere in the children's quarrels. 'Let
'em fight it out among theirselves,' the woman would say; and
if a child complained the only response would be: 'You must've

been doin' summat to them. If you'd've left them alone, they'd've left you alone; so don't come bringing your tales home to me!' It was harsh schooling; but the majority seemed to thrive upon it, and the few quieter and more sensitive children soon learned either to start early and get to school first, or to linger behind, dipping under bushes and lurking inside field gates until the main body had passed.

Flora Thompson, *Lark Rise to Candleford*, 1939

SOLITARY ROADSTER

The little hedge-row birds,
That peck along the road, regard him not.
He travels on, and in his face, his step,
His gait, is one expression; every limb,
His look and bending figure, all bespeak
A man who does not move with pain, but moves
With thought – He is insensibly subdued
To settled quiet: he is one by whom
All effort seems forgotten, one to whom
Long patience has such mild composure given,
That patience now doth seem a thing, of which
He hath no need. He is by nature led
To peace so perfect, that the young behold
With envy, what the old man hardly feels.
　　I asked him whither he was bound, and what
The object of his journey; he replied
'Sir! I am going many miles to take
'A last leave of my son, a mariner,
'Who from a sea-fight has been brought to Plymouth,
'And there is dying in hospital.'

William Wordsworth, 'Old Man Travelling', 1798

ROADSTER IN A TRANCE

My last special feat was turning out of bed at two, after a hard day, pedestrian and otherwise, and walking thirty miles into the country to breakfast. The road was so lonely in the night, that I fell asleep to the monotonous sound of my own feet, doing their regular four miles an hour. Mile after mile I walked, without the slightest sense of exertion, dozing heavily and dreaming constantly. It was only when I made stumble like a drunken man, or struck out into the road to avoid a horseman close upon me on the path – who had no existence – that I came to myself and looked about. The day broke mistily (it was autumn time), and I could not disembarrass myself of the idea that I had to climb those heights and bands of clouds, and that there was an Alpine convent somewhere behind the sun, where I was going to breakfast. This sleepy notion was so much stronger than such substantial objects as villages and haystacks, that, after the sun was up and bright, and when I was sufficiently awake to have a sense of pleasure in the prospect, I still occasionally caught myself looking out for wooden arms to point the right road up the mountain, and wondering there was no snow yet. It is a curiosity of broken sleep that I made immense quantities of verses on that pedestrian occasion (of course I never make any when I am in right senses), and that I spoke a certain language once pretty familiar to me, but which I have forgotten from disuse, with fluency. Of both these phenomena I have such frequent experience in the state between sleeping and waking, that I sometimes argue with myself that I cannot be awake, for, if I were, I should not be half so ready. The readiness is not imaginary, because I often recall long strings of the verses, and many turns of the fluent speech, after I am broad awake.

Charles Dickens, 'Shy Neighbourhoods', 1860

WHITE AND WINDEN

An' when the winden road so white
A-climmen up the hill in zight,
Da lead to pliazen, east ar west
The vuse a-know'd an' lov'd the best,
How touchen in the zunsheen's glow
Ar in the shiades that clouds da drow
Upon the zundurn'd down below,
's the white road up athirt the hill.

William Barnes, 'The White Road Upathirt the Hill', 1879

MILESTONES

(i)

The little English roads are delightful to walk; you are so glad to be able to put a mile behind you so quickly; but as all miles are miles the smallness of the English mile is a deception. I reckon that if I walk at a normal pace I can cover six English miles in two hours and expend in the process almost the same effort as going one German mile – taking into consideration the specially good quality of the English roads. But it is a pleasant deception to see that one has gone twelve miles in only a few hours.

Karl Philipp Moritz, *Journeys of a German in England*, 1782
(trans. Reginald Nettel, 1965)

(ii)

Next morning a friend of the commercial room kindly showed me the road to Limerick, and his genial company made the miles fly past. Presently he had to turn back and attend the markets, but still the milestones seemed to fly by. I got out my watch, and found I was walking an Irish mile in twelve minutes.

Impossible! – they must be English miles. So they were. The roads of this country (I was now in Limerick) are of recent construction. The Irish mile is, like the language, dying out, and so in out-of-the-way parts of Limerick you come into splendid roads accurately marked out with English miles.

The Reverend A. N. Cooper, MA, Vicar of Filey, Yorks.,
Tramps of the 'Walking Parson', 1902

(iii)

I have known a man who was painfully affected by the sight of one. He was used to spending strenuous days in the pursuit of a weary profession and in his brief walks would fall in with these inscriptions. So many miles to such and such a place he would read; so many miles to Arcady it sounded; and to dwell on the long road stretching away from his feet past little hamlets and moorland farms would give him a regretful pleasure. And when the time came to 'buckle on his pack' then he would linger lovingly over each stone as it told him of the steps of his journey towards El Dorado – surely the most futile of messages.

John Buchan, *Scholar Gypsies*, 1896

THE ROADSIDE LUNCH

The best roadside lunch in England is a split piece of toast with a rasher of bacon slipped inside, followed by bread and cheese and beer. On the Continent I am content with bread, raw onion, and a bottle of wine; but I make it a rule never to pass a little restaurant when hungry, in the hope of finding a better one further on. I like to have a pocketful of raisins to munch at odd times and a little chocolate or chewing gum.

Frank Tatchell, *The Happy Traveller*, 1923

IT IS A LIVING ROAD

Much has been written of travel, much less of the road. Writers have treated the road as a passive means to an end, and honoured it most when it has been an obstacle; they leave the impression that a road is a connection between two points which only exists when the traveller is upon it. Though there is much travel in the Old Testament, 'the way' is used chiefly as a metaphor. 'Abram journeyed, going on still toward the south', says the historian, who would have used the same words had the patriarch employed wings. Yet to a nomadic people the road was as important as anything upon it. The earliest roads wandered like rivers through the land, having, like rivers, one necessity, to keep in motion. We still say that a road 'goes' to London, as we 'go' ourselves. We point out a white snake on a green hill-side, and tell a man: 'That is going to Chichester.' At our inn we think when recollecting the day: 'That road must have gone to Strata Florida.' We could not attribute more life to them if we had moving roads with platforms on the sidewalks. We may go or stay, but the road will go up over the mountains to Llandovery, and then up over again to Tregaron. It is a silent companion always ready for us, whether it is night or day, wet or fine, whether we are calm or desperate, well or sick. It is always going: it has never gone right away, and no man is too late. Only a humorist could doubt this, like the boy in the lane who was asked: 'Where does this lane go to, boy?' and answered: 'I have been living here these sixteen years and it has never moved to my knowledge.' Some roads creep, some continue merely; some advance with majesty, some mount a hill in curves like a soaring sea-gull.

Edward Thomas, *The Icknield Way*, 1916

MADE OF CRYSTAL

The road wound before me like a pink ribbon, but looked at closely it was not pink at all, but of many hues. The chippings used are neither limestone nor granite, but of a substance like mica or quartz, remarkable for its tranparency and delicate tints. I picked a handful at random from a pile by the roadside and studied them. There were crystals of purple and turquoise and emerald and pink, and others that glittered like cut glass. Beautiful pearls, a few shillings a ton. I carried a pocketful about with me for the rest of the holiday.

Arthur Wainwright, *The Pennine Way*, 1986

A STROLLING MARQUIS ENCOUNTERS CHILDREN AND AUTOMOBILES

In my bright yellow English suit, which I had received as a present, I really seemed to myself, I must frankly admit, a great lord and grand seigneur, a marquis strolling up and down his park, though it was only a semi-rural, semi-surburban, neat, modest, nice little poor-quarter and country road I walked on, and on no account a noble park, as I have been so arrogant as to suppose, a presumption I gently withdraw, because all that is parklike is pure invention and does not fit here at all. Factories both great and small and mechanical workshops lay scattered agreeably in green countryside. Fat cozy farms meanwhile kindly offered their arms to knocking and hammering industry, which always has something skinny and worn-out about it. Nut trees, cherry trees, and plum trees gave the soft rounded road an attractive, entertaining, and delicate character. A dog lay across the middle of the road which I found as a matter of fact quite beautiful and loved. I loved in fact almost everything I saw as I proceeded, and with a fiery love. Another pretty little dog scene and child scene was as follows. A large but thoroughly comical, humorous, not at all dangerous fellow of a dog was quietly watching a wee scrap of a boy who crouched on some porch steps and bawled on account of the attention which the good-natured yet still somewhat terrifying-looking animal chose to pay him, bawled miserably with fear, setting up a loud and childish wail. I found the scene enchanting; but another childish scene in this country-road theater I found almost more delightful and enchanting. Two very small children were lying on the rather dusty road, as in a garden. One child said to the other: 'Now give me a nice little kiss.' The other child gave what was so pressingly demanded. Then said the first: 'All right, now you may get up.' So without a sweet little kiss he would probably never have allowed the other what he now permitted it. 'How well this naïve little scene goes with the lovely blue sky, which laughs down so divinely upon the gay, nimble, and bright earth!' I said to myself. 'Children are heavenly because they are always in a kind of heaven. When they grow older and grow up, their heaven vanishes and then they fall out of their childishness into the dry calculating manner and tedious perceptions of adults. For the children of poor folk the country road in summer is like a playroom. Where else can they go, seeing that the gardens are selfishly closed to them? Woe to the automobiles blustering by, as they ride coldly and maliciously into the children's games, into the child's heaven, so that small innocent human beings are in danger of being crushed to a pulp. The terrible thought that a child actually can be run over by such a clumsy triumphal car, I dare not think it, otherwise my wrath will seduce me to coarse expressions, with which it is well known nothing much ever gets done.'

To people sitting in a blustering dust-churning automobile I always present my austere and angry face, and they do not deserve a better one. Then they believe that I am a spy, a plainclothes policeman, delegated by high officials and authorities to spy on the traffic, to note down the numbers of vehicles, and later to report them. I always then look darkly at the wheels, at the car as a whole, but never at its occupants, whom I despise, and this in no way personally, but purely on principle; for I do not understand, and I never shall understand, how it can be a pleasure to hurtle past all the images and objects which our beautiful earth displays, as if one had gone mad and had to accelerate for fear of misery and despair. In fact, I love repose and all that reposes. I love thrift and moderation and am in my inmost self, in God's name, unfriendly toward any agitation and haste. More than what is true I need not say. And because of these words the driving of automobiles will certainly not be discontinued, nor its evil air-polluting smell, which nobody for sure particularly loves or esteems. It would be unnatural if someone's nostrils were to love and inhale with relish that which for all correct nostrils, at times, depending perhaps on the mood one is in, outrages and evokes revulsion. Enough, and no harm meant. And now walk on.

Robert Walser, *The Walk*, 1917
(trans. Christopher Middleton, 1957)

GO!

I'll take those old roads once more. Let's go! Route march, burden, desert, boredom, anger.

Arthur Rimbaud, *A Season in Hell*, 1873

SONGS YES, VERSE NO

Song is universal in Germany; it causes no dismay; *Shuffle off to Buffalo*; *Bye bye blackbird*; or *Shenandoah*; or *The Raggle Taggle* sung as I moved along, evoked nothing but tolerant smiles. But verse was different. Murmuring on the highway caused raised eyebrows and a look of anxious pity. Passages uttered with gestures and sometimes quite loud, provoked, if one was caught in the act, stares of alarm. Regulus brushing the delaying population aside as he headed for the Carthaginian executioner, as though to Lacedaemonian Terentum or the Venafrian fields, called for a fairly mild flourish; but urging the assault at Harfleur to fill the wall up with English dead would automatically bring on a heightened pitch of voice and action and double one's embarrassment if caught. When this happened I would try to taper off in a cough or weave the words into a tuneless hum and reduce all gestures to a feint at hair-tidying. But some passages demand an empty road as far as the eye can see before letting fly. The terrible boxing match, for instance, at the funeral games of Anchises when Entellus sends Dares reeling and spitting blood and teeth across the Sicilian shore, and then, with his thronged fist scatters a steer's brains with one blow between the horns – this needs care. As for the sword thrust at the bridge head that brings the great lord of Luna crashing among the augurs like an oak tree on Mount Alvernus – here the shouts, the walking stick slashes, the staggering gait and the arms upflung should never be indulged if there is anyone within miles, if then. To a strange eye, one is drunk or lunatic.

So it was today. I was at this very moment of crescendo and climax, when an old woman tottered out of a wood where she had been gathering sticks. Dropping and scattering them, she took to her heels. I would have liked the earth to have swallowed me, or to have been plucked into the clouds.

Patrick Leigh Fermor, A Time of Gifts, 1977

CROSSROADS

He came where four roads met
He chose a narrow one;
Spring thorns the way beset
But at the end there shone
The bright reward that pilgrims get

And Heaven's unsetting sun.

John Davidson, 1893

Once on the road it was all downhill.

Samuel Beckett, *The End*, 1967

I'M NO ROADSTER

Some do not walk at all; some walk in the highways; a few walk across lots. Roads are made for horses and men of business. I do not travel in them much, comparatively, because I am not in a hurry to get to any tavern or grocery or livery-stable or depot to which they lead. I am a good horse to travel but not from choice a roadster. The landscape-painter uses the figures of men to mark a road. He would not make the use of my figure. I walk out into a Nature such as the old prophets and poets, Menu, Homer, Chaucer, walked in. You may name it America but it is not America: neither Americus Vespucious, nor Columbus, nor the rest were the discoverers of it. At present, in this vicinity, the best part of the land is not private property; the landscape is not owned, and the walker enjoys comparative freedom. But possibly the day will come when it will not be partitioned off into so-called pleasure grounds, in which a few will take a narrow

and exclusive pleasure only – when fences shall be multiplied,
and mantraps and other engines invented to confine men to
the *road*.

Henry David Thoreau, 'Walking', 1843

ROADSTERS UNITE

Thoreau said he was a good horse, but a poor roadster as well.
I chant the virtues of the roadster. I sing of the sweetness of
gravel, good sharp quartz-grit. It is the proper condiment for
the sterner seasons, and many a human gizzard would be
cured of half its ills by a suitable daily allowance of it. I think
Thoreau would have profited immensely by it. His diet was
too exclusively vegetable. A man cannot live on grass alone.
If one has been a lotus eater all summer, he must turn gravel
eater in the fall and winter. Those who have tried it know that
gravel possesses an equal though an opposite charm. It spurs
to action.

John Burroughs, *The Exhilarations of the Road*, 1875

STOP DRINK THINK

Glowing with answers in the aromatic dark,
I walk, so wise,
Under the final problem of lit skies.

I reach the bridge, where the road turns north to Stoer,
And there perch me
Under the final problem of a tree.

I'm in my Li Po mood. I've half a mind
To sit and drink

Until the moon, that's just arisen, should sink.

The whisky's good, it constellates. How wise
Can a man be,
I think, inside that final problem, me.

If you are short of answers, I've got them all
As clear as day ...
I blink at the moon and put the bottle away

And then walk on (for there are miles to go
And friends to meet)
Above the final problem of my feet.

Norman MacCaig, 'The Road to Inveruplan', 1969

UP-HILL

Does the road wind up-hill all the way?
Yes, to the very end.
Will the day's journey take the whole long day?
From morn to night, my friend.

But is there for the night a resting place?
A roof for when the slow dark hours begin.
May not the darkness hide it from my face?
You cannot miss that inn.

Shall I meet other wayfarers at night?
Those who have gone before.
Then must I knock, or call when just in sight?
They will not keep you standing at that Door.

Shall I find comfort, travel-sore and weak?

Of labour you shall find the sum.
Will there be beds for me and all who seek?
Yes, beds for all who come.

Christina Rossetti, 'Up-hill', 1858

THE PASSION FOR WHAT IS BEYOND

And now we come to that last and most subtle quality of all, to that sense of prospect, of outlook, that is brought so powerfully to our minds by a road. In real nature as in old landscapes, beneath that impartial daylight in which a whole variegated plain is plunged and saturated, the line of the road leads the eye forth with the vague sense of desire up to the green limit of the horizon. Travel is brought home to us, and we visit in spirit every grove and hamlet that tempts us in the distance. *Sehnsucht* – the passion for what is ever beyond – is livingly expressed in that white riband of possible travel that severs the uneven country; not a ploughman following his plough up the shining furrow, not the blue smoke of any cottage in a hollow, but is brought to us with a sense of nearness and attainability by this wavering line of junction. Every little vista, every little glimpse that we have of what lies before us, gives the impatient imagination rein, so that it can outstrip the body and already plunge into the shadow of the woods, and overlook from the hill-top the plain beyond it, and wander in the windings of the valleys that are still far in front. The road is already there – we shall not be long behind. It is as if we were marching with the rear of a great army, and, from far before, heard the acclamation of the people as the vanguard entered some friendly and jubilant city. Would not every man, through all the long miles of the march, feel as if he were also within the gates?

Robert Louis Stevenson, 'Roads', 1873

ALL ROADS LEAD TO THE CITY

So I turned my back on the sea and headed north for London, still over fifty miles away. It was the third week in June, and the landscape was frosty with pollen and still coated with elder-blossom. The wide-open Downs, the sheep-nibbled grass, the beech hangers on the edge of the valleys, the smell of chalk, purple orchids, blue butterflies, and thistles recalled the Cotswolds I'd so carelessly left. Indeed Chanctonbury Ring, where I slept that night, could have been any of the beacons round Painswick or Haresfield; yet I felt farther from home, by the very familiarity of my surroundings, than I ever did later in a foreign country.

But next day, getting back on to the London road, I forgot everything but the way ahead. I walked steadily, effortlessly, hour after hour, in a kind of swinging, weightless dream. I was at that age which feels neither strain nor friction, when the body burns magic fuels, so that it seems to glide in warm air, about a foot off the ground, smoothly obeying its intuitions. Even exhaustion, when it came, had a voluptuous quality, and sleep was caressive and deep, like oil. It was the peak of the curve of the body's total extravagance, before the accounts start coming in.

I was living at that time on pressed dates and biscuits, rationing them daily, as though crossing a desert. Sussex, of course, offered other diets, but I preferred to stick to this affectation. I pretended I was T. E. Lawrence, engaged in some self-punishing odyssey, burning up my youth in some pitiless Hadhramaut, eyes narrowing to the sandstorms blowing out of the wadis of Godalming in a mirage of solitary endurance.

But I was not the only one on the road; I soon noticed there were many others, all trudging northwards in a sombre proces-sion. Some, of course, were professional tramps, but the majority belonged to that host of unemployed who wandered aimlessly about England at that time.

One could pick out the professionals; they brewed tea by the roadside, took it easy, and studied their feet. But the others, the majority, went on their way like somnambulists, walking alone and seldom speaking to each other. There seemed to be more of them inland than on the coast – maybe the police had seen to that. They were like a broken army walking away from a war, cheeks sunken, eyes dead with fatigue. Some carried bags of tools, or shabby cardboard suitcases; some wore the ghosts of city suits; some, when they stopped to rest, carefully removed their shoes and polished them vaguely with handfuls of grass. Among them were carpenters, clerks, engineers from the Midlands; many had been on the road for months, walking up and down the country in a maze of jobless refusals, the tread-mill of the mid-Thirties ...

Then, for a couple of days, I got a companion. I was picked up by the veteran Alf. I'd turned off the road to set up camp for the night, when he came filtering through the bushes.

I'd seen him before; he was about five feet high and was clearly one of the brotherhood. He wore a deerstalker hat, so sodden and shredded it looked like a helping of breakfast food, and round the waist of his mackintosh, which was belted with string, hung a collection of pots and spoons.

Ratting like a dustbin, he sat down beside me and began pulling off his boots.

'Well,' he said, eyeing my dates with disgust, 'you're a poor little bleeder, en't you?'

He shook out his boots and put them on again, then gave my supper another look.

'You can't live on terrible tack like that – you'll depress the lot of us. What you want is a billy. A-boil yerself up. 'Ere, 'ang on – jus' wait a minute ...'

Rummaging through the hardware around his waist, he produced a battered can, the kind of thing my uncles brought home from the war – square, with a triangular handle. It was a miniature cauldron, smoke-blackened outside and dark, tannin-stained within.

''Ere, take it,' he said. 'You make me miserable.' He started to build a fire. 'I'm goin' to boil you a bit of tea and tatters.' And that is what he did.

We stayed together as far as Guildford, and I shared more of his pungent brews. He was a tramp to his bones, always wrapping and unwrapping himself, and picking over his bits and pieces. He wasn't looking for work; this was simply his life, and he carefully rationed his energies – never passing a patch of grass that looked good for a shakedown, nor a cottage that seemed ripe for charity. He said his name was Alf, but one couldn't be sure, as he called me Alf, and everyone else. 'Couple of Alfs got jugged in this town last year,' he'd say. 'Hookin' the shops – you know, with fish-hooks.' Or: 'An Alf I knew used to do twenty-mile a day. One of the looniest Alfs on the road. Said he got round it quicker. And so he did. But folks got sick of his face.'

Alf talked all day, but was garrulously secretive, and never revealed his origins. I suppose that in the shared exposure of the open road he needed this loose verbal hedge around him. At the same time, he never asked me about myself, though he took it for granted that I was a greenhorn, and gave me careful advice about insulation from weather, flannelling housewives, and dodging the cops.

As for his own technique of roadwork, he wasn't slow out of laziness but because he moved to a deliberate timetable, making a professional grand tour in a twelve-months' rhythm, which seemed to him fast enough. During the winter he'd hole up in a London dosshouse, then restart his leisurely cycle of England, turning up every year in each particular district with the regularity of the seasons. Thus he was the spring tramp of the Midlands, the summer bird of the south, the first touch of autumn to the Kentish Weald – indeed, I think he firmly believed that his constancy of motion spread a kind of reassurance among the housewives, so that he was looked for and welcomed as one of the recurring phenomena of nature, and was suitably rewarded therefore.

Certainly his begging was profitable, and he never popped through a gate without returning with fistfuls of food – screws of tea, sugar, meat bones, and cake, which he'd then boil in one awful mess. He was clean, down-at-heel, warm-hearted, and cunning; and he showed me genuine if supercilious kindness. 'You're a bleedin' disgrace,' he used to say, 'a miserable little burden.'

Alf had one strange habit – a passion for nursery rhymes, which he'd mutter as he walked along.

> Sing a song of sixpence,
> Pocketful of rye,
> Four-an'-twenny blackbirds
> Bakes in an oven.
>
> Ba-ba, black sheep.
> Have you any wool?
> Yes, sir, yes, sir,
> I got plenty …

The effect of a dozen of these, left hanging in the air, was enough to dislocate the senses.

At Guildford we parted, Alf turning east for the Weald, which for him still lay three months away.

'So long, Alf,' I said.

'So long, Alf,' he answered. 'Try not to be too much of a nuisance.'

He passed under the railway bridge and out of my life, a shuffling rattle of old tin cans, looking very small and triangular with his pointed hat on his head, and black mackintosh trailing the ground.

London was now quite near, not more than a two-days' walk, but I was still in no particular hurry. So I turned north-west and began a detour round it, rather like a wasp sidling up to a jam jar. After leaving Guildford, I slept on Bagshot Heath – all birches, sand, and horseflies – which to me seemed a sinister and wasted place like some vast dead land of Russia. Then next morning, only a few miles farther up the road, everything suddenly changed back again, and I was walking through parkland as green as a fable, smothered with beeches and creamy grass.

Every motor car on the road was now either a Rolls-Royce or a Daimler – a gliding succession of silver sighs – their crystal interiors packed with girls and hampers and erect top-hatted men. Previously, I'd not seen more than two such cars in my life; now they seemed to be the only kind in the world, and I began to wonder if they were intimations of treasures to come, whether all London was as rich as this.

Tramping in the dust of this splendour, I wasn't surprised when one of the Daimlers pulled up and an arm beckoned to me from the window. I hurried towards it, thinking it might be full of long-lost relations, but in fact there was no one I knew. 'Want a pheasant, my man?' asked a voice from inside. 'We just knocked over a beauty a hundred yards back.'

A quarter of an hour later I arrived at Ascot. It was race week, and I'd walked right into it. White pavilions and flags; little grooms and jockeys dodging among the long glossy legs of thoroughbreds; and the pedigree owners dipping their long cool necks into baskets of paté and gulls' eggs.

I went round to the entrance, thinking I might get in, but was stared at by a couple of policemen. So I stared, in turn, at a beautiful woman by the gate, who for a moment paused dazzlingly near me – her face as silkily finished as a Persian miniature, her body sheathed in swathes like a tulip, and her sandalled feet wrapped in a kind of transparent rice-paper so that I could count every clean little separate toe.

Wealth and beauty were the common order of things now, and I felt I had entered another realm. It would have been no good busking or touting here, indeed outlandish in such a place. Alf, and the tattered lines of the workless, were far away in another country ... So I left Ascot, and came presently to another park, full of oak trees and grazing deer, and saw Windsor Castle standing on its green-baize hill like a battered silver cruet. I slept that stifling night in a field near Stoke Poges, having spent the evening in the village churchyard, sitting on a mossy gravestone and listening to the rooks, and wondering why the place seemed so familiar.

A few mornings later, coming out of a wood near Beaconsfield, I suddenly saw London at last – a long smoky skyline hazed by the morning sun and filling the whole of the eastern horizon. Dry, rusty-red, it lay like a huge flat crust, like ash from some spent volcano, simmering gently in the summer morning and emitting a faint, metallic roar.

No architectural glories, no towers or palaces, just a creeping insidious presence, its vast horizontal broken here and there by a gasholder or factory chimney. Even so, I could already feel its intense radiation – an electric charge in the sky – that rose from its million roofs in a quivering mirage, magnetically, almost visibly, dilating.

Cleo, my girl-friend, was somewhere out there; hoarding my letters (I hoped) and waiting. Also mystery, promise, chance, and fortune – all I had come to this city to find. I hurried towards it, impatient now, its sulphur stinging my nostrils. I had been a month on the road, and the suburbs were long and empty. In the end I took a tube.

Laurie Lee, *As I Walked Out One Midsummer Morning*, 1969

SIX

In the City

Walk fast in the country and stroll about in towns.

Frank Tatchell

YOU PAVEMENTS!

You flagg'd walks of the cities! you strong curbs at the
    edges!
You ferries! you planks and posts of wharves! you
    timber-lined sides! you distant ships!
You rows of houses! you window pierc'd facades! you
    roofs!
You porches and entrances! you copings and iron
    guards!
You windows whose transparent shells might expose
    so much!

You doors and ascending steps! you arches!
You gray stones of interminable pavements! you
    trodden crossings!
From all that has touch'd you I believe you have
    imparted to yourselves, and now would impart the
    same secretly to me,
From the living and the dead you have peopled your
    impassive surfaces, and the spirits thereof would be
    evident and amicable with me.

Walt Whitman, 'Song of the Open Road', 1860

ARCHITECTURE, FASHIONS, FREQUENCIE
OF PEOPLE

The fairest place of all the citie (which is indeed of that
admirable and incomparable beauty, that I think no place
whatever, eyther in Christendome or Paganisme may compare
with it) is the Piazza, that is, the market place of St. Marke, or
(as our english merchants commorant in Venice, doe call it)
the place of St. Marke, in Latin Forumor Platea Di Marci. Truly

such is the stupendous glory of it, that in my first walke thereof it did even amaze or ravish my senses. For here is the greatest magnificance of architecture to be seene, that any place under the sunne does yeelde. Here you may both see all manner of fashions of attire, and heare all the languages of Christendome, besides those that are spoken by the barbarous Ethnickes; the frequencie of people being so great twise a day, betwixt sixe of the clock in the morning and eleven, and againe betwixt five in the afternoon and eight, that a man may very properly call it rather Orbis then Urbis forum – that is, a market place of the world, not of the citie.

Thomas Coryate, *Coryats Crudities*, 1611

THE PAVEMENTS ARE ALIVE

For ease and for dispatch, the morning's best;
No tides of passengers the street molest.
You'll see a draggled damsel, here and there,
From Billingsgate her fishy traffic bear;
On doors the sallow milk-maid chalks her gains;
Ah! how unlike the milk-maid of the plains!
Before proud gates attending asses bray,
Or arrogate with solemn pace the way;
These grave physicians with their milky cheer,
The love-sick maid and dwindling beau repair;
Here rows of drummers stand in martial file,
And with their vellum thunder shake the pile,
To greet the new-made bride. Are sounds like these
The proper prelude to a state of peace?
Now industry awakes her busy sons,
Full charg'd with news the breathless hawker runs:
Shops open, coaches roll, carts shake the ground,
And all the streets with passing cries resound.

If cloth'd in black, you tread the busy town
Or if distinguish'd by the rev'rend gown,
Three trades avoid; oft in the mingling press,
The barber's apron soils the sable dress;
Shun the perfumer's touch with cautious eye,
Nor let the baker's step advance too nigh;
Ye walkers too that youthful colours wear,
Three sullying trades avoid with equal care;
The little chimney-sweeper skulks along,
And marks with sooty stains the heedless throng;
When small-coal murmurs in the hoarser throat,
From smutty dangers guard thy threaten'd coat:
The dust-man's cart offends thy clothes and eyes,
When through the street a cloud of ashes flies;
But whether black or lighter dyes are worn,
The chandler's basket, on his shoulder borne,
With tallow spots thy coat; resign the way,
To shun the surly butcher's greasy tray,
Butcher's, whose hands are dy'd with blood's foul stain,
And always foremost in the hangman's train.

Let due civilities be strictly paid.
The wall surrender to the hooded maid;
Nor let thy sturdy elbow's hasty rage
Jostle the feeble steps of trembling age;
And when the porter bends beneath his load,
And pants for breath, clear thou the crowded road.
But, above all, the groping blind direct,
And from the pressing throng the lane protect.
You'll sometimes meet a fop, of nicest tread,
Whose mantling peruke veils his empty head;
At ev'ry step he dreads the wall to lose,
And risks, to save a coach, his red-heel'd shoes;
Him, like the miller, pass with caution by,

Lest from his shoulder clouds of powder fly.
But when the bully, with assuming pace,
Cocks his broad hat, edg'd round with tarnish'd lace,
Yield not the way; defy his strutting pride,
And thrust him to the muddy kennel's side;
He never turns again, nor dares oppose,
But mutters coward curses as he goes.

If drawn by bus'ness to a street unknown,
Let the sworn porter point thee through the town;
Be sure observe the signs, for signs remain,
Like faithful land-marks to the walking train.
Seek not from prentices to learn the way,
Those fabling boys will turn thy steps astray;
Ask the grave tradesman to direct thee right,
He ne'er deceives, but when he profits by 't.

John Gay, *Trivia; or, The Art of Walking the Streets of London*, 1716

DANGEROUS PAVEMENTS: OBSTACLES

I went into the city for a walk, and dined there with a private man; and coming home this evening broke my shin in the Strand over a tub of sand left just in the way. I got home dirty enough, and went straight to bed, where I have been cooking it with gold-beaters skin, and have been peevish enough with Patrick, who was near an hour bringing a rag from next door. It is my right shin, where never any humour fell when t'other used to swell; so I approached it less: however I shall not stir till 'tis well, which I reckon will be in a week.

I am very careful in these sorts of things; but I wish I had Mrs Johnson's water: she is out of town and I must make a shift with allum. I will dine with Mrs Vanhomrigh till I am well, who lives but five doors off; and that I may venture.

Jonathan Swift, *Journal to Stella*, 1710–13

DANGEROUS PAVEMENTS: EFFLUVIA

Mr. Johnson and I walked arm-in-arm up the high-street, to my house in James's Court: it was a dusky night: I could not prevent his being assailed by the evening effluvia of Edinburgh. I heard a late baronet, of some distinction in the political world in the beginning of the present reign, observe, that 'walking the streets of Edinburgh at night was pretty perilous and a good deal odoriferous'. The peril is much abated, by the care which the city magistrates have taken to enforce the city laws against throwing foul water from the windows; but, from the structure of the houses in the old town, which consist of many stories, in each of which a different family lives, and there being no covered sewers, the odour still continues. A zealous Scotsman would have wished Mr. Johnson to be without one of his five senses on this occasion. As we marched slowly along, he grumbled in my ear, 'I smell you in the dark!' but he acknowledged that the breadth of the street, and the loftiness of the buildings on each side, made a noble appearance ...

James Boswell, *Journal of a Tour to the Hebrides*, 1785

DANGEROUS PAVEMENTS: YOBBERY

Prepare for death, if here at night you roam,
And sign your will before you sup from home,
Some fiery fop, with new commission vain,
Who sleeps on brambles till he kills his man,
Some frolick drunkard, reeling from a feast,
Provokes a broil, and stabs you for a jest,
Yet ev'n these heroes, mischievously gay,
Lords of the street, and terrors of the way;
Flush'd as they are with folly, youth, and wine,
Their prudent insults to the poor confine;

Afar they mark the flambeau's bright approach,
And shun the shining train, and golden coach.

Samuel Johnson, 'London', 1738

THOSE PAVEMENTS ABROAD

The very walk of the Parisians, that light, jerking, fidgeting trip
on which they pride themselves, and think it grace and spirit,
is the effect of the awful construction of their streets or, of the
round, flat, slippery stones, over which you are obliged to make
your way on tiptoe, as over a succession of stepping stones,
and where natural ease and steadiness are out of the question.
On the same principle, French women shew their legs (it is a
pity, for they are often handsome, and a stolen glimpse of them
would often be charming) sooner than get draggle-tailed; and
you see an old French beau generally walk like a crab nearly
side-ways, from having been so often stuck up in a lateral
position between a coach-wheel, that threatened the wholeness
of his bones, and a stone-wall that might endanger the cleanli-
ness of his person. In winter, you are splashed all over with
mud; in summer, you are knocked down with the smells. If
you pass along the middle of the street, you are hurried out
of your breath; if on one side, you must pick your way no less
cautiously.

Paris is a vast pile of tall and dirty alleys, of slaughter-houses
and barbers' shops – an immense suburb huddled together
within the walls so close, that you cannot see the loftiness of
the buildings for the narrowness of the streets, and where all
that is fit to live in, and best worth looking at, is turned out
upon the quays, the boulevards, and their immediate vicinity.

William Hazlitt, *Notes of a Journey through
France and Italy*, 1826

CONGESTION

They wandered endless boulevards, some bustling, some dingy, some tawdry and flaring, some melancholy and mean; rows of garden gods, planted on the walls of yards full of vases and divinities of concrete, huge railway halls, monster hotels, dissenting chapels in the form of Gothic churches, quaint ancient almshouses that were once built in fields, and tea gardens and beer houses and knackers' yards. They were in a district far from the experience of Lothair, which indeed had been exhausted when he had passed Eustonia, and from which he had long been separated. The way was broad but ill-lit, with houses of irregular size but generally of low elevation, and sometimes detached in smoke-dried gardens. The road was becoming a bridge which crossed a canal, with barges and wharves and timber yards, when their progress was arrested by a crowd.

Benjamin Disraeli, *Lothair*, 1870

ALL THOSE FACES

How oft, amid those overflowing streets,
Have I gone forward with the crowd, and said
Unto myself, 'The face of every one
That passes by me is a mystery!'

William Wordsworth, *The Prelude*, 1850

OUT OF THE CROWD CAME . . .

Not long ago, about the closing in of an evening in autumn, I sat at the large bow-window of the D—— Coffee-House in London. For some months I had been ill in health, but was

now convalescent, and, with returning strength, found myself
in one of those happy moods which are so precisely the converse
of *ennui* ... I felt a calm but inquisitive interest in every thing.
With a cigar in my mouth and a newspaper in my lap, I had
been amusing myself for the greater part of the afternoon, now
in poring over advertisements, now in observing the promis-
cuous company in the room, and now in peering through the
smoky panes into the street.

This latter is one of the principal thoroughfares of the city,
and had been very much crowded during the whole day. But,
as the darkness came on, the throng momently increased; and,
by the time the lamps were well lighted, two dense and
continuous tides of population were rushing past the door. At
this particular period of the evening I had never before been
in a similar situation, and the tumultuous sea of human heads
filled me, therefore, with a delicious novelty of emotion. I gave
up, at length, all care of things within the hotel, and became
absorbed in contemplation of the scene without.

At first my observations took an abstract and generalizing
turn. I looked at the passengers in masses, and thought of them
in their aggregate relations. Soon, however, I descended to
details, and regarded with minute interest the innumerable
varieties of figure, dress, air, gait, visage, and expression of
countenance.

By far the greater number of those who went by had a satisfied, business-like demeanor, and seemed to be thinking only
of making their way through the press. Their brows were knit,
and their eyes rolled quickly; when pushed against by fellow-
wayfarers they evinced no symptom of impatience, but adjusted
their clothes and hurried on. Others, still a numerous class,
were restless in their movements, had flushed faces, and talked
and gesticulated to themselves, as if feeling in solitude on
account of the very denseness of the company around. When
impeded in their progress, these people suddenly ceased

muttering, but redoubled their gesticulations, and awaited, with an absent and overdone smile upon the lips, the course of the persons impeding them. If jostled, they bowed profusely to the jostlers, and appeared overwhelmed with confusion ... They were undoubtedly noblemen, merchants, attorneys, tradesmen, stock-jobbers ... They did not greatly excite my attention.

The tribe of clerks was an obvious one; and here I discerned two remarkable divisions. There were the junior clerks of flash houses – young gentlemen with tight coats, bright boots, well-oiled hair, and supercilious lips. Setting aside a certain dapperness of carriage, which may be termed *deskism* for want of a better word, the manner of these persons seemed to be an exact fac-simile of what had been the perfection of *bon ton* about twelve or eighteen months before. They wore the cast-off graces of the gentry; – and this, I believe, involves the best definition of the class.

The division of the upper clerks of staunch firms, or of the 'steady old fellows,' it was not possible to mistake. These were known by their coats and pantaloons of black or brown, made to sit comfortably, with white cravats and waistcoats, broad solid-looking shoes, and thick hose or gaiters. They had all slightly bald heads, from which the right ears, long used to pen-holding, had an odd habit of standing off on end. I observed that they always removed or settled their hats with both hands, and wore watches, with short gold chains of substantial and ancient pattern. Theirs was the affectation of respectability – if indeed there be an affectation so honorable.

There were many individuals of dashing appearance, whom I easily understood as belonging to the race of swell pick-pockets, with which all great cities are infested ...

The gamblers, of whom I descried not a few, were still more easily recognizable. They wore every variety of dress, from that of the desperate thimble-rig bully, with velvet waistcoat, fancy neckerchief, gilt chains, and filigreed buttons, to that of the scrupulously inornate clergyman, than which nothing could be less liable to suspicion ... Very often, in company with these sharpers, I observed an order of men somewhat different in habits, but still birds of a kindred feather. They may be defined as the gentlemen who live by their wits. They seem to prey upon the public in two battalions – that of the dandies and that of the military men. Of the first grade the leading features are long locks and smiles; of the second, frogged coats and frowns.

Descending in the scale of what is termed gentility, I found darker and deeper themes for speculation. I saw Jew peddlers, with hawk eyes flashing from countenances whose every other feature wore only an expression of abject humility; sturdy professional street beggars scowling upon mendicants of a better stamp, whom despair alone had driven forth into the night for charity ... Women of the town of all kinds and of all ages – the unequivocal beauty in the prime of her womanhood, putting one in mind of the statue in Lucian, with the surface of Parian marble, and the interior filled with filth, the loathsome and utterly lost leper in rags, the wrinkled, bejewelled, and paint-begrimed beldame, making a last effort at youth, and the mere child of immature form, yet, from long association, an adept in the dreadful coquetries of her trade ... beside these, piemen, porters, coal-heavers, sweeps; organ-grinders, monkey-exhibitors, and ballad-mongers, those who vended with those who sang; ragged artizans and exhausted laborers of every description, and all full of a noisy and inordinate vivacity which jarred discordantly upon the ear, and gave an aching sensation to the eye.

As the night deepened, so deepened to me the interest of the scene; for not only did the general character of the crowd materially alter ... but the rays of the gas-lamps, feeble at first in their struggle with the dying day, had now at length gained ascendency, and threw over every thing a fitful and garish lustre. All was dark yet splendid ...

With my brow to the glass, I was thus occupied in scrutinizing the mob, when suddenly there came into view a countenance (that of a decrepid old man, some sixty-five or seventy years of age) – a countenance which at once arrested and absorbed my whole attention, on account of the absolute idiosyncrasy of its expression. Any thing even remotely resembling that expression I had never seen before ... As I endeavoured, during the brief minute of my original survey, to form some analysis of the meaning conveyed, there arose confusedly and paradoxically within my mind, the ideas of vast mental power, of caution, of penuriousness, of avarice, of coolness, of malice, of blood-thirstiness, of triumph, of merriment, of excessive terror, of intense – of supreme despair. I felt singularly aroused, startled, fascinated. 'How wild a history,' I said to myself, 'is written within that bosom!' Then came a craving desire to keep the man in view – to know more of him. Hurriedly putting on an overcoat, and seizing my hat and cane, I made my way into the street, and pushed through the crowd in the direction which I had seen him take; for he had already disappeared. With some little difficulty I at length came within sight of him, approached, and followed him closely, yet cautiously, so as not to attract his attention.

I had now a good opportunity of examining his person. He was short in stature, very thin, and apparently very feeble. His clothes, generally, were filthy and ragged; but as he came, now and then, within the strong glare of a lamp, I perceived that his linen, although dirty, was of beautiful texture; and my vision deceived me, or, through a rent in a closely-buttoned and evidently second-handed *roquelaire* which enveloped him, I caught a glimpse both of a diamond and of a dagger. These observations heightened my curiosity, and I resolved to follow the stranger whithersoever he should go.

It was now fully night-fall, and a thick humid fog hung over the city, soon ending in a settled and heavy rain. This change of weather had an odd effect upon the crowd, the whole of which was at once put into new commotion, and overshadowed by a world of umbrellas. The waver, the jostle, and the hum increased in a tenfold degree. For my own part I did not much regard the rain – the lurking of an old fever in my system rendering the moisture somewhat too dangerously pleasant. Tying a handkerchief about my mouth, I kept on. For half an hour the old man held his way with difficulty along the great thoroughfare; and I here walked close at his elbow through fear of losing sight of him. Never once turning his head to look back, he did not observe me. By and by he passed into a cross street, which, although densely filled with people, was not quite so much thronged as the main one he had quitted. Here a change in his demeanor became evident. He walked more slowly and with less object than before – more hesitatingly. He crossed and re-crossed the way repeatedly, without apparent aim; and the press was still so thick, that, at every such movement, I was obliged to follow him closely. The street was a narrow and long one, and his course lay within it for nearly an hour, during which the passengers had gradually diminished to about that number which is ordinarily seen at noon on Broadway near the park – so vast a difference is there between a London populace and that of the most frequented American city. A second turn brought us into a square, brilliantly lighted, and overflowing with life. The old manner of the stranger re-appeared. His chin fell upon his breast, while his eyes rolled wildly from under his knit brows, in every direction, upon those who hemmed him in. He urged his way steadily and perseveringly. I was surprised, however, to find, upon his having made the circuit of the square, that he turned and retraced his steps. Still more was I astonished to see him repeat the same walk several times – once nearly detecting me as he came round with a sudden movement.

In this exercise he spent another hour, at the end of which

we met with far less interruption from passengers than at first. The rain fell fast; the air grew cool; and the people were retiring to their homes. With a gesture of impatience, the wanderer passed into a by-street comparatively deserted. Down this, some quarter of a mile long, he rushed with an activity I could not have dreamed of seeing in one so aged, and which put me to much trouble in pursuit. A few minutes brought us to a large and busy bazaar, with the localities of which the stranger appeared well acquainted, and where his original demeanor again became apparent, as he forced his way to and fro, without aim, among the host of buyers and sellers.

During the hour and a half, or thereabouts, which we passed in this place, it required much caution on my part to keep him within reach without attracting his observation. Luckily I wore a pair of caout-chouc overshoes, and could move about in perfect silence. At no moment did he see that I watched him. He entered shop after shop, priced nothing, spoke no word, and looked at all objects with a wild and vacant stare. I was now utterly amazed at his behavior, and firmly resolved that we should not part until I had satisfied myself in some measure respecting him.

A loud-toned clock struck eleven, and the company were fast deserting the bazaar. A shop-keeper, in putting up a shutter, jostled the old man, and at the instant I saw a strong shudder come over his frame. He hurried into the street, looked anxiously around him for an instant, and then ran with incredible swiftness through many crooked and peopleless lanes, until we emerged once more upon the great thoroughfare whence we had started – the street of the D—— Hotel. It no longer wore, however, the same aspect. It was still brilliant with gas; but the rain fell fiercely, and there were few persons to be seen. The stranger grew pale. He walked moodily some paces up the once populous avenue, then, with a heavy sigh, turned in the direction of the river, and, plunging through a great variety of devious ways, came out, at length, in view of one of the principal theatres.

It was about being closed, and the audience were thronging from the doors. I saw the old man gasp as if for breath while he threw himself amid the crowd; but I thought that the intense agony of his countenance had, in some measure, abated. His head again fell upon his breast; he appeared as I had seen him at first. I observed that he now took the course in which had gone the greater number of the audience – but, upon the whole, I was at a loss to comprehend the waywardness of his actions.

As he proceeded, the company grew more scattered, and his old uneasiness and vacillation were resumed. For some time he followed closely a party of some ten or twelve roisterers; but from this number one by one dropped off, until three only remained together, in a narrow and gloomy lane, little frequented. The stranger paused, and, for a moment, seemed lost in thought; then, with every mark of agitation, pursued rapidly a route which brought us to the verge of the city, amid regions very different from those we had hitherto traversed. It was the most noisome quarter of London, where every thing wore the worst impress of the most deplorable poverty, and of the most desperate crime. By the dim light of an accidental lamp, tall, antique, worm-eaten, wooden tenements were seen tottering to their fall, in directions so many and capricious, that scarce the semblance of a passage was discernible between them. The paving-stones lay at random, displaced from their beds by the rankly-growing grass. Horrible filth festered in the dammed-up gutters. The whole atmosphere teemed with desolation. Yet, as we proceeded, the sounds of human life revived by sure degrees, and at length large bands of the most abandoned of a London populace were seen reeling to and fro. The spirits of the old man again flickered up, as a lamp which is near its death-hour. Once more he strode onward with elastic tread. Suddenly a corner was turned, a blaze of light burst upon our sight, and we stood before one of the huge suburban temples of Intemperance – one of the palaces of the fiend. Gin.

It was now nearly daybreak; but a number of wretched inebriates still pressed in and out of the flaunting entrance. With a half shriek of joy the old man forced a passage within, resumed at once his original bearing, and stalked backward and forward, without apparent object, among the throng. He had not been thus long occupied, however, before a rush to the doors gave token that the host was closing them for the night. It was something even more intense than despair that I then observed upon the countenance of the singular being whom I had watched so pertinaciously. Yet he did not hesitate in his career, but, with a mad energy, retraced his steps at once, to the heart of the mighty London. Long and swiftly he fled, while I followed him in the wildest amazement, resolute not to abandon a scrutiny in which I now felt an interest all-absorbing. The sun arose while we proceeded, and, when we had once again reached the most thronged mart of the populous town, the street of the D. Hotel, it presented an appearance of human bustle and activity scarcely inferior to what I had seen on the evening before. And here, long, amid the momently increasing confusion, did I persist in my pursuit of the stranger. But, as usual, he walked to and fro, and during the day did not pass from out the turmoil of that street. And, as the shades of the second evening came on, I grew wearied unto death, and, stopping fully in front of the wanderer, gazed at him steadfastly in the face. He noticed me not, but resumed his solemn walk, while I, ceasing to follow, remained absorbed in contemplation. 'This old man,' I said at length, 'is the type and the genius of deep crime. He refuses to be alone. *He is the man of the crowd.* It will be in vain to follow; for I shall learn no more of him, nor of his deeds ...'

Edgar Allan Poe, 'The Man of the Crowd', 1841

DEAD PAVEMENTS

I wander thro' each dirty street,
Near where the dirty Thames does flow,
And mark in every face I meet
Marks of weakness, marks of woe.

In every cry of every Man
In every Infant's cry of fear,
In every voice, in every ban,
The mind-forg'd manacles I hear.

How the Chimney-sweeper's cry
Blackens o'.er the churches' walls
And the hapless Soldier's sigh
Runs in blood down Palace walls.

But most the midnight harlot's curse
From every dismal street I hear,
Weaves around the marriage hearse
And blasts the new born infant's tear.

William Blake, 'London', 1793

INTO THE UNDERWORLD

Some say that phantoms haunt those shadowy streets,
    And mingle freely there with sparse mankind;
And tell of ancient woes and black defeats,
    And murmur mysteries in the grave enshrined:
But others think them visions of illusion,
Or even men gone far in self-confusion;
    No man there being wholly sane in mind.

And yet a man who raves, however mad,
　Who bares his heart and tells of his own fall,
Reserves some inmost secret good or bad:
　The phantoms have no reticence at all:
The nudity of flesh will blush though tameless,
The extreme nudity of bone grins shameless,
　The unsexed skeleton mocks shroud and pall.

I have seen phantoms there that were as men
　And men that were as phantoms flit and roam;
Marked shapes that were not living to my ken,
　Caught breathings acrid as with Dead Sea foam:
The City rests for man so weird and awful,
That his intrusion there might seem unlawful,
　And phantoms there may have their proper home.

James Thomson, 'The City of Dreadful Night', 1874

What peculiarities one finds in big cities when one knows how to roam and to search.

Charles Baudelaire, Intimate Journals, 1887

HOME OF THE STROLLER (1)

One day when we were strolling along the busy streets of Arcueil, a friend came up to us and asked us a question: 'To where are your steps directed?' We were really at a loss in replying for we were just strolling anywhere without any definite goal; but this question, however banal it seemed, plunged Satie into deep reflection. Several days later, he was still thinking about it and racking his brains to know why this passing friend wanted to know the object of our walk. Our questioner was a Freemason, which explains a lot.

Léon Louis Veyssière, Les bulles du parcier, 1991

HOME OF THE STROLLER (2)

The leisurely quality ... fits the style of the *flâneur* who goes botanizing on the asphalt. But even in those days it was not possible to stroll about everywhere in the city. Before Haussmann wide pavements were rare, and the narrow ones afforded little protection from vehicles. Strolling could hardly have assumed the importance it did without the arcades. 'The arcades, a rather recent invention of industrial luxury', so says an illustrated guide to Paris of 1852, 'are glass-covered, marble-panelled passageways through entire complexes of houses whose proprietors have combined for such speculations. Both sides of these passageways, which are lighted from above, are lined with the most elegant shops, so that such an arcade is a city, even a world, in miniature.' It is in this world that the *flâneur* is at home; he provides 'the favourite sojourn of the strollers and the smokers, the stamping ground of all sorts of little *métiers*', with its chronicler and its philosopher. As for himself, he obtains there the unfailing remedy for the kind of boredom that easily arises under the baleful eyes of a satiated reactionary regime. In the words of Guys as quoted by Baudelaire, 'Anyone who is capable of being bored in a crowd is a blockhead. I repeat: a blockhead, and a contemptible one.' The arcades were a cross between a street and an *intérieur* ... The street becomes a dwelling for the *flâneur*; he is as much at home among the façades of houses as a citizen is in his four walls. To him the shiny, enamelled signs of businesses are at least as good a wall ornament as an oil painting is to a bourgeois in his salon. The walls are the desk against which he presses his notebooks; news-stands are his libraries and the terraces of cafés are the balconies from which he looks down on his household after his work is done.

Walter Benjamin, *Charles Baudelaire: A Lyric Poet in the Era of High Capitalism*, 1973 (trans. Henry Zotin, 1983)

HOME OF THE STROLLER (3)

Toni and I were strolling along Oxford Street, trying to look like *flâneurs*. This wasn't as easy as it might sound. For a start, you usually needed a *quai*, or at the very least, a *boulevard*; and, however much we might be able to imitate the aimlessness of the *flânerie* itself, we always felt that we hadn't quite mastered what happened at each end of the stroll. In Paris, you would be leaving behind some rumpled couch in a *chambre particulière*; over here, we had just left behind Tottenham Court Road Underground station and were heading for Bond Street.

Julian Barnes, Metroland, 1980

A UNE PASSANTE

La rue assourdissante autour de moi hurlait
Longue, mince, en grand deuil, douleur majestueuse,
Une femme passa, d'une main fastueuse
Soulevant, balançant le feston et l'ourlet;

Agile et noble, avec sa jambe de statue.
Moi, je buvais, crispé comme un extravagant,
Dans son oeil, ciel livide où germe l'ouragan,
La douceur qui fascine et le plaisir qui tue.

Un éclair . . . puis la nuit! – Fugitive beauté
Dont le regard m'a fait soudainement renaître,
Ne te verrai-je plus que dans l'éternité?

Ailleurs, bien loin d'ici! trop tard! *jamais* peut-être!
Car j'ignore où tu fuis, tu ne sais où je vais,
Ô toi que j'eusse aimée, ô toi qui le savais!

Charles Baudelaire, Les fleurs du mal, 1857

DECORATIVE GIRLS

Our way back took us along the Graben and the Kärntnerstrasse. About lamplighting time, I had noticed a small, drifting population of decorative girls who shot unmistakable glances of invitation at passers-by. Konrad shook his head. 'You must beware, dear young,' he said in a solemn voice. 'These are wenches and they are always seeking only pelf. They are wanton, and it is only their wont.'

Patrick Leigh Fermor, *A Time of Gifts*, 1977

VI GOES SHOPPING

She walked along, looking at the shops and rubbing shoulders with the plain, hard-working women of the neighbourhood who were out buying bread and soap.

'*If I had a lot of money,*' she thought, '*I'd buy a lot of furniture for cash, and have a flat ... and get fifty evening dresses, and five day dresses, and a hundred pairs of shoes, and send my father ten shillings a week regular, and have champagne, and chicken, and whisky, and tongue sandwiches for breakfast every afternoon...*'

She stopped to look at a pair of orange-and-silver dance-slippers, priced at six-and-elevenpence. With the impulse, she went straight into the shop.

'I want those orange-and-silver shoes in the window.'

'What size, madam?'

'Um ... er, fours.'

'Oh, I'm awfully sorry, madam, but those slippers are the last of a range; we only have them in threes and fives.'

'Oh. . . . Well, can I try on a three?'

'Yes, certainly; but they're a very small fitting three.'

Vi felt like a woman on the verge of a terrible bereavement;

without those orange-and-silver slippers there would be nothing left for her to live for; nothing.

'I'll try 'em on.'

She squeezed her feet into them, and hobbled three paces in agony.

'Perhaps the five, madam?'

'No, I don't *take* size five. ... Could you stretch these?'

'Just a little, madam; but I'd try the five if I were you – it's a very small-fitting five.'

'Stretch these.' She followed the assistant with her eyes; she was afraid to let the orange-and-silver slippers out of her sight. They were as dear to her as life itself. She needed them more than anything else on earth.

'Now you might find them a little easier, madam.'

'Ooooo!' Vi put them on. This time she could walk five paces in them. 'Yes, that's better. They'll stretch a bit when I've worn them once or twice, won't they?'

'Oh, yes, madam.'

'All right, I'll take them.' The girl put the slippers in a box. Vi blinked: it seemed to her that they were far too beautiful to cover up. She left the shop, hugging the box to her bosom.

Two doors farther on she paused at the window of a stationer's shop in which there was displayed a range of coloured inks – red ink, yellow ink, blue ink, orange ink –

'*Orange ink! Then I could write letters to match my shoes!*' She almost ran into the shop.

'How much is orange ink?'

'Sixpence and ninepence, miss.'

'I'll have a sixpenny bottle.'

Vi put the ink in her bag. Then she remembered that she had come out to buy stockings and a brassiere. Well, the brassiere would have to wait; but stockings were a necessity. Grossman's had good stockings for one-and-eleven. ... But next door to the stationer's there was a Woolworth's store. She went in – not to buy anything, but only to look around. Nobody goes into Woolworth's shops to buy anything: one visits Woolworth's as a kind of museum, merely to look …

The cosmetics counter drew Vi as a magnet.

DARK ALLURE PERFUMES said a show-card. Vi clutched at a bottle as a starving man might clutch at a loaf. 'Oh, Miss!' … *Ting* went the cash-register. Vi placed the perfume-bottle in her pocket. Then her conscience muttered: '*Wasting money on scent when you've got a dozen bottles already! Get the stockings before all your money is gone!*' She set her jaw resolutely. But Woolworth is a tempter, a devil with women; a genius of shelf appeal, he displays feminine trimmings near the door; he catches them as they go in, and, as they go out cashes in on their afterthoughts. Vi saw a display of artificial flowers.

These were things she could not resist – canvas camelias, cotton roses, velveteen violets – they were somehow close to her soul. She bought something resembling a sprig of yellow pansies. '*Stockings! Stockings!*' cried her conscience. She grasped the paper bag with the artificial flowers. Now she would go to Grossman's, she really and truly would.…

Glass emeralds set in gilt metal on the jewellery counter, winked at her like satanic eyes. She handled a pair of ear-rings: forty medium-sized diamonds set in solid lumps of platinum, complete with clasps on a card – sixpence the lot. Woolworth must be mad to sell such lovely things so cheap. 'These, miss!' 'Thank you, madam.' *Ting.*

'*After all,*' thought Vi, '*I've still got about half a crown left.…*' She went out and crossed the road, determined to buy her stockings. But she had to go out of her way to avoid a 'bus, and found herself outside the '*Black Horse.*'

Outside a public-house!

The swing-doors opened and shut like snapping jaws, and swallowed her.

'Johnnie Walker,' she said to the barmaid. She drank it, and felt better. 'Same again.'

'*Oh Jesus, my stockings!*' she thought, abruptly. But there was only a shilling left in her purse. Still, there was always Woolworth's. A pair of stockings, sixpence each stocking; just for this one evening.... She finished her second drink, and went back to Woolworth's.

As she walked to the stocking-counter she looked neither to the right nor to the left. Stockings, stockings, stockings, stockin –

A spotted silk handkerchief caught her eye. She hesitated and advanced a hand towards it. '*No, no!*' cried the muffled voice of reason. Well, she would just feel it. She touched it, lingered over it, paused –

'Can I help you, madam?' asked a sales-girl.

'I'll have this one,' said Vi. She wanted to kick herself. Then an idea struck her, an inspiration. '*Coo! I can wear my sandals and paint my toenails –*'

She returned to the cosmetics counter. Varnish for toenails ... dark red....

Ting! ... 'Thank you, madam.'

Having no more money, she walked home, and laid out her parcels on Helen's bed.

'Well, did you get your stuff?' asked Helen.

'Oh, yes.'

'What's in that box? Shoes?'

'Uh?' Vi opened the box, took out the shoes, held them up, made a grimace, threw them down, and said: 'Oh Christ, aren't they lousy!'

Gerald Kersch, *Night and the City*, 1938

'FIRE FIRE!'

The evening was very beautiful, and we walked as far as Canal Street and back. During our promenade, two fire engines passed us, attended by the usual retinue of shouting children; this is about the sixth time since yesterday evening. They are so frequent here, that the cry: 'Fire, Fire!' seems to excite neither alarm nor curiosity, and except the above mentioned pains-taking juveniles, none of the inhabitants seem in the least bit disturbed by it.

Fanny Kemble, *Mrs. Butler's Diary*, 1835

TOWN OR COUNTRY?

There is a map of Washington accurately laid down; and taking that map with him in his journeyings a man may lose himself in the streets, not as one loses oneself in London between Shoreditch and Russell Square, but as one does so in the deserts of the Holy Land, between Emmaus and Arimathea. In the first place no one knows where the places are, or is sure of their existence, and then between their presumed localities the country is wild, trackless, unbridged, uninhabited, and desolate. Massachusetts Avenue runs the whole length of the city, and is inserted on the maps as a full-blown street, about four miles in length. Go there, and you will find yourself not only out of town, away among the fields, but you will find yourself beyond the fields, in an uncultivated wilderness. Tucking your trousers up to your knees you will wade through bogs, you will lose yourself amongst rude hillocks, you will be out of reach of humanity. The unfinished dome of the Capitol will loom before you in the distance, and you will think that you approach the ruins of some western Palmyra. If you are a sportsman, you will desire to shoot snipe within sight of the President's house. There is much unsettled land within the States of America, but I think none so desolate in its state of nature as three fourths of the ground on which is supposed to stand the city of Washington.

Anthony Trollope, *North America*, 1862

LIVERPOOL?

Free Town is on the northern base of the mountain, and extends along the sea-front with most business like wharves, quays and warehouses. Viewed from the harbour, 'The Liverpool of West Africa', as it is called, looks as if it were built of grey stone, which it is not. When you get ashore, you will find that most of the stores and houses – the majority of which, it may be remarked, are in a state of acute dilapidation – are of painted wood, with corrugated iron roofs.

There is one central street, and the others are neatly planned at right angles to it. None of them are in any way paved or metalled. They are covered in much prettier fashion, and in a way more suitable for naked feet, by green Bahama grass, save and except those which are so nearly perpendicular that they have got every bit of earth and grass cleared off them down to the bed-rock, by the heavy rain of the wet season.

In every direction natives are walking at a brisk pace, their naked feet making no sound on the springy turf of the streets, carrying on their heads huge burdens which are usually crowned by the hat of the bearer, a large limpet-shaped affair made of palm trees. While some carry these enormous bundles, others bear logs or planks of wood, blocks of building stone, vessels containing palm-oil, baskets of vegetables, or tin-trays on which are folded shawls. As the great majority of the native inhabitants of Sierra Leone pay no attention whatever to where they are going, either in this world or the next, the confusion and noise are out of all proportion to the size of the town; and when, as frequently happens, a section of actively perambulating burden bearers charge recklessly into a sedentary section, the members of which have dismounted their loads and squatted themselves down beside them, right in the middle of the fairway, to have a friendly yell with some acquaintances, the row becomes terrific. In among these crowds of county folk walk stately Mohammedans, Mandingoes, Akers, and Fulahs of the Arabised tribes of the Western Soudan. These are lithe, well-made men, and walk with a peculiarly fine, elastic carriage.

Mary Kingsley, *Travels in West Africa*, 1897

LIVERPOOL

I walked on, down Princes Road. There was shabby gentility mixed with unobtrusive ruin. There was something gothic about stately old buildings half burned to the ground, or turned into brothels (surely door-bells labelled *Fiona* and *Janine* and *Miss Tress* meant that?). Loud music came from the open windows of the 'Nigeria Social Club' and at the 'Sierra Leone Social Club' there were fat blacks in bowler hats and shabby business suits on the steps, drinking beer out of cans. I assumed that the 'social club' was a way of evading Britain's strict drinking hours, and the names suggested not racism but rather nationalism or even tribalism – I could not imagine anyone from Upper Volta or Nigeria being welcome in the 'Ghana Social Club'.

Princes Road was a wide boulevard lined with trees. I followed it down to Granby, counting policemen – eight in a matter of minutes. They walked in pairs carrying steel-tipped canes about a yard long, the sort of weapon that usually has a poetic name, like 'wog-basher'. The policemen gave the impression of friendliness and deliberately chatted to bystanders and small children, seeming to ignore the graffiti which said PIGS OUT and *Why are coppers like bananas – coz they yellow, they bent, and they come in bunches.*

The shops on side streets had either boarded-up windows or else steel mesh grates, and the same grates sheathed the public phone-boxes. I stepped into one of these phone-boxes and called the Central Police Station and asked the information officer how many black policemen there were in Liverpool.

'Who wants to know?' he asked.

'Just a curious American,' I said.

'I should have known,' he said. 'I'll tell you something – Liverpool is nothing like America. I know about the trouble you've got over there, and compared to that this is nothing. I could give you figures –'

'For starters, how many black policemen?'

'Twelve coloured officers,' he said. And the entire force was 4600.

'*Twelve!*' I laughed and hung up.

And the 'coloured' was interesting, too. Policemen were 'coloured', convicted criminals were 'West Indian', and purse-snatchers were 'nig-nogs'. But when a black runner came first in a race against foreigners he was 'English'. If he came second he was 'British'. If he lost he was 'coloured'. If he cheated he was 'West Indian'.

I kept walking. The riots had left marks on Liverpool Eight that were visible a year later: the broken windows had not been fixed, there were signs of scorching on walls and doors, and temporary barricades had been left in place. And there were posters advertising lectures by members of the Communist Party and the Socialist Workers Party – very angry lectures, judging by the titles ('Fight Back!', 'We Demand Action!' and so forth). And yet this area was not the ruin I had expected. I had been promised a wasteland, but it was no more than fine decaying houses and rotting odours.

In a ploy to gain entrance to a house I asked a shopkeeper (Manubhai Patel, formerly of Kampala, Uganda; drygoods and sundries) if he knew of a person who might sew a button on my leather jacket. Yes, he knew a *karia* – Gujerati for black – just around the corner.

'Thanks very much,' I said.

'*Kwaheri, bwana.*'

God, I thought, that feels good. It had been years since anyone had called me *bwana*.

Paul Theroux, *The Kingdom by the Sea*, 1983

THE STROLLER AND THE BYE-LAW

At three o'clock Cummings and Gowing called for a good long walk over Hampstead and Finchley, and brought with them a friend named Stillbrook. We walked and chatted together, except Stillbrook, who was always a few yards behind us staring at the ground and cutting at the grass with his stick.

As it was getting on for five, we four held a consultation, and Gowing suggested that we should make for 'The Cow and Hedge' and get some tea. Stillbrook said: 'A brandy and soda was good enough for him.' I reminded them that all public-houses were closed till six o'clock. Stillbrook said, 'That's all right – *bona fide travellers.*'

We arrived; as I was trying to pass, the man in charge of the gate said, 'Where from?' I replied: 'Holloway.' He immediately put up his arm, and declined to let me pass. I turned back for a moment, when I saw Stillbrook closely followed by Cummings and Gowing, make for the entrance. I watched them, and thought I would have a good laugh at their expense. I heard the porter say, 'Where from?' When to my surprise, in fact disgust, Stillbrook replied: 'Blackheath,' and the three were immediately admitted. Gowing called to me across the gate, and said: 'We shan't be a minute.' I waited for them the best part of an hour. When they appeared they were all in most excellent spirits, and the only one who made an effort to apologize was Stillbrook, who said to me, 'It was very rough on you to be kept waiting but we had another spin for S. and B's.' I walked home in silence; I couldn't speak to them. I felt very dull the whole evening.

George and Weedon Grossmith, *The Diary of a Nobody*, 1894

STRANGE STROLLS (1)

And such a magnificent hippodrome that I could not resist trying to go round it just once in Vincenti's fashion. It proved frightfully difficult. After my fourteenth fall I was pulled up by a policeman. 'What are you doing here?' he said, keeping fast hold of me. 'I 'bin watching you for the last five minutes.' I explained eloquently and enthusiastically. He hesitated a moment, and then said, 'Would you mind holding my helmet while I have a try? It dont look so hard.' Next moment his head was buried in the macadam and his right knee was out through its torn garment. 'I never was beaten yet,' he said, 'and I wont be beaten now. It was my coat that tripped me.' We both hung our coats on the railings and went at it again. If each round of the square had been a round in a prize-fight we should have been less damaged and disfigured; but we persevered in getting round twice without a rest or a fall, when an inspector arrived and asked him bitterly whether that was his notion of fixed point duty. 'I allow it aint fixed point,' said the constable, emboldened by his new accomplishment, 'but I'll lay half a sovereign you cant do it.' The inspector could not resist the temptation to try (I was whirling round before his eyes in a most fascinating manner); and he made rapid progress after half an hour or so. We were subsequently joined by an early postman and by a milkman, who unfortunately broke his leg and had to be carried to hospital by the other three.

George Bernard Shaw, *The Star*, 1890

STRANGE STROLLS (2)

One day in New York, wishing to explore that great city in a truly haphazard way, I hit on the following device – a zigzag walk. The first turning to the left is the way of the heart. Take it at random and you are sure to find something pleasant and diverting. Take the left again and the piquancy may be repeated. But reason must come to the rescue, and you must turn to the right in order to save yourself from a mere uninteresting circle. To make a zigzag walk you take the first turning to the left, the first to the right, then the first to the left again, and so on.

I had a wonderful night walking thus in New York, taking cross-sections of that marvellous cosmopolitan city. And many were the surprises and delights and curiosities that the city unfolded to me in its purlieus and alleys and highways and quays.

Stephen Graham, *The Gentle Art of Tramping*, 1926

STRANGE STROLLS (3)

I think I may have invented it myself – certainly I have been doing it for years – though there is nothing particularly ingenious about it. It consists of walking back and forth across the Thames, crossing every pedestrian bridge from Tower to Hammersmith (it can be done the other way, of course, but if the route is traversed westwards, and the walker starts on the northern side of Tower Bridge, he has the most beautiful section of the entire march – the southern shore between Putney and Hammersmith – to finish with).

There are sixteen walkable bridges on the route: Tower, London, Southwark, Blackfriars, Waterloo, Hungerford, Westminster, Lambeth, Vauxhall, Chelsea, Albert, Battersea, Wandsworth, Fulham (a railway bridge, but, like Hungerford, with a pedestrian walkway stuck on the side), Putney and Hammersmith. There is no signboard, German fashion, on the northern approach to Tower Bridge, with an estimate of the time the walk will take; this will depend not only on the speed of the walker but on the policy regarding rests and refreshment.

Bernard Levin, *Enthusiasms*, 1985

STRANGE STROLLS (4)

Some of the special pleasures the city has to offer are the sort you might as well enjoy because they are unavoidable. Take crossing the street in the Old Quarter. This you do by lifting your elbows high, as if fording a furious stream. The street is narrow but the traffic torrential. The trick is to walk forward slowly enough for drivers to see you in time to avoid you, but fast enough to gain the centre without being knocked down. Then, with a quick glance left and right, the same deliberate steps carry you on to the other side.

It is an enormous thrill, like whitewater rafting. The important thing is to take the plunge. I've seen tourists standing for ten minutes staring into the hurtling traffic, unable to put a toe into the stream, hoping perhaps that the passing flood will stop. But it never stops.

Christopher Hope, *The Hanoi Hug*, 1998

PAVEMENT REVERIES . . .

After the strings of houses, after the unvarying streets through which I gently accompany you, the walls rise up ... the warehouses, all-brick giant ramparts ... Treasure cliffs! ... monster shops ... phantasmagoric storehouses, citadels of merchandise, mountains of tanned goatskins enough to stink all the way to

Kamchatka! Forest of mahogany in thousands of piles, tied up like asparagus, in pyramids, miles of materials! ... rugs enough to cover the Moon, the whole world ... all the floors in the Universe! ... Enough wool to smother Europe beneath heaps of cuddly warmth ... Herrings to fill the seas! Himalayas of powdered sugar ... Matches to fry the poles! ... Enormous avalanches of pepper, enough to make the Seven Floods sneeze! ... A thousand boatloads of onions, enough to cry through five hundred wars ... Three thousand six hundred trains of beans drying in covered hangars more colossal than the Charing Cross, North and Saint Lazare stations put together ... Coffee for the whole planet! ... enough to give a lift during their forced marches to the four hundred thousand avenging conflicts of the fight-ingest armies in the world ... never again sitting, snoring, exempt from sleep and eating, hypertense, storming, exalted, dying in the charge, hearts unfolded, borne off to superdeath by the hyperpalpitating superglory of powdered coffee! ... The dream of the three hundred fifteen emperors! ...

Still more buildings, more enormous, for the loads of cheap meat, preserved carcasses in dry freezers, in mustard sauce, in prodigious venison, myriads of sausages with chopped rind as high as the Alps! ... Corned-beef fat, giant masses that would cover Parliament and Leicester and Waterloo so that you wouldn't see them stuck underneath, they'd be swamped so fast! two mammoths all stuffed with truffles just transported from the River Love, preserved, intact in ice, refrigerated for twelve thousand years! ...

I'm now talking about jam, really colossal sweetness, forums of jars of mirabelle plums, surging oceans of oranges, rising up on all sides, overflowing the roofs, fleetloads from Afghanistan, sweet golden loukoums from Istanbul, pure sugar, all in acacia leaves ... Myrtles from Smyrna and Karachi ... sloes from Finland ... Chaos, vales of precious fruits stored behind triple-doors, incredible choice of flavors, exquisite sugared Arabian Nights' magic in amphora jars, eternal joys for childhood promised from the depths of the Scriptures, so dense, so eager that sometimes they crack the wall, they're squeezed in so thick, burst the sheet metal, roll into the street, cascade right into the gutter! in pleasant torrents and delights! ... Then the mounted police come charging in, clear the area, the view, lash the looters with blackjacks ... It's the end of a dream! ...

Immediately on the other side of these docks there's the big violent sweep of air whirling in from the green heights of the valley in Greenwich ... the big bend in the river ... the gusts from the sea ... from the pale-dawn estuaries below ... after Barking ... lying just below the clouds ... where the tiny cargoes come up ... where the waves break against the jetties, splash, fall back, swoon into the mud ... The ebbing tide. It all depends on the kind of thing you like! ... I say it in all simplicity! ... The sky ... the gray water ... the purplish shores ... it's all so soothing ... No control of one or the other ... gently drawn round ... in slow circles and eddies, you're always charmed further off toward other dreams ... all to expire in lovely secrets, toward other worlds getting ready in veils and mists with big pale and fuzzy designs among the whispering mosses ... Are you following me?

Louis-Ferdinand Céline, *Guignol's Band*, 1934
(trans. Bernard Frechtman and Jack T. Nile, 1954)

STOP AND LOOK

She walked through the streets with Thomas, feeling the life of the city. 'I know what's on your mind,' he was saying; 'I've felt it myself. You stop in front of the monuments and palaces ... everything else seems like a hum, a background noise.'

Giuliana Morandini, *Berlin Angel*, 1987 (trans. Liz Heron, 1993)

ARCHITECTURE, FASHIONS, FREQUENCIE OF
PEOPLE EXHAUST HIM

In the afternoon he spent two hours in his room, then took the *vaporetto* to Venice, across the foul-smelling lagoon. He got out at San Marco, had his tea in the Piazza, and then, as his custom was, took a walk through the streets. But this walk of his brought about nothing less than a revolution in his mood and an entire change in all his plans. There was a hateful sultriness in the narrow streets. The air was so heavy that all the manifold smells wafted out of houses, shops, and cook shops – smells of oil, perfumery, and so forth – hung low, like exhalations, not dissipating. Cigarette smoke seemed to stand in the air, it drifted so slowly away. To-day the crowd in these narrow lanes oppressed the stroller instead of diverting him. The longer he walked, the more was he in tortures under that state, which is the product of the sea air and the sirocco and which excites and enervates at once. He perspired painfully. His eyes rebelled, his chest was heavy, he felt feverish, the blood throbbed in his temples. He fled from the huddled, narrow streets of the commercial city, crossed many bridges, and came into the poor quarter of Venice. Beggars waylaid him, the canals sickened him with their evil exhalations. He reached a quiet square, one of those that exist at the city's heart, forsaken of God and man; there he rested awhile on the margin of a fountain, wiped his brow, and admitted that he must be gone.

Thomas Mann, *Death in Venice*, 1912
(trans. H. T. Lowe Porter, 1928)

IT GOES QUIET

In this late attempt to recapture the town, I seemed to have cleared the streets. They are as empty as the thoroughfares in an architectural print. Nothing but a few historical phantoms survive; a muffled drum, a figure from a book and an echo of Utraquists rioting a few squares away – the milling citizens, the rushing traffic vanish and the voices of the bilingual city sink to a whisper. I can just remember a chestnut-woman in a kerchief stamping beside a brazier to keep warm and a hurrying Franciscan with a dozen loaves under his arm. Three cab-drivers nursing their tall whips and drinking schnapps in the outside-bar of a wine cellar materialise for a moment above the sawdust, their noses scarlet from the cold or drink or both and evaporate again, red noses last, like rear lamps fading through a fog.

Patrick Leigh Fermor, *A Time of Gifts*, 1977

THEN COME THE COMMUTING DEAD

Walking through the city, there is no encouragement to look up at the sky. Historically, for most of this century – from the time of T. S. Eliot's 'unreal city/under the brown fog of winter noon', his upright dead, to Robert Frank's bankers, photo-graphed in 1951, uniform drudges purposely scuttling under the lee of tall buildings (the lids of their polished top hats, their bowlers, shading the eyes from the heavens) – it has been forbidden to tilt back the neck. An unfocussed stare into the middle distance has been cultivated; Adam's apples bobbling, lips tight with swallowed secrets. It's forbidden to stop, to slow down, to admit changes in atmospheric pressure. There's no weather here: lightweight suits, loose rain-coats, at all seasons. The City never was a place for through traffic – where else was there to go? Within the walls, it's a zone of other-directed zombies, procurers of fog, scurrying ants who have flakes of ancient dirt from the high cliff walls of banks and brokerages and temples of finance. The gargoyles keep watch: dragons, griffins, lions, eagles. They check to make sure that eyes stay on pavements, on the legs in front of them. An enclosure of high heels and extravagant stockings. Walkers who make walking impossible.

Iain Sinclair, *Lights Out for the Territory*, 1997

WALK, DON'T WALK

I always get depressed after lunch. It figures, I hear you say. I go to my room and sometimes I have a drink (I don't smoke, so dope's out). Other days I play guitar or else work on my screen-play. It's called 'WALK DON'T WALK'. I get a lot of good ideas after lunch for some reason. That's when I got the idea for my screen-play. It just came to me. I remembered how I'd been stuck one day at the corner of Arteria boulevard and Normandie avenue. There was a pile of traffic and the pedestrian signs were going berserk. 'WALK' would come on so I'd start across. Two seconds later 'DON'T WALK' so I go back. Then on comes 'WALK' again. This went on for ten minutes. 'WALK. DON'T WALK. WALK. DON'T WALK.' I was practically out of my box. But what really stunned me was the way I just stayed there and obeyed the goddam machine for so long – I never even thought about going it alone. Then one afternoon it came to me that it was a neat image for life; just the right kind of metaphor for the whole can of worms. The final scene of this movie is going to be a slow crane shot away from this malfunctioning traffic sign going 'WALK. DON'T WALK.' Then the camera pulls further up and away in a helicopter and you see that in fact the whole city is fouled up because of this one sign flashing. They don't know what to do; the programming's gone wrong. It's a great final scene.

William Boyd, 'Not Yet, Jayette', 1981

SEVEN

Tough Tracks

I choose to walk at all risks.

Elizabeth Barrett Browning

THE TRIALS OF AN EARLY WANDERER

'A little further, O my father, yet a little further, and we shall come into the open moonlight.' Their road was through a forest of fir-trees; at its entrance the trees stood at distances from each other, and the path was broad, and the moonlight and the moonlight shadows reposed upon it, and appeared quietly to inhabit that solitude. But soon the path winded and became narrow; the sun at high noon sometimes speckled, but never illumined it, and now it was dark as a cavern.

'It is dark, O my father!' said Enos, 'but the path under our feet is smooth and soft, and we shall soon come out into the open moonlight.'

'Lead on, my child!' said Cain; 'guide me, little child!' And the innocent little child clasped a finger of the hand which had murdered the righteous Abel, and he guided his father. 'The fir branches drip upon thee, my son.' 'Yea, pleasantly, father, for I ran fast and eagerly to bring thee the pitcher and the cake, and my body is not yet cool. How happy the squirrels are that feed on these fir-trees! they leap from bough to bough, and the old squirrels play round their young ones in the nest. I clomb a tree yesterday at noon, O my father, that I might play with them, but they leaped away from the branches, even to the slender twigs did they leap, and in a moment I beheld them on another tree. Why, O my father, would they not play with me? … Then Cain stopped, and stifling his groans he sank to the earth, and the child Enos stood in the darkness beside him.

And Cain lifted up his voice and cried bitterly, and said, 'The Mighty One that persecuteth me is on this side and on that; he pursueth my soul like the wind, like the sand-blast he passeth through me; he is around me even as the air! O that I might be utterly no more! I desire to die – yea, the things that never had life, neither move they upon the earth – behold! they seem precious to mine eyes. O that a man might live without the

breath of his nostrils. So I might abide in darkness, and blackness, and an empty space! Yea, I would lie down. I would not
rise, neither would I stir my limbs till I became as the rock in
the den of the lion, on which the young lion resteth his head
whilst he sleepeth ...' Then Enos spake to his father, 'Arise, my
father, arise, we are but a little way from the place where I found
the cake and the pitcher.' And Cain said, 'How knowest thou!'
and the child answered – 'Behold the bare rocks are a few of
thy strides distant from the forest; and while even now thou
wert lifting up thy voice, I heard the echo.' Then the child took
hold of his father, as if he would raise him: and Cain being faint
and feeble rose slowly on his knees and pressed himself against
the trunk of a fir, and stood upright and followed the child.

The path was dark till within three strides' length of its
termination, when it turned suddenly; the thick black trees
formed a low arch, and the moonlight appeared for a moment
like a dazzling portal. Enos ran before and stood in the open
air; and when Cain, his father, emerged from the darkness, the
child was affrighted. For the mighty limbs of Cain were wasted
as by fire; his hair was as the matted curls on the bison's forehead, and so glared his fierce and sullen eye beneath: and the
black abundant locks on either side, a rank and tangled mass,
were stained and scorched, as though the grasp of a burning
iron hand had striven to rend them; and his countenance told
in a strange and terrible language of agonies that had been,
and were, and were still to continue to be.

The scene around was desolate; as far as the eye could reach
it was desolate: the bare rocks faced each other, and left a long
and wide interval of thin white sand. You might wander on
and look round and round, and peep into the crevices of the
rocks and discover nothing that acknowledged the influence
of the seasons. There was no spring, no summer, no autumn:
and the winter's snow, that would have been lovely, fell not on
these hot rocks and scorching sands ... The pointed and

shattered summits of the ridges of the rocks made a rude mimicry of human concerns, and seemed to prophecy mutely of things that then were not; steeples, and battlements, and ships with naked masts. As far from the wood as a boy might sling a pebble of the brook, there was one rock by itself at a small distance from the main ridge. It had been precipitated there perhaps by the groan which the Earth uttered when our first father fell. Before you approached, it appeared to lie flat on the ground, but its base slanted from its point, and between its point and the sands a tall man might stand upright. It was here that Enos had found the pitcher and cake, and to this place he led his father. But ere they had reached the rock they beheld a human shape: his back was towards them, and they were advancing unperceived, when they heard him smite his breast and cry aloud, 'Woe is me! woe is me! I must never die again, and yet I am perishing with thirst and hunger.'

Pallid, as the reflection of the sheeted lightning on the heavy-sailing night-cloud, became the face of Cain; but the child Enos took hold of the shaggy skin, his father's robe, and raised his eyes to his father, and listening whispered, 'Ere yet I could speak, I am sure, O my father, that I heard that voice. Have not I often said that I remembered a sweet voice? O my father! this is it': and Cain trembled exceedingly. The voice was sweet indeed, but it was thin and querulous, like that of a feeble slave in misery, who despairs altogether, yet can not refrain himself from weeping and lamentation. And, behold! Enos glided forward, and creeping softly around the base of the rock, stood before the stranger, and looked up into his face. And the Shape shrieked, and turned round, and Cain beheld him, that his limbs and his face were those of his brother Abel whom he had killed! And Cain stood like one who struggles in his sleep because of the exceeding terribleness of a dream.

Thus as he stood in silence and darkness of soul, the Shape fell at his feet, and embraced his knees, and cried out with a bitter outcry, 'Thou eldest born of Adam, whom Eve, my mother, brought forth, cease to torment me! I was feeding my flocks in green pastures by the side of quiet rivers, and thou killedst me; and now I am in misery.' Then Cain closed his eyes, and hid them with his hands; and again he opened his eyes, and looked around him, and said to Enos, 'What beholdest thou? Didst thou hear a voice, my son?' 'Yes, my father, I beheld a man in unclean garments and he uttered a sweet voice, full of lamentation.' Then Cain raised up the Shape that was like Abel, and said: – 'The Creator of our father, who had respect unto thee, and unto thy offering, wherefore hath he forsaken thee?' Then the Shape shrieked a second time, and rent his garment, and his naked skin was like the white sands beneath their feet; and he shrieked yet a third time, and threw himself on his face upon the sand that was black with the shadow of the rock, and Cain and Enos sate beside him; the child by his right hand, and Cain by his left. They were all three under the rock, and within the shadow. The Shape that was like Abel raised himself up, and spake to the child, 'I know where the cold waters are, but I may not drink, wherefore didst thou then take away my pitcher?' But Cain said, 'Didst thou not find favour in the sight of the Lord thy God?' The Shape answered, 'The Lord is God of the Living only; the dead have another God.' Then the child Enos lifted up his eyes and prayed; but Cain rejoiced secretly in his heart. 'Wretched shall they be all the days of their mortal life,' exclaimed the Shape, 'who sacrifice worthy and acceptable sacrifices to the God of the dead; but after death their toil ceaseth. Woe is me, for I was well beloved by the God of the living, and cruel wert thou, O my brother, who didst snatch me away from his power and his dominion.' Having uttered these words, he rose suddenly, and fled over the sands, and Cain said in his heart, 'The curse of the Lord is on me; but who is the God of the dead?' and he ran after the Shape, and the Shape fled shrieking over the sands, and the sands rose like white mists behind the steps of Cain, but the feet of him that was like Abel disturbed not the sands. He greatly outrun Cain, and turning short, he wheeled round, and came again to the rock where they had been sitting, and where Enos still stood; and the child caught hold of his garment as he passed by, and he fell upon the ground. And Cain stopped, and beholding him not, said, 'he has passed into the dark woods,' and he walked slowly back to the rocks; and when he reached it the child told him that he had caught hold of his garment as he passed by, and that the man had fallen upon the ground: and Cain once more sate beside him, and said, 'Abel, my brother, I would lament for thee, but that the spirit within me is withered, and burnt up with extreme agony. Now, I pray thee, by thy flocks, and by thy pastures, and by the quiet rivers which thou lovedst, that thou tell me all that thou knowest. Who is the God of the dead? where doth he make his dwelling? what sacrifices are acceptable unto him? for I have offered, but have not been received; I have prayed, and have not been heard; and how can I be afflicted more than I already am?' The Shape arose and answered, 'O that thou hadst had pity on me as I will have pity on thee. Follow me, Son of Adam! and bring thy child with thee!'

And they three passed over the white sands between the rocks, silent as the shadows.

Samuel Taylor Coleridge, *The Wanderings of Cain*, Canto II, 1798

WALKING IN THE MIDST OF THE SEA

And the LORD said unto Moses, Wherefore criest thou unto me? speak unto the children of Israel, that they go forward:

But lift thou up thy rod, and stretch out thine hand over the sea, and divide it: and the children of Israel shall go on dry ground through the midst of the sea.

And I, behold, I will harden the hearts of the Egyptians, and they shall follow them: and I will get me honour upon Pharaoh, and upon all his host ...

And Moses stretched out his hand over the sea; and the LORD caused the sea to go back by a strong east wind all that night, and made the sea dry land, and the waters were divided.

And the children of Israel went into the midst of the sea upon the dry ground: and the waters were a wall unto them on their right hand, and on their left.

And the Egyptians pursued, and went in after them to the midst of the sea, even all Pharaoh's horses, his chariots, and his horsemen ...

And the LORD said unto Moses, Stretch out thine hand over the sea, that the waters may come again upon the Egyptians, upon their chariots, and upon their horsemen.

And Moses stretched forth his hand over the sea, and the sea returned to his strength when the morning appeared; and the Egyptians fled against it; and the LORD overthrew the Egyptians in the midst of the sea.

And the waters returned, and covered the chariots, and the horsemen, and all the host of Pharaoh that came into the sea after them; there remained not so much as one of them.

But the children of Israel walked upon dry land in the midst of the sea; and the waters were a wall unto them on their right hand, and on their left.

Exodus 14:15–29

Try to sleep. But sleep does not come.
Gut knots.
Get up. Walk one hundred rounds.
Sigh hard.
In one night dark hair
Turns to third season's hoar frost.

Lu Yu, 1117

THE WALKER IS TEMPTED BY THE EASY WAY

Upon starting on again we went more slowly, and I especially advanced along the rocky way with a more deliberate step. While my brother chose a direct path straight up the ridge, I weakly took an easier one which really descended. When I was called back, and the right road was shown me, I replied that I hoped to find a better way around on the other side, and that I did not mind going farther if the path were only less steep. This was just an excuse for my laziness; and when the others had already reached a considerable height I was still wandering in the valleys. I had failed to find an easier path, and had only increased the distance and difficulty of the ascent. At last I became disgusted with the intricate way I had chosen, and resolved to ascend without more ado. When I reached my brother, who, while waiting for me, had had ample opportunity for rest, I was tired and irritated. We walked along together for a time, but hardly had we passed the first spur when I forgot about the circuitous route which I had just tried, and took a lower one again. Once more I followed an easy, roundabout path through winding valleys, only to find myself soon in my old difficulty. I was simply trying to avoid the exertion of the ascent; but no human ingenuity can alter the nature of things, or cause anything to reach a height by going down. Suffice it to say that, much to my vexation and my brother's amusement, I made this same mistake three times or more during a few hours.

Petrarch, *The Ascent of Mount Ventoux*, 1336

THE EASY WAY WILL ALWAYS TEMPT

I saw then that they went on their way to a pleasant river, which David the king called 'the river of God;' but John, 'the river of the water of life.' (Ps. xlvi. 4. Ezek. xlvii. 1–9. Rev. xxii. 1.) Now, their way lay just upon the bank of this river: here, therefore, Christian and his companion walked with great delight; they drank also of the water of the river, which was pleasant and enlivening to their weary spirits. Besides, on the banks of this river, on either side, were green trees with all manner of fruit; and the leaves they ate to prevent surfeits and other diseases that are incident to those that heat their blood by travel. On either side of the river was also a meadow, curiously beautified with lilies; and it was green all the year long. In this meadow they lay down and slept, for here they might lie safely. (Ps. xxiii. 2. Isa. xiv. 30.) When they awoke, they gathered again of the fruit of the trees, and drank again of the water of the river, and then lay down again to sleep. Thus they did several days and nights. Then they sang, –

> Behold ye how these crystal streams do glide,
> To comfort pilgrims by the highway-side.
> The meadows green, besides their fragrant smell,
> Yield dainties for them; and he who can tell
> What pleasant fruit, yea, leaves, these trees do yield,
> Will soon sell all, that he may buy this field.

So when they were disposed to go on (for they were not as yet at their journey's end), they ate, and drank, and departed.

Now, I beheld in my dream that they had not journeyed far, but the river and the way for a time parted, at which they were not a little sorry; yet they durst not go out of the way. Now the way from the river was rough, and their feet tender by reason of their travel; so the souls of the pilgrims were much discouraged because of the way. (Num. xxi. 4.) Wherefore, still as they went on, they wished for a better way. Now, a little before them, there was on the left hand of the road a meadow, and a stile to go over into it, and that meadow is called By-path Meadow. Then said Christian to his fellow, If this meadow lieth along by our wayside, let us go over into it. Then he went to the stile to see, and behold a path lay along by the way on the other side of the fence. 'Tis according to my wish, said Christian. Here is the easiest going; come, good Hopeful, and let us go over.

Hope. But how if this path should lead us out of the way?

Chr. That is not likely, said the other. Look, doth it not go along by the wayside? So Hopeful, being persuaded by his fellow, went after him over the stile. When they were gone over, and were got into the path, they found it very easy for their feet; and withal they, looking before them, espied a man walking as they did, and his name was Vain-confidence: so they called after him, and asked him whither that way led. He said, To the Celestial Gate. Look, said Christian, did not I tell you so? By this you may see we are right. So they followed, and he went before them. But, behold, the night came on, and it grew very dark; so that they that were behind lost sight of him that went before.

He therefore that went before (Vain-confidence by name), not seeing the way before him, fell into a deep pit (Isa. ix. 16), which was on purpose there made by the prince of those grounds, to catch vainglorious fools withal, and was dashed in pieces with his fall.

Now Christian and his fellow heard him fall, so they called to know the matter; but there was none to answer, only they heard a groaning. Then said Hopeful, Where are we now? Then was his fellow silent, as mistrusting that he had led him out of the way; and now it began to rain, and thunder, and lighten, in a most dreadful manner, and the water rose amain.

Then Hopeful groaned within himself, saying, Oh that I had kept on my way!

Chr. Who could have thought that this path should have led us out of the way?

Hope. I was afraid on't at the very first, and therefore gave you that gentle caution. I would have spoken plainer, but that you are older than I.

Chr. Good brother, be not offended. I am sorry I have brought thee out of the way, and that I have put thee into such imminent danger. Pray, my brother, forgive me; I did not do it of an evil intent.

Hope. Be comforted, my brother, for I forgive thee; and believe, too, that this shall be for our good.

Chr. I am glad I have with me a merciful brother. But we must not stand here; let us try to go back again.

Hope. But, good brother, let me go before.

Chr. No, if you please, let me go first, that, if there be any danger, I may be first therein; because by my means we are both gone out of the way.

Hope. No, said Hopeful, you shall not go first; for your mind being troubled, may lead you out of the way again. – Then for their encouragment they heard the voice of one saying, 'Let thine heart be towards the highway, even the way that thou wentest: turn again.' (Jer. xxxi. 21.) But by this time the waters were greatly risen, by reason of which the way of going back was very dangerous. (Then I thought that it is easier going out of the way when we are in, than going in when we are out.) Yet they adventured to go back; but it was so dark, and the flood so high, that in their going back they had like to have been drowned nine or ten times.

Neither could they, with all the skill they had, get again to the stile that night. Wherefore at last, lighting under a little shelter, they sat down there until daybreak; but being weary, they fell asleep. Now there was not far from the place where they lay, a castle, called Doubting Castle, the owner whereof was Giant Despair; and it was in his grounds they now were sleeping. Wherefore he, getting up in the morning early, and walking up and down in his fields, caught Christian and Hopeful asleep in his grounds. Then with a grim and surly voice he bid them awake, and asked them whence they were, and what they did in his grounds. They told him they were pilgrims, and that they had lost their way. Then said the giant, You have this night trespassed on me, by trampling in and lying on my grounds, and therefore you must go along with me. So they were forced to go, because he was stronger than they. They also had but little to say, for they knew themselves in a fault. The giant, therefore, drove them before him, and put them into his castle, in a very dark dungeon, nasty and stinking to the spirits of these two men. Here, then, they lay from Wednesday morning till Saturday night, without one bit of bread, or drop of drink, or light, or any to ask how they did: they were, therefore, here in evil case, and were far from friends and acquaintance. (Ps. lxxxviii. 8.) Now in this place Christian had double sorrow, because it was through his unadvised counsel that they were brought into this distress.

John Bunyan, The Pilgrim's Progress, 1678

A WALK AROUND THE WORLD

Meanwhile, upon the firm opacous globe
Of this round World, whose first convex divides
The luminous inferior orbs, enclosed
From Chaos and th'inroad of Darkness old,
Satan alighted walks. A globe far off
It seemed, now seems a boundless Continent
Dark, waste and wild, under the frown of Night
Starless exposed, and ever-threatening storms
Of Chaos blustering round, inclement sky;
Save on that side which from the wall of Heaven,
Though distant far, some small reflection gains
Of glimmering air less vexed with tempest loud.
Here walked the Fiend at large in spacious field.
As when a vulture on Imaus bred,
Whose snowy ridge the roving Tartar bounds,

Dislodging from a region scarce of prey
To gorge the flesh of lambs or yeanling kids
On hills where flocks are fed, flies towards the Springs
Of Ganges or Hydaspes, Indian streams,
But in his way lights on the barren plains
Of Sericana, where Chineses drive
With sails and wind their cany wagons light:
So on this windy sea of land, the Fiend
Walked up and down alone bent on his prey,
Alone, for other creature in this place,
Living or lifeless, to be found was none,
None yet.

John Milton, Paradise Lost, Book III, 1667

A MAN'S NAKED FOOT

It happened one day, about noon, going towards my boat, I was exceedingly surprised with the print of a man's naked foot on the shore, which was very plain to see on the sand. I stood like one thunder-struck, or as if I had seen an apparition. I listened, I looked round me, but I could hear nothing, nor see anything. I went up to a rising-ground to look further; I went up to the shore, and down the shore, but it was all one: I could see no other impression but that one. I went to it again to see if there was any more, and to observe it might not be my fancy; but there was no room for that, for there was exactly the print of a foot – toes, heel and every part of a foot. How it came thither I knew not, nor could I in the least imagine; but after innumerable fluttering thoughts, like a man perfectly confused and out of myself, I came home to my fortification, not feeling, as we say, the ground I went on.

Daniel Defoe, Robinson Crusoe, 1719

MISSES SMITH AND BICKERTON BRAVE THE RICHMOND ROAD

Emma was just turning to the house, with spirits freshened up for the demands of the two little boys, as well as of their grandpapa, when the great iron sweep-gate opened, and two persons entered whom she had never less expected to see together – Frank Churchill with Harriet leaning on his arm – actually Harriet! – A moment sufficed to convince her that something extraordinary had happened. Harriet looked white and frightened, and he was trying to cheer her. – The iron gates and the front-door were not twenty yards asunder; – they were all three soon in the hall, and Harriet immediately sinking into a chair fainted away.

A young lady who faints, must be recovered; questions must be answered, and surprises be explained. Such events are very interesting, but the suspense of them cannot last long. A few minutes made Emma acquainted with the whole.

Miss Smith, and Miss Bickerton, another parlour boarder at Mrs. Goddard's, who had been also at the ball, had walked out together, and taken a road – the Richmond road, which, though apparently public enough for safety, had led them into alarm. – About half a mile beyond Highbury, making a sudden turn, and deeply shaded by elms on each side, it became for a considerable stretch very retired; and when the young ladies had advanced some way into it, they had suddenly perceived at a small distance before them, on a broader patch of greensward by the side, a party of gipsies. A child on the watch, came towards them to beg; and Miss Bickerton, excessively frightened, gave a great scream, and calling on Harriet to follow her, ran up a steep bank, cleared a slight hedge at the top, and made the best of her way by a short cut back to Highbury. But poor Harriet could not follow. She had suffered very much from cramp after dancing, and her first attempt to mount the bank brought on such a return of it as made her absolutely powerless – and in this state, and exceedingly terrified, she had been obliged to remain.

How the trampers might have behaved, had the young ladies been more courageous, must be doubtful; but such an invitation for attack could not be resisted; and Harriet was soon assailed by half a dozen children, headed by a stout woman and a great boy, all clamorous, and impertinent in look, though not absolutely in word. – More and more frightened, she immediately promised them money, and taking out her purse, gave them a shilling, and begged them not to want more, or to use her ill. – She was then able to walk, though but slowly, and was moving away – but her terror and her purse were too tempting, and she was followed, or rather surrounded, by the whole gang, demanding more.

In this state Frank Churchill had found her, she trembling and conditioning, they loud and insolent. By a most fortunate chance his leaving Highbury had been delayed so as to bring him to her assistance at this critical moment. The pleasantness of the morning had induced him to walk forward, and leave his horses to meet him by another road, a mile or two beyond Highbury – and happened to have borrowed a pair of scissors the night before of Miss Bates, and to have forgotten to restore them, he had been obliged to stop at her door, and go in for a few minutes: he was therefore later than he had intended; and being on foot, was unseen by the whole party till almost close to them. The terror which the woman and boy had been creating in Harriet was then their own portion. He had left them completely frightened; and Harriet eagerly clinging to him, and hardly able to speak, had just strength enough to reach Hartfield, before her spirits were quite overcome. It was his idea to bring her to Hartfield: he had thought of no other place.

This was the amount of the whole story, – of his communication and of Harriet's as soon as she had recovered her senses and speech. – He dared not stay longer than to see her well; these several delays left him not another minute to lose; and Emma engaging to give assurance of her safety to Mrs. Goddard, and notice of there being such a set of people in the neighbourhood to Mr. Knightley, he set off, with all the grateful blessings that she could utter for her friend and herself.

Jane Austen, *Emma*, 1814

THIS WALKER IS LEFT NAKED IN THE WORLD

I passed the night in the cottage of a farmer, resigning myself to the attacks and annoyance of such vermin as generally haunt impoverished dwellings. I was proportionably pleased in the morning to pursue my journey. My route was towards Liubane, at about the ninth mile-stone from which I sat down, to smoke a segar, or pipe, as fancy might dictate, when I was suddenly seized from behind, by two ruffians, whose visages were as much concealed as the oddness of their dress would permit. One of them, who held an iron bar in his hand, dragged me by the collar towards the forest, while the other, with a bayonetted musket, pushed me on, in such a manner, as to make me move with more than ordinary celerity; while a boy, auxiliary to these vagabonds, was stationed on the road side to keep a look out.

We had got some sixty or eighty paces into the thickest part of the forest, when I was desired to undress, and having stript off my trowsers and jacket, then my shirt, and, finally, my shoes and stockings, they proceeded to tie me to a tree. From this ceremony, and from the manner of it, I fully concluded that they intended to try the effect of a musket upon me, by firing at me as they would at a mark. I was, however, reserved for fresh scenes: the villains, with much *sang froid* seated themselves at my feet, and rifled my knapsack and pockets, even cutting out the linings of the clothes in search of bank bills or some other valuable articles. They then compelled me to take at least a pound of black bread, and a glass of rum poured from a small flask which had been suspended from my neck. Having appropriated my trowsers, shirts, stockings and shoes (the last I regretted most of all, as they were a present from Sir D. Bailey) – as also my spectacles, watch, compass, thermometer, and small pocket-sextant, with one hundred and sixty roubles, they at length released me from the tree, and at the point of a stiletto made me swear that I would not inform against them, – such, at least, I conjectured to be their meaning, though of their language I understood not a word.

Having received my promise, I was again treated to bread and rum, and once more fastened to the tree, in which condition they finally abandoned me. Not long after, a boy who was passing heard my cries, and set me at liberty. I did not doubt he was sent by my late companions upon so considerate an errand, and felt so far grateful: though it might require something more than common charity to forgive their depriving me of my shirt and trowsers, and leaving me almost as naked as I came into the world.

John Dundas Cochrane, *Narrative of a
Pedestrian Journey*, 1824

I WILL TAKE THE HARD WAY

The rain keeps on pouring down. I presently see one of my men sitting right in the middle of the road on a rock, totally unsheltered, and a feeling of shame comes over me in the face of this black man's aquatic courage. Besides, Herr von Lucke had said I was sure to get half-drowned and catch an awful cold, so there is no use delaying. Into the rain I go, and off we start. I may remark I subsequently found that my aquatic underling was drunk. I conscientiously attempt to keep dry, by holding up an umbrella, knowing that though hopeless it is the proper thing to do.

We leave the road about fifty yards above the hut, turning into the unbroken forest on the right-hand side, and following a narrow, slippery, muddy, root-beset bush-path that was a comfort after the road. Presently we come to a lovely mountain torrent flying down over red-brown rocks in white foam; exquisitely lovely, and only a shade damper than the rest of things. Seeing this I solemnly fold up my umbrella and give it to Kefalla. My relations, nay, even Mrs. Roy, who is blind to a large percentage of my imperfections, say the most scathing things about my behaviour with regard to water. But really my conduct is founded on sound principles. I know from a series of carefully conducted experiments, carried out on the Devonshire Lynn, that I cannot go across a river on slippery stepping-stones; therefore, knowing that attempts to keep my feet out of water only end in my placing the rest of my anatomy violently in, I take charge of Fate and wade.

This particular stream, too, requires careful wading, the rocks over which it flows being arranged in picturesque, but perilous confusion; however all goes well, and getting to the other side I decide to 'chuck it,' as Captain Davis would say, as to keeping dry, for the rain comes down heavier than ever.

Now we are evidently dealing with a foot-hillside, but the rain is too thick for one to see yards in any direction, and we seem to be in a ghost-land forest, for the great palms and red-woods rise up in the mist before us, and fade in the mist behind, as we pass on. The rocks which edge and strew the path at our feet are covered with exquisite ferns and mosses – all the most delicate shades of green imaginable, and here and there of absolute gold colour, looking as if some ray of sunshine had lingered too long playing on the earth, and had got shut off from heaven by the mist, and so lay nestling among the rocks until it might rejoin the sun.

The path now becomes an absolute torrent, with mud-thickened water, which cascades round one's ankles in a sportive way, and round one's knees in the hollows in the path. Five seconds after abandoning the umbrella I am wet through, but it is not uncomfortable at this temperature, something like that of a cucumber frame with the lights on, if you can clear your mind of all prejudice, as Dr. Johnson says, and forget the risk of fever which saturation entails.

Mary Kingsley, *Travels in West Africa*, 1897

MR TWAIN?

I have nothing remarkable to tell of the ascent. We soon got into a cloud, and never got out of it.

Anthony Trollope, *The West Indies and the Spanish Main*, 1860

ARE WE NEARLY TO THE TOP?

The Rigi-Kulm is an imposing Alpine mass, 6,000 feet high, which stands by itself, and commands a mighty prospect of blue lakes, green valleys, and snowy mountains – a compact and magnificent picture three hundred miles in circumference. The ascent is made by rail, or horseback, or on foot, as one may prefer. I and my agent panoplied ourselves in walking costume, one bright morning, and started down the lake on the steamboat; we got ashore at the village of Wäggis, three-quarters of an hour distant from Lucerne. This village is at the foot of the mountain.

We were soon tramping leisurely up the leafy mule-path, and then the talk began to flow, as usual. It was twelve o'clock noon, and a breezy, cloudless day; the ascent was gradual, and the glimpses, from under the curtaining boughs, of blue water, and tiny sail-boats, and beetling cliffs, were as charming as glimpses of dreamland. All the circumstances were perfect

– and the anticipation, too, for we should soon be enjoying, for the first time, that wonderful spectacle, an Alpine sunrise – the object of our journey. There was (apparently) no real need to hurry, for the guide-book made the walking distance from Wäggis to the summit only three hours and a quarter. I say 'apparently,' because the guide-book had already fooled us once – about the distance for Allerheiligen to Oppenau – and for aught I knew it might be getting ready to fool us again. We were only certain as to the altitudes – we calculated to find out for ourselves how many hours it is from the bottom to the top. The summit is 6,000 feet above the sea, but only 4,500 feet above the lake. When we had walked half an hour we were fairly into the swing and humour of the undertaking, so we cleared for action; that is to say, we got a boy whom we met to carry our alpenstocks, and satchels, and overcoats and things for us; that left us free for business.

I suppose we must have stopped oftener to stretch out on the grass in the shade and take a bit of a smoke than this boy was used to, for presently he asked if it had been our idea to hire him by the job or by the year. We told him he could move along if he was in a hurry. He said he wasn't in such a very particular hurry, but he wanted to get to the top while he was young. We told him to clear out then, and leave the things at the uppermost hotel and say we should be along presently. He said he would secure us a hotel if he could, but if they were all full he would ask them to build another one and hurry up and get the paint and plaster dry against we arrived. Still gently chaffing us, he pushed ahead, up the trail, and soon disappeared. By six o'clock we were pretty high up in the air, and the view of lake and mountains had greatly grown in breadth and interest. We halted a while at a little public-house, where we had bread and cheese and a quart or two of fresh milk, out on the porch, with the big panorama all before us – and then moved on again.

Ten minutes afterwards we met a hot, red-faced man plunging down the mountain, with mighty strides, swinging his alpenstock ahead of him and taking a grip on the ground with its iron point to support these big strides. He stopped, fanned himself with his hat, swabbed the perspiration from his face and neck with a red handkerchief, panted a moment or two, and asked how far it was to Wäggis. I said three hours. He looked surprised and said –

'Why, it seems as if I could toss a biscuit into the lake from here, it's so close by. Is that an inn there?'

I said it was.

'Well,' said he, 'I can't stand another three hours, I've had enough for to-day. I'll take a bed there.'

'Are we nearly to the top?'

'Nearly to the *top*! Why, bless your soul, you haven't really started yet.'

I said we would put up at the inn, too. So we turned back and ordered a hot supper, and had quite a jolly evening of it with this Englishman.

The German landlady gave us neat rooms and nice beds, and when I and my agent turned in, it was with the resolution to be up early and make the utmost of our first Alpine sunrise. But of course we were dead tired, and slept like policemen; so when we awoke in the morning and ran to the window it was already too late, because it was half-past eleven. It was a sharp disappointment. However, we ordered breakfast and told the landlady to call the Englishman, but she said he was already up and off at daybreak – and swearing mad about something or other. We could not find out what the matter was. He had asked the landlady the altitude of her place above the level of the lake, and she had told him fourteen hundred and ninety-five feet. That was all that was said; then he lost his temper. He said that between —— fools and guide-books, a man could acquire ignorance enough in twenty-four hours in a country like this to last him a year. Harris believed our boy had been loading him up with misinformation; and this was probably the case, for his epithet described that boy to a dot.

We got under way about the turn of noon, and pulled out for the summit again, with a fresh and vigorous step ...

In the course of a couple of hours we reached a fine breezy altitude where the little shepherd-huts had big stones all over the roofs to hold them down to earth when the great storms rage. The country was wild and rocky here, but there were plenty of trees, plenty of moss, and grass.

Presently we came upon half a dozen sheep nibbling grass in the spray of a stream of clear water that sprang from a rock wall a hundred feet high, and all at once our ears were startled with a melodious 'Lul ... 1 ... 1 ... lul-lul-*la*hee-o-o-o!' pealing joyously from a near but invisible source, and recognised that we were hearing for the first time the famous Alpine *jodel* in its own native wilds. And we recognised, also, that it was that sort of quaint commingling of baritone and falsetto which at home we call 'Tyrolese warbling.'

The jodling (pronounced *yodling* – emphasis on the *o*) continued, and was very pleasant and inspiriting to hear. Now the jodler appeared – a shepherd boy of sixteen – and in our gladness and gratitude we gave him a franc to jodel some more. So he jodeled, and we listened. We moved on presently, and he generously jodeled us out of sight. After about fifteen minutes, we came across another shepherd boy who was jodeling, and gave him half a franc to keep it up. He also jodeled us out of sight. After that, we found a jodler every ten minutes; we gave the first one eight cents, the second one six cents, the third one four cents, the fourth one a penny, contributed nothing to Nos. 5, 6, 7, and during the remainder of the day hired the rest of the jodlers, at a franc apiece, not to jodel any more. There is somewhat too much of this jodling in the Alps.

About the middle of the afternoon we passed through a

prodigious natural gateway called the Felsenthor, formed by two enormous upright rocks, with a third lying across the top. There was a very attractive little hotel close by, but our energies were not conquered yet, so we went on.

Three hours afterward we came to the railway track. It was slanted straight up the mountain with the slant of a ladder that leans against a house and it seemed to us that a man would need good nerves who proposed to travel up it or down it either ...

At ten minutes past six we reached the Kaltbad station, where there is a spacious hotel with great verandahs which command a majestic expanse of lake and mountain scenery. We were pretty well fagged out now, but as we did not wish to miss the Alpine sunrise, we got through with our dinner as quickly as possible and hurried off to bed. It was unspeakably comfortable to stretch our weary limbs between the cool damp sheets. And how we did sleep! – for there is no opiate like Alpine pedestrianism.

In the morning we both awoke and leaped out of bed at the same instant and ran and stripped aside the window curtains, but we suffered a bitter disappointment again: it was already half-past three in the afternoon.

We dressed sullenly and in ill spirits, each accusing the other of over-sleeping. Harris said if we had brought the courier along, as we ought to have done, we should not have missed these sunrises. I said he knew very well that one of us would have had to sit up and wake the courier; and I added that we were having trouble enough to take care of ourselves on this climb, without having to take care of a courier besides.

During breakfast our spirits came up a little, since we found by the guide-book that in the hotels on the summit the tourist is not left to trust to luck for his sunrise, but is roused betimes by a man who goes through the halls with a great Alpine horn, blowing blasts that would raise the dead. And there was another consoling thing: the guide-book said that up there on the summit the guests did not wait to dress much, but seized a red bed-blanket and sailed out arrayed like an Indian. This was good: this would be romantic: two hundred and fifty people grouped on the windy summit, with their hair flying and their red blankets flapping, in the solemn presence of the snowy ranges and the messenger splendours of the coming sun, would be a striking and memorable spectacle. So it was good luck, not ill luck, that we had missed those other sunrises.

We were informed by the guide-book that we were now 3,228 feet above the level of the lake – therefore full two-thirds of our journey had been accomplished. We got away at a quarter past four p.m. . . .

We climbed and climbed; and we kept on climbing; we reached about forty summits; but there was always another one just ahead. It came on to rain, and it rained in dead earnest. We were soaked through, and it was bitter cold. Next a smoky fog of clouds covered the whole region densely, and we took to the railway ties to keep from getting lost. Sometimes we slopped along in a narrow path on the left-hand side of the track but by-and-by, when the fog blew aside a little and we saw that we were treading the rampart of a precipice, and that our left elbows were projecting over a perfectly boundless and bottomless vacancy, we gasped and jumped for the ties again.

The night shut down, dark, and drizzly, and cold. About eight in the evening the fog lifted and showed us a well-worn path which led up a very steep rise to the left. We took it, and as soon as we had got far enough from the railway to render the finding it again an impossibility, the fog shut down on us once more.

We were in a bleak unsheltered place now, and had to trudge right along in order to keep warm, though we rather expected to go over a precipice sooner or later. About nine o'clock we made an important discovery – that we were not in any path. We groped around a while on our hands and knees, but could not find it; so we sat down in the mud and the wet scant grass to wait. We were terrified into this by being suddenly confronted with a vast body which showed itself vaguely for an instant, and in the next instant was smothered in the fog again. It was really the hotel we were after, monstrously magnified by the fog, but we took it for the face of a precipice and decided not to try to claw up it.

We sat there an hour, with chattering teeth and quivering bodies, and quarrelled over all sorts of trifles, but gave most of our attention to abusing each other for the stupidity of deserting the railway track. We sat with our backs to the precipice, because what little wind there was came from that quarter. At some time or other the fog thinned a little; we did not know when, for we were facing the empty universe and the thinness could not show; but at last Harris happened to look around, and there stood a huge, dim, spectral hotel where the precipice had been. One could faintly discern the windows and chimneys, and a dull blur of lights. Our first emotion was deep, unutterable gratitude, our next was a foolish rage, born of the suspicion that possibly the hotel had been visible three-quarters of an hour while we sat there in those cold puddles quarrelling.

Yes, it was the Rigi-Kulm hotel – the one that occupies the extreme summit, and whose remote little sparkle of lights we had often seen glinting high aloft among the stars from our balcony away down yonder in Lucerne. The crusty portier and the crusty clerks gave us the surly reception which their kind deal in in prosperous times, but by mollifying them with an extra display of obsequiousness and servility we finally got them to show us to the room which our boy had engaged for us.

We got into some dry clothing, and while our supper was preparing we loafed forsakenly through a couple of vast cavernous drawing-rooms, one of which had a stove in it. This stove was in a corner, and densely walled around with people … There were some Americans, and some Germans, but one could see that the great majority were English.

We lounged into an apartment where there was a great crowd, to see what was going on. It was a memento-magazine. The tourists were eagerly buying all sorts and styles of paper-cutters, marked 'Souvenir of the Rigi,' with handles made of the little curved horn of the ostensible chamois; there were all manner of wooden goblets and such things, similarly marked. I was going to buy a paper-cutter, but I believed I could remember the cold comfort of the Rigi-Kulm without it, so I smothered the impulse.

Supper warmed us, and we went immediately to bed; but first, as Mr. Baedeker requests all tourists to call his attention to any errors which they may find in his guide-books, I dropped him a line to inform him that when he said the foot journey from Wäggis to the summit was only three hours and a quarter, he missed it by just about three days …

We curled up in the clammy beds, and went to sleep without recking. We were so sodden with fatigue that we never stirred. Much later on Alpine horn aroused us. It may well be imagined that we did not lose any time. We snatched on a few odds and ends of clothing, cocooned ourselves in the proper red blankets and plunged along the halls and out into the whistling wind bare-headed. We saw a tall wooden scaffolding on the very peak of the summit, a hundred yards away, and made for it. We rushed up the stairs to the top of this scaffolding, and stood there, above the vast outlying world, with hair flying and ruddy blankets waving and cracking in the fierce breeze.

'Fifteen minutes too late, at least!' said Harris, in a vexed voice. 'The sun is clear above the horizon.'

'No matter,' I said, 'it is a most magnificent spectacle, and we will see it do the rest of its rising, anyway.'

In a moment we were deeply absorbed in the marvel before us, and dead to everything else. The great cloud-barred disk of the sun stood just above a limitless expanse of tossing white-caps – so to speak – a billowy chaos of massy mountain domes and peaks draped in imperishable snow, and flooded with an opaline glory of changing and dissolving splendours ...

We could not speak. We could hardly breathe. We could only gaze in drunken ecstasy and drink it in. Presently Harris exclaimed –

'Why, ——nation, it's going *down!*'

Perfectly true. We had missed the *morning* horn-blow, and slept all day. This was stupefying. Harris said, –

'Look here, the sun isn't the spectacle – it's *us* – stacked up here on top of this gallows, in these idiotic blankets, and two hundred and fifty well dressed men and women down here gawking up at us and not caring a straw whether the sun rises or sets, as long as they've got such a ridiculous spectacle as this to set down in their memorandum-books. They seem to be laughing their ribs loose, and there's one girl there that appears to be going all to pieces. I never saw such a man as you before. I think you are the very last possibility in the way of an ass.'

'What have *I* done?' I answered with heat.

'What have you done? You've got up at half-past seven o'clock in the evening to see the sun rise, that's what you've done.'

'And have you done any better, I'd like to know? I always used to get up with the lark, till I came under the petrifying influence of your turgid intellect.'

... And so the customary quarrel went on. When the sun was fairly down, we slipped back to the hotel in the charitable gloaming, and went to bed again. We had encountered the hornblower on the way, and he had tried to collect compensation, not only for announcing the sunset, which we did see, but for the sunrise, which we had totally missed, but we said no, we only took our solar rations on the 'European plain'

– pay for what you get. He promised to make us hear his horn in the morning, if we were alive.

Mark Twain, 'The Rigi-Kulm', A Tramp Abroad, 1880

WE WERE BUT TINY BLACK SPECKS

It falls to a lot of men to view land not previously seen by human eyes, and it was with feelings of keen curiosity, not un-mingled with awe, that we watched the new mountains rise from the great unknown that lay ahead of us. Mighty peaks they were, the eternal snows at their bases, and their rough-hewn forms rising high towards the sky. No man of us could tell us what we would discover in our march south, what wonders might not be revealed to us, and our imaginations would take wings until a stumble in the snow, the sharp pangs of hunger, or the dull ache of physical weariness brought back our attention to the needs of the immediate present. As these days wore on, and mountain after mountain came into view, grimly majestic, the consciousness of our insignificance seemed to grow upon us. We were but tiny black specks crawling slowly and painfully across the white plain, and bending our puny strength to the task of wresting from nature secrets preserved inviolate through all the ages.

Ernest Shackleton, Heart of the Antarctic, 1909

FESTINATION!

From dawn until about ten o'clock I felt fine. The wind rose with the sun but we had some protection from the wall and only an occasional gust raked us with sand. The full force was spent on the desert to the west where a veil of orange-coloured gauze rose and fell with curious regularity. After ten o'clock I began to be irritated by the usual trivialities. I began to imagine that the camels were spread too far apart in their groups of three. Sometimes I had to wait until Mezek caught up with us and it was impossible to see whether all was well from a quick glance backwards. I told Lelean to slow down so that we could march along together. At this he began to dawdle to such an extent that the camels were bunched under each other's tails and a frisky movement from the leader rippled through the whole string. I told him to get a move on again and felt that he should have known what I meant the first time. In giving orders in Swahili I found it extremely difficult to express niceties of action and irritation arose only too often through a splutter of words. This caused even more confusion.

For hour after hour we trudged south in a long-drawn-out line that, from afar, must have borne some resemblance to a trail of ants. Lelean was heading for a distant mound which he took to be a hill on the north side of the Kalacha and the rest of us followed in his footprints. After vainly trying to get a fix on our position in the dawn light I put the compass away convinced that the louring mass of Kulal away to the right was the only land mass I could recognize with any certainty. The Huri Hills swam hazily through the mirage. Sidamticha, the Rageh and half a dozen other little hills might have been outliers of the Andes for all the navigational help they afforded. They appeared as if they were beginning to melt.

On one occasion I pointed out a possible route on the map to Lelean, but Mezek had to hold the sheet down in the wind and I doubt whether Lelean had much idea what he was looking at. Even when I orientated the map and showed him where the sun rose and where his home, Mount Kulal, was ('Manyatta yako eh?') he said 'Yes' (n'dio, n'dio), but he could not understand the conceptual relationship between symbols and reality. To him it must have been a rather dull line-drawing in pink and black.

'Is this Kalacha?' I asked, pointing to the minute blue circle of the water-point.

'N'dio.'

'Do you *know* Kalacha?'

'N'dio.'

'So we go *this* way?'

'N'dio.'

'So tonight' – this triumphantly – 'we shall be *there*!' And I stabbed the smudgy-brown symbol of lava at a point where it was intersected by the interrupted line of a *lugga*.

'No, no!' he said. 'Hapana! We shall be *there*!' He stood up and pointed roughly in the same direction. Clearly, Lelean was no cartographer and I, for that matter, was unlikely to gain many prizes in a navigation school. The marvel is that we got anywhere.

More trudging. Nothing to look at. Only sand and the wraiths on the horizon. A waste land. Nothing to think about except whether the camels would last out and whether we should find a shelter at dusk. Nothing to listen to except the high-pitched whine of the wind, the flat-footed *thoomp thoomp* of the camels' hooves and the plash of water in the jerricans. When the animals faltered or tossed their heads and splashed froth, Mezek grunted 'Hodai!' but he said it rarely and with no especial conviction. We were all of us very tired.

In the absence of shade and with no prospect of any lessening in the intensity of the heat before nightfall we plodded on through a series of irregular stages broken only by brief halts to rest the camels. On these occasions we stopped in what appeared to be the exact centre of an enormous bowl of sand. On the horizon we could see the flanks of Kulal but, due to our southerly progress, the long narrow mountain resembled a range of hills. Somewhere to the south I hoped we should again strike the lava wall and find shelter there but, after following it closely for several hours that morning, we parted company when it swung east in what I took to be an extensive bay. I wanted to get as far south as I could by nightfall.

During these brief halts I sat with my back to a camel, pulled my hat over my eyes and tried to think of something to think about. The important thing was not to think about tea; we had no wood for a fire. I also tried to keep my thoughts off the unprofitable subjects of navigation and how long the camels would last out. The name of Cassian, one of the Desert Fathers, came to mind. What had he said about the white melancholy and the demons of noontide? That they 'mounted at a regular time, like a fever, bringing their highest tide of inflammation at definite accustomed hours'? I dismissed Cassian and tried another tack.

What were the names of the Muses? Through some almost forgotten association with a girl in a pantomime chorus I remembered Terpsichore; Clio became mixed up with asps and Egypt and I was unsure about Erato's association with sacred hymns. It seemed improbable. I dismissed the Muses.

How far had we walked? I remembered that a man can outwalk a horse – I had this evocative but useless piece of information from an old copy of the *New Yorker*. I also remembered that Roman soldiers used to average twenty miles a day with a pack, and that a man called Barclay once walked a thousand miles in a thousand hours. What was the medical term for exceptionally fast walking? Festination! Was it a symptom of good health or neurosis? Probably the latter. Sitting there with my back pressed up against the rumbling chest wall of a camel I reflected that nobody but a fool would walk in the desert. The sand continued to blow. For the most part it drifted past without touching us, like a veil of rain across a lakeland valley. In the distance the streamers appeared to be motionless; they had the feathery appearance of wind clouds and I wondered whether they foreshadowed wind.

John Hillaby, *Journey to the Jade Sea*, 1964

WALKING WOUNDED: MR YOUNG'S DISLOCATION

Mr Young was perhaps a dozen or two yards behind me, but out of sight. I afterwards reproached myself for not stopping and lending him a steadying hand, and showing him the slight footsteps I had made by kicking out little blocks of the crumbling surface, instead of simply warning him to be careful. Only a few seconds after giving this warning, I was startled by a scream for help, and hurrying back, found the missionary face downward, his arms outstretched, clutching little crumbling knobs on the brink of a gully that plunges down a thousand feet or more to a small residual glacier. I managed to get below him, touched one of his feet, and tried to encourage him by saying, 'I am below you. You are in no danger. You can't slip past me and I will soon get you out of this.'

He then told me that both of his arms were dislocated. It was almost impossible to find available footholds on the treacherous rock, and I was at my wits' end to know how to get him rolled or dragged to a place where I could get about him, find out how much he was hurt, and a way back down the mountain. After narrowly scanning the cliff and making footholds, I managed to roll and lift him a few yards to a place where the slope was less steep, and there I attempted to set his arms. I found, however, that this was impossible in such a place. I therefore tied his arms to his sides with my suspenders and necktie, to prevent as much as possible inflammation from movement. I then left him, telling him to lie still, that I would be back in a few minutes, and that he was now safe from slipping. I hastily examined the ground and saw no way of getting him down except by the steep glacier gully. After scrambling to an outstanding point that commands a view of it from top to bottom, to make sure that it was not interrupted by sheer precipices, I concluded that with great care and the digging of slight footholds he could be slid down to the glacier, where I could lay him on his back and perhaps be able to set his arms. Accordingly, I cheered him up, telling him I had found a way, but that it would require lots of time and patience. Digging a footstep in the sand or crumbling rock five or six feet beneath him, I reached up, took hold of him by one of his feet, and gently slid him down on his back, placed his heels in the step, then descended another five or six feet, dug heel notches, and slid him down to them. Thus the whole distance was made by a succession of narrow steps at very short intervals, and the glacier was reached perhaps about midnight. Here I took off one of my boots, tied a handkerchief around his wrist for a good hold, placed my heel in his arm pit, and succeeded in getting one of his arms in place, but my utmost strength was insufficient to reduce the dislocation of the other. I therefore bound it closely to his side, and asked him if in his exhausted and trembling condition he was still able to walk.

'Yes', he bravely replied.

John Muir, Travels in Alaska, 1915

WALKING WOUNDED: 'THE RIGHT CALF MIGHT BE A PROBLEM'

Saturday 23rd November

In a rain-sodden field a man catches a woman. The grass is flat with mud. The right calf might be a problem, possibly the left boot as well, up front on the instep. While walking, so many things pass through one's head, the brain rages.

Sunday 24th November

Mythical hills in the mist, built from sugar beets, lining the path through the field. A hoarse dog.

Holzhausen: the road emerges. By the first farm, something

harvested, covered with a plastic tarp anchored with old tyres. You pass a lot of discarded rubbish as you walk.

Monday 25th November

A brief rest in a stretch of woodland. I can look into the valley, as I take the short cut over wet, slushy meadows; the road here makes a wide loop. What a snowstorm; now everything's calm again, I'm slowly drying out. Mickenhausen ahead of me, wherever the hell it is. Raindrops are still falling from the fir trees to the needle-covered ground. My thighs are steaming like a horse. Hill country, lots of woodland now, everything seems foreign to me now. The villages feign death as I approach.

Just before Mickenhausen (Munster?), turning further west, following my instincts. Blisters on the balls of my toes give me trouble; had no idea walking could hurt so much.

Obergessertshausen: no break, since it is almost completely dark. I'm rambling more than walking. Both legs hurt so much that I can barely put one in front of the other. How much is one million steps?

Tuesday 26th November

Things are somewhat clearer having bought a Shell map in Kirchheim. During the night there was a bad storm; in the morning, snow was melting everywhere in tatters. Rain, snow and hail, those are the Lower Orders.

The cigarette packets on the roadside fascinate me greatly, even more when left uncrushed, then blown up slightly to take on a corpse-like quality.

Wednesday 27th November

Laupenheim, train station restaurant: bought a Sud-deutsche newspaper, having no idea what's going on in the world. It confirmed that today is only Wednesday, as I've had my doubts. Untersulmetingen, then through a forest, a quiet forest with clover leaves on the snowy wet ground. While I was taking a shit, a hare came by at arm's length without noticing me. Pale brandy on my left thigh, which hurts from my groin down with every step. Why is walking so full of woe?

Werner Herzog, *Of Walking in Ice*, 1978
(trans. Alan Greenberg and Martje Herzog, 1980)

WALKING WOUNDED: MY BLOODY BOOTS

At six-thirty we arrived at the village of Marz Robat itself. We had been on the road for three hours and during this time had covered perhaps ten miles but, nevertheless, I felt utterly exhausted. By the look on Hugh's face he was experiencing somewhat similar sensations.

Outstripped by the *Mirgun* and his companion, whose opinions of our powers of locomotion were plain enough, we followed them into a narrow enclosure on the right of the road and sank down on the scruffy grass.

'You know,' said Hugh, 'I feel rather done up, I can't think why.'

'It must be the change of air.'

We were in a little garden high above the river, on the outskirts of the village, which belonged to a *chaie khana* across the road. The *chaie khana* was really only a hole in a wall with a sagging roof of dead vegetation strung on some long poles. Standing in a wooden cradle, looking like a medieval siege mortar and equally defunct, was a Russian samovar made of copper and decorated with the Imperial eagles. It was splendid but unfortunately it was not working. Deciding that it would take a long time to get up a head of steam in a thing of this size, I closed my eyes in a coma of fatigue.

When I next opened them I was covered with a thick blanket of flies. They were somnolent in the cool of the evening and, when I thumped myself, squashing dozens of them, they simply rose a foot in the air and fell back on me with an audible 'plop', closing the ranks left by the slaughtered like well-drilled infantry.

Now the samovar was belching steam, jumping up and down on its wooden cradle in its eagerness to deliver the goods. It no longer resembled a cannon; it was more like an engine emerging from its shed anxious to be off up the line and away.

Bending over us was the proprietor, a curious-looking giant in a long brown cloak reaching to his feet, which stuck out coyly from under it. He was an object of nightmare but he brought with him all the apparatus of tea.

My teeth were chattering like castanets and without a word the giant took off his verminous cloak and wrapped me in it, leaving himself in a thin cotton shift. Another cloak was brought for Hugh. Here, when the sun went down, it was cold.

Regarding us silently from the walls of the little garden there was an immense audience. The male population of Marz Robat, all but the bedridden, come to view these extraordinary beings who to them must have had all the strangeness of visitors from outer space. To appreciate their point of view one would have to imagine a Tajik stretched out in a garden in Wimbledon.

It was green tea and delicious but the cups were too small; pretty things of fine porcelain. After we had each drunk two entire pots we still had need of more liquid. Ours was not a thirst that proceeded from dry throats but a deep internal need to replace what had been sucked out of us in our unfit state by the power of the sun.

'I shouldn't do that,' Hugh croaked, as I demanded water. 'You'll be sorry.'

My powers of restraint, never great, had been broken. Now

our roles were reversed.

'I thought you wanted me to drink it.'

'Not when you're tired. It's too cold.'

He was too late; the giant had already sent down to the river for a *chatti* of water. Somewhere I had read that salt was the thing for a person suffering from dehydration, so I called for salt too; a rock of it was produced and I put it in the pot, sluiced it round and drank deep. It was a nasty mixture but at least I felt that in some way I was justifying my lack of self-control.

All this time the crowd had been quietly slipping down off the wall and closing in on us; now they were all round us gorging with their eyes. We were the cynosure. Hugh was the first to crack.

'– !' He got up and stalked to the far end of the garden, tripping over his *chapan*. The crowd followed him but he barked at them so violently that they sheered off then settled on me.

With the intention of splitting them, I made for the only available corner (the other was occupied by the *Mirgun* and his friend), but as soon as I started to walk I found that there was something very wrong with my feet inside the Italian boots. It was as if a tram had gone over them. I sat down hastily, took the boots off and found that my socks were full of blood.

It seemed impossible that such damage could have been done in the space of three hours and some ten miles. My feet looked as though they had been flayed, as indeed they had.

How it had happened was a mystery; the boots were not tight, rather there was an excess of living-room inside them. The real trouble was that they were slightly pointed, whether because pointed shoes were the current Italian fashion and the designers thought that the appearance was improved or whether to facilitate rock climbing was not clear. What was certain was that for me pointed boots were excruciatingly painful.

Hugh tottered over to look and the villagers made little

whistling sounds when they saw the extent of the damage. All of them knew the value of feet in the Hindu Kush. For some time Hugh said nothing. There was nothing to say and nothing to be done until Abdul Ghiyas arrived with the horses and the medicine chest.

'They're very bad,' he said at last. 'What do you want to do, go back to Kabul?'

To return to Kabul was useless; yet to go on seemed madness.

There was no question of my feet healing, the daily quota of miles would ensure that. I thought of all the difficulties we had overcome to get even as far as Marz Robat: the children uprooted from school; our flat let; my job gone; the money that Hugh and myself had expended; his own dotty dream of climbing Mir Samir to be frustrated at the last moment; my own dream, equally balmy, of becoming an explorer in the same way going up in smoke. I thought of the old inhabitant at Kabul. 'They're always setting off,' he had chuckled, 'that's as far as they get.' Were we to join this select body who had travelled only in their cups? There seemed to be no alternative but to go on. The fact that there was none rallied me considerably.

'We might be able to get you a horse,' Hugh said.

He could not have said anything better. I am completely ignorant of horses. The last time I had attempted to mount one I faced the wrong way when putting my foot in the stirrup and found myself in the saddle facing the creature's tail. Worse, being nervous of horses, I emanate a smell of death when close to them so that, sniffing it, they take fright themselves and attempt to destroy me. A horse would certainly have destroyed me on the road we had traversed that afternoon. At some places it had been only a couple of feet wide with a sheer drop to the river below.

'I think I'll carry on as I am. Another horse means another driver.'

'It would be *your* horse. We wouldn't need another driver.'
'If I walk they may harden up.' It was a phrase that I was
to use constantly from now on.

Eric Newby, A Short Walk in the Hindu Kush, 1972

I AM ENJOYING MYSELF

I am going to cross the ferry for Fort William, for I have resolved
to eke out my cash by all sorts of self-denial, and to walk along
the whole line of forts. I am unfortunately shoeless; there is
no town where I can get a pair, and I have no money spare to
buy them, so I expect to enter Perth barefoot. I burnt my shoes
in drying them at the boatman's hovel on Loch Katrine, and I
have by this means hurt my heel. Likewise my left leg is a little
inflamed, and the rheumatism in the right of my head afflicts
my right eye, ear, cheek, and the three teeth – but, nevertheless,
I am enjoying myself.

Samuel Taylor Coleridge, Letter, 1803

SHE ENCOURAGED US TO GO ON . . .

While my fellow-traveller and I were walking by the side of
Loch Ketterine, one fine evening after sunset, in our road to a
Hut where, in the course of our Tour, we had been hospitably
entertained some weeks before, we met, in one of the loneliest
parts of that solitary region, two well-dressed Women, one of
whom said to us, by way of greeting, 'What, you are stepping
westward?'

> *'What, you are stepping westward?'* – *'Yea.'*
> – 'Twould be a *wildish* destiny,
> If we, who thus together roam

In a strange Land, and far from home,
Were in this place the guests of Chance:
Yet who would stop, or fear to advance,
Though home or shelter he had none,
With such a sky to lead him on?

The dewy ground was dark and cold;
Behind, all gloomy to behold;
And stepping westward seemed to be
A kind of *heavenly* destiny:
I liked the greeting; 'twas a sound
Of something without place or bound;
And seemed to give me spiritual right
To travel through that region bright.

The voice was soft, and she who spake
Was walking by her native lake:
The salutation had to me
The very sound of courtesy:
Its power was felt; and while my eye
Was fixed upon the glowing Sky,
The echo of the voice enwrought
A human sweetness with the thought
Of travelling through the world that lay
Before me in my endless way.

William Wordsworth, 'Stepping Westward', 1807

PINCELOUP THE SHOEBREAKER IS LOSING HIS TOUCH

'Where is Pinceloup?'
    'I don't know sir,' replied the clerk.
    'Baron,' the owner said, as he turned to speak to the client

who had just come in, 'my staff and I saw him leave early this morning on your behalf.'

'What I see,' retorted the other, 'is that I was counting on my shoes being ready at four o'clock. You assured me they would be. It is now six o'clock and the dinner is at eight. I don't intend to stand here cooling my heels.'

'But, sir ...'

'Don't tell me you're sorry. It is I, my dear man, who am sorry. You can't depend on anyone nowadays.'

The baron looked down at his feet and wiggled his toes under the worn calfskin. He'd have to go to the dinner party in his old shoes, bulging from his bunions and bubbled by his corns. Obviously he was comfortable in them, but aren't we always anxious to try out our latest purchase? The pair of dress shoes that he had bought the day before that tortured him so when he first put them on were still walking the streets of Paris, being broken in by a fellow named Pinceloup.

'May I make a suggestion?' ventured the owner. 'I know the man well. I have used him for more than thirty years, sir. He has broken in over twelve thousand pairs of shoes for me, following the customers' directives. He figures a morning per pair for normal feet, but an entire afternoon should there be any deformity. Our exceptional patrons ...'

The baron didn't readily count himself among the latter.

'... I mean those whom it was nature's whim to deform, and God knows I pity them, will sometimes cost Pinceloup an entire day.'

With the tip of his cane, the baron maliciously applied pressure to the corn crowning the big toe of his right foot, swollen by gout.

'Pinceloup is, moreover, a great judge of physiognomy and I shall miss him. He knows at a glance whether to walk pigeon-toed or duck-footed, or to stuff a wad of cotton in the shoe at just the right place, that is to say at the place that ... Baron, sir?'

'Yes?'

'People like Pinceloup will be hard to come by in the future. Love for one's work is a thing of the past. Love for art is disappearing. But please sit down, he should be here any time now.'

'Art?' cried out the baron. 'Indeed I shall sit down.'

'Pinceloup,' the owner continued, 'belonged to my father before I took over the business.'

This sort of talk the baron savored, and time wore on. The salesmen, meanwhile, were coming and going, carrying piles of boxes, kneeling, wielding their shoehorns, here lacing up an Oxford, there vaunting the quality of the alligator and, over in the women's section, assuming feminine poses as they side-saddled their fitting stools, clamping their knees together like women in bathing suits, not hesitating to look away should gaping thighs offer them the forbidden view. The owner kept a watchful eye on his people without diverting his attention from the baron who, though not a particularly good customer, was a man of great renown. The Petit-Chablis clan, lest one forget, still owned half of the country's railroads, and that is indeed what drew a good part of the clientele.

'Honestly, I can't understand what's keeping him.'

'And it's getting dark,' the baron sighed.

They were about to give up when the door opened and Pinceloup appeared, green around the gills and dragging at the heels.

'Ah! There you are.'

The baron looked at his dress shoes now gracing the shoe-breaker's feet. They no longer bore a resemblance to the ones the Baron had purchased, but rather to the good old pair he now wore. His eyes wandered from the one to the other.

'My dear fellow,' he exclaimed, putting his hand on Pinceloup's shoulder, 'did everything go well?'

'Everything, Baron, sir. There might still be a hint of stiffness in the reinforcement of the outer left heel. I apologize for that.'

Am I getting old, Pinceloup wondered. Is the leather less supple due to the new fangled methods of tanning and splicing? Or might the stitching or the lining be too heavy?

'Unshoe him,' the owner told a clerk.

'I'd appreciate it,' Pinceloup uttered feebly.

'Are you otherwise satisfied?' Baron Petit-Chablis inquired.

With the tip of his cane, he pointed to the already bloated shoes, now emptied of Pinceloup's feet, as well as of the scraps of cardboard, cotton balls, strips of cork, rubber disks and the like.

'They've put in eighteen kilometers,' Pinceloup declared. 'I advise you to put them on right away while they're still warm. We'll obtain a more generous contact. Talcum powder ...'

'The talc,' shouted the owner.

The talcum powder will save the day, mused Pinceloup.

The baron had himself shod, laced up and helped to his feet. He shook hands with the owner. At the same time, he extended his left hand which held his cane, trying discreetly to offer Pinceloup a coin. He nearly blinded the poor devil in the process.

The breaker watched the baron as he left with short and hesitant steps.

Seeing him stop in the middle of the street for relief, Pinceloup felt the pain and even a twinge of shame.

'Monsieur,' he said to the owner, 'I just can't do it any more.'

'What's that?'

'I've lost my touch. Look!' They could see the baron limping off.

'I did what I could,' Pinceloup muttered as he examined his lacerated feet. His socks were embedded in his flesh and darkened in spots with blood stains.

'Come on now, don't give up for heaven's sake. You're the best breaker in all of Paris, Pinceloup. The main thing in life is to be tops at something. Remember ...'

'And tomorrow?' interrupted Pinceloup, his sense of honor reviving.

'You'll do two pairs for me. They'll be a snap.'

'But I didn't see them on the customers' feet.' The owner went to his file and pulled two sheets of vellum.

'Here.' He knows that Pinceloup can't read and Pinceloup knows that he knows. If the boss is being mean again, it's because he esteems him, needs him, and can boast that no one else in all of Paris can break in shoes as well as Pinceloup.

'See you tomorrow,' Pinceloup murmured.

Since his feet hurt him so, he put on his espadrilles, which he saved for the bad evenings. The boss, despite the fact that it was closing time, asked him to leave through the back service door.

Daniel Boulanger, *The Shoebreaker*, 1963 (trans. Penny Million Pucelik and Marijo Despereaux Schneider, 1989)

MOONSTRUCK . . .

The stars shone clear in the strip of sky between the huge dark cliffs, and as I rambled recalling the lessons of the day, the full moon suddenly looked down over the canyon wall, her face apparently filled with eager concern, which had a startling effect as if she had left her place in the sky and had come down to gaze on me alone. The effect was frighteningly impressive and made me forget the Indians and the great black rocks above me ...

John Muir, *My First Summer in the Sierra*, 1911

INTO THE NIGHT (1)

As the Thernadier hostelry was in the part of the village which is near the church, it was to the spring in the forest in the direction of Chelles that Cossette was obliged to go for her water.

She made as much motion as possible with the handle of the bucket as she walked along. This made a noise which afforded her company. Cossette traversed the labyrinth of tortuous and deserted streets which terminate in the village of Montfermeil on the side of Chelles. From time to time she caught the flicker of a candle through the crack of a shutter – this was life and light; there were people there, and it reassured her. But in proportion as she advanced, her pace slackened mechanically, as it were. When she had passed the corner of the last house, Cossette paused. It had been hard to advance further than the last stall; it had become impossible to proceed further than the last house. She set her bucket on the ground, thrust her hand into her hair, and began slowly to scratch her head – a gesture peculiar to children when terrified and undecided what to do. It was no longer Montfermeil; it was open fields. Black and desert space was before her. She gazed in despair at that darkness, where there was no longer any one, where there were beasts, where there were spectres, possibly. Then she seized her bucket again; fear had lent her audacity. "Bah! I will tell him that there was no more water!" and she resolutely re-entered Montfermeil.

Hardly had she gone a hundred paces when she paused and began to scratch her head again. Now it was the Thenardier who appeared to her, with her hideous, hyena mouth, wrath flashing in her eyes. The child cast a melancholy glance before her and behind her. What was she to do? It was before the Thenardier that she recoiled. She resumed her path to the spring and began to run. She emerged from the village, she entered the forest at a run, no longer looking or listening to anything. She only paused in her course when her breath failed her; but she did not halt in her advance. She went straight before her in desperation. As she ran she felt like crying.

The nocturnal quivering of the forest surrounded her completely.

It was only seven or eight minutes walk from the edge of the woods to the spring. Cossette knew the way, through having gone over it many times in daylight. She did not get lost. A remnant of instinct guided her vaguely. In this manner she reached the spring. It was a narrow, natural basin, hollowed out by the water in a clayey soil, about two feet deep, surrounded with moss and with those tall, crimped grasses which are called Henry IV's frills, and paved with several large stones. A brook ran out of it, with a tranquil little noise.

Cossette did not take time to breathe. She felt with her left hand in the dark for a young oak which leaned over the spring, and which usually served to support her, found one of its branches, clung to it, bent down, and plunged the bucket in the water. She drew out the bucket nearly full, and set it on the grass. That done, she perceived that she was worn out with fatigue. She would have liked to set out again at once, but the effort to fill the bucket had been such that she found it impossible to take a step. She was forced to sit down. She dropped on the grass, and remained crouching there.

Overhead, the sky was covered with vast black clouds, like masses of smoke. The tragic mask of shadow seemed to bend over the child.

Jupiter was setting in the depths. The child stared with great bewilderment at this great star, which terrified her.

A cold wind was blowing from the plain. The forest was dark, not a leaf was moving; there was none of the vague, fresh gleams of summertide. Great boughs uplifted themselves in frightful wise. Slender and misshapen bushes whistled in the clearings. The darkness was confusing. Man requires light. Whoever buries himself in the opposite of day feels his heart contract. When the eye sees black, the heart sees trouble. In an eclipse in the night, in the sooty opacity, there is anxiety even for the stoutest of hearts. No one walks alone in the forest at night without trembling.

Without misunderstanding her sensations, Cossette was conscious that she was seized upon by that black enormity of nature; it was no longer terror alone which was gaining possession of her; it was something more terrible even than terror; she shivered.

Then by some sort of instinct, she began to count out aloud, one, two, three, four, and so on up to ten, in order to escape from that singular state which she did not understand, but which terrified her, and, when she had finished, she began again; this restored her to a true perception of the things about her. Her hands, which had been drawing in the water, felt cold. She rose. She had but one thought now – to flee at full speed through the forest, across the fields to the houses, to the windows, to the lighted candles.

She advanced a dozen paces, but the bucket was full; it was heavy; she was forced to set it on the ground once more. She took breath for an instant, then lifted the handle of the bucket again, and resumed her march, proceeding a little further this time, but again she was obliged to pause. After some moment of repose she set out again. She walked bent forward, with drooping head, like an old woman.

But she could not make much headway in this manner, and she went on very slowly. In spite of diminishing the length of her stops, and walking as long as possible between them, she reflected with anguish that it would take her more than an hour to return to Montfermeil at this rate, and the Thenardier would beat her. On arriving at an old chestnut tree, with which she was acquainted, she made a last halt, summoned up a last energy, picked up the bucket, and resumed her march. But the poor little creature couldn't help crying "Oh my God! my God!"

At that moment she became conscious that her bucket no

longer weighed anything at all. A hand, which seemed to her enormous, had seized the handle, and lifted it vigorously. She raised her head. A large black form, straight and erect, was walking beside her through the darkness; it was a man who had come up behind her, whose approach she had not heard. This man, without a word, had taken her bucket.

There are instincts for all the encounters of life.

The child was not afraid.

Victor Hugo, *Les Miserables*, 1897 (trans. Isabel F. Hapgood)

INTO THE NIGHT (2)

In those silences which came too frequently the identity of the figure walking beside one seemed to merge in the night; one strode on alone, conscious of the pressure of the dark all around, conscious, too, that by degrees resistance to it grew less and less; that the body carried forward over the ground was some thing separate from the mind which floated away as though in a swoon. The road, even, had been left behind, and we had struck – if a word implying definite action can be used of anything as indefinite as our course now became, across the fields of the daytime – the trackless ocean of the night. From time to time it was advisable to test the ground beneath the feet in order that its substance might be proved indisputably. Both eyes and ears were fast sealed, or, for the pressure on them was of something intangible, had grown numb insensibly, so that the apparition of several lights beneath us had to be realised almost with conscious effort. Could one really see, as in the daytime, or was this some vision within the brain like those stars which a blow scatters before the eye? There they hung, floating without anchorage, in soft depths of darkness in a valley beneath us; for directly that the eye had proved them true the brain woke and constructed a scheme of the world in which to place them. There, too, must be a hill, a town beneath it, the road winding round as we remembered it; a dozen lights can do much to solidify the world. The strangest part of our pilgrimage was over, for something visible had emerged; we had a proof before us. Moreover, we found ourselves upon a road, and walked forward more freely. There were human beings down here too, though they were not as the people of the daytime are. Suddenly a light burnt close at our side, and even as we saw it bearing down upon us a wheel crunched, and a man in a cart was lit up before us; in a second his lights were out and his wheels were dumb; no voice of ours could have reached him. Again, as though scenes were passed swiftly before us and withdrawn, we found ourselves in a farm-yard, where a lantern swung an unsteady disc of light over the huddled shapes of cattle, and even discovered parts of our submerged persons. The voice of the farmer bidding us good-night recalled us as though a firm hand had grasped ours, to the shores of the world, but in two strides the immense flood of darkness and silence was over us again. Yet once more lights stood beside us, as though they had approached with silent steps like the lights of ships passing at sea – the lamps that we had seen from the hill-top. The village was quiet, but not asleep, as though it lay wide-eyed in tacit conflict with the dark; we could distinguish forms leaning against the house-walls, men apparently, who could not sleep with that weight of night pressing against their windows, but must come forth and stretch their arms in it. How puny were the rays of the lamp against the immeasurable waves of darkness surging round them! A ship at sea is a lonely thing, but far lonelier it seemed was this little village anchored to the desolate earth and exposed every night, alone, to the unfathomed waters of darkness.

And yet, once accustomed to the strange element, there was great peace and beauty in it. It seemed as though only the phantoms and spirits of substantial things were now abroad;

clouds floated where the hills had been, and the houses were sparks of fire. The eye might bathe and refresh itself in the depths of the night, without grating upon any harsh outline of reality; the earth with its infinity of detail was dissolved into ambiguous space. The walls of the house were too narrow, the glare of the lamps too fierce for those thus refreshed and made sensitive; we were as birds lately winged that have been caught and caged.

Virginia Woolf, *The Guardian*, 1905

INTO THE NIGHT (3)

When Cousin Liza pounded at the door on that February morning in 1931, it was still the time of day when everyone whispered. Dark and cold in the kind of way it never was when the sun came up. It was still the time that the trees claimed as their own as they whispered secrets against the sky. They whispered something when Cousin Liza knocked, and she looked around nervously, but they became silent then.

The walk from St David's to River Sallee was a long and arduous one. It was best started early. Queen was still half-asleep when they left. But the way Cousin Liza walked, sleep didn't stay around for long. It departed with a frown and an irritated yawn. Wide awake after the first few minutes, Queen pushed the straw hat more firmly on to her hand, held the cloth bag securely on her shoulder, and kept running to keep up.

Cousin Liza had planned to start at five a.m. She must have made a mistake, though. Day was a long time coming, and the trees and the shadows and the frogs shouting in the drains kept insisting that it was still their time. They had been walking for more than two hours when the first glimmers of dawn appeared. At one time they had passed a house in which a light burned brightly. The man inside may have seen them, for the door was open. Into the darkness he shouted, 'Wey dis two woman goin at this hour?' and his feet pounded on the floor as though he were coming out to get them. If she had known who he was, Cousin Liza wouldn't be afraid, but you never knew the people who were up that late. They could be doing all sorts of things with the supernatural. So Cousin Liza pulled Queen and they pelted off down the road, feet flying on the broken pavement. After this, Queen was afraid, for she realized that Cousin Liza, too, walked with fear.

At one point, when they got to a place where the road forked in three directions, Queen did not find it strange to see a cock standing in the middle of the crossroads. She was accustomed to fowls. It was only when she felt Cousin Liza jerk her towards the drain that she froze. They passed in the drain at the side of the road and walked without looking back. Cousin Liza did not have to tell Queen it would be dangerous to look back. She *knew*! Queen's whole body was heart. It pounded with a painful thump that resounded in her step. Her bare feet felt neither the stones in the road nor the effect of the miles. Suspended in a twilight between conscious thought and puppetry, she knew neither where she was nor where she was going to. And worse was yet to come.

They were making their way through a track in Hope, St Andrew's, which could cut down on the distance to Grenville town, when Queen pulled convulsively on Cousin Liza's hand. Liza's twenty-eight years on what she knew of earth had not given her the fearlessness that Queen expected her to possess. Queen stood, one hand now on top of the straw hat the brim of which framed her round face, the thick black plaits sticking out on both sides, the other hand lifted towards the distance. Liza froze. With a taut, tense movement she boxed down the child's shaking finger.

'Don't point,' she whispered hoarsely. 'Bite you finger,' she remembered to add.

On the hill next to the gravestone, something moved. No house was in sight. Above the watching women, the branches of the trees leaned across and linked leaves, touching each other caressingly in the stillness of the morning. The thing moved again. A pale light from a wandering, waning moon flashed across it and the thing bent towards them, beckoning, encouraging them forward. Queen's arms were thrown around Liza and she clung tightly, mouth open, the breath pushed from her throat to her lips in audible sobs, eyes wide with terror. Liza, body and hands hard with fear, held on to the child. She uttered no prayer with her lips, none in her heart. Her whole body was a throbbing prayer. Papa God! Papa God!

Whatever it was was quiet now. Still, no longer beckoning. The leaves above, too, had stopped their furtive caressing. Liza's feet moved. One quiet dragging step. Two, the left foot following because it couldn't go off on its own in a different direction. T-h-r-ee. Queen's body, with no will or separate identity of its own, did whatever Liza's did. The thing bent towards them. Queen screamed. With sudden decision, Liza dragged Queen along the edge of the track. And as this living fear drew level with the taunting thing above, it stopped in unbelief.

'Jesus!' said Cousin Liza. 'Jesus!'

The plantain leaf bowed again.

Queen, sobbing now with the release of terror, clung to Cousin Liza's hand and was dragged along the track. Her destination was daylight. It was only when the sky lightened and she could hear cocks crowing and see people moving about the yards that she became once more a conscious being. She started to feel tired and told Cousin Liza that she wanted to rest.

They had been walking for seven hours and were in Paradise with the sun blazing down upon their heads when the bus from St David's passed them on its way to Sauteurs. Queen ate her coconut-drops and stretched out her tongue at the people looking back from the back seat of the bus. Years later, an older

Queen learnt that the threepence she and Cousin Liza had spent to buy things to eat along the way could have paid a bus fare. Even though she had known then, the knowledge would have been of little use. Faith would have called her damn lazy if she had suggested going by bus.

'Liza, girl, you must be tired. How you do? Come, come, come girl. Come an sit down. Queenie, child, me mind did tell you me mother would send you up today.'

Cousin Kamay accepted their arrival as a matter of course.

'Constance, put some food in the bowl for Cousin Liza. Go in the kitchen an see what you get to eat, Queen. It have food dey. Help yourself to what you want. How you mother?'

'She well, tanks.'

'"Well, tanks" *who*?'

'She well tanks, Cousin Kamay.'

Cousin Kamay watched her. 'Hm! You gettin big! These children nowadays you have to keep a eye on them yes. Go an see what you get to eat!'

The journey was over. In two days' time, after being about her mother's business, eleven-year-old Queen would leave again with Cousin Liza or whoever else happened to be making the trip to St David's. The one thing that remained to haunt her was the knowledge that the return trip would have to be made in darkness, when the sun was down, and when those who had to walk always made their journeys.

Merle Collins, The Walk, 1990

BEHIND HIM

Like one, that on a lonely road
    Doth walk in fear and dread,
And having once turn'd round, walks on,
    And turns no more his head:

> Because he knows, a frightful fiend
> Doth close behind him tread.

Samuel Taylor Coleridge, *The Rime of the*
Ancient Mariner, 1798

IN FRONT OF YOU (1)

You climb the green slope to another wood, and passing through it, come unexpectedly to a gap – no, to a ditch, no a country road, a lane, leading from you do not know where to you do not know what. You go down into it; you climb up on the other side. You have entered a different kind of property. You are in a turnip field, which you skirt. In the next field you see a fearsome animal all by himself, grazing at leisure. Upon seeing a bull you decide to pass him in the spirit of an escaping torero – or you make a rule to meet your danger.

Stephen Graham, *The Gentle Art of Tramping*, 1926

AROUND THE WORLD AGAIN

September 30, 1954. The condition of Neurath and Raeder, and the peril for my friend, weigh heavily on my mind. I have a new idea to make myself exercise regularly to the point of exhaustion: I have begun, along with the garden work, to walk the distance from Berlin to Heidelberg – 620 kilometers! For that purpose, I have marked out a circular course in the garden. Lacking a tape measure, I measured my shoe, paced off the distance step by step, and multiplied by the number of paces. Placing one foot ahead of the other 870 times, thirty-one centimeters to a step, yields 270 meters for a round. If I had taken a different route, along the prison wall, I could have made my track 350 meters. But because of the better view, I prefer this other track. This project is a training of the will, a battle against the endless boredom; but it is also an expression of the last remnants of my urge toward status and activity.

Hess often sits on his garden bench for hours. For some time the guards have been letting him alone. Today I stopped briefly in front of his bench. Hess remarked, 'By the way, I've stopped thinking that my food is doctored to give me stomach cramps. After all, I can take any one of the seven bowls that are standing on the table for all of us.'

I nodded my appreciation. 'Well, well, so you've got over your obsession at last.'

Hess smiled. 'No, of course not. If I did, it wouldn't be an obsession.'

The logic of his reply so staggered me that I made a confession. 'Oh well, I have my own eccentricities,' I said. 'Do you know that I'm collecting kilometers? Isn't that crazy, writing down the kilometers I've walked every day?'

Hess shook his head. 'Why not, if you enjoy it?'

I insisted on my claim to having a screw loose: 'But every week I add up the kilometers, calculate the weekly average, enter the kilometers for the week in a table with various columns, one column for the general average, another for the total number of kilometers.'

'That just happens to be your pastime,' Hess said consolingly. 'Others have others.'

I went on. 'Besides all that, in addition to the garden work I have to reach seven times seven kilometers by the end of the week. If I don't achieve this goal, I have to make up for it the following week. And I've been doing this for ten days.'

I asked Hess, since he was sitting so comfortably on his bench, to note each of my rounds on the walk to Heidelberg by drawing a line in the sand. He stood up, walked slowly over to our bean rows, and gave me thirty beans. 'Put these in your left pocket, and after every round drop one in the right pocket.

At night you can count them. Clear?' Then he walked back into the building.

March 19, 1955. My fiftieth birthday.

By sheer chance, on this day I completed the last stage on the walk to Heidelberg. While I was still tramping my rounds in the garden, Hess came out and sat down on his bench. It consists of two brick pedestals with a narrow board laid across them. He leaned against two tomato stakes to keep his back from touching the cold wall. 'Now I am setting out for Munich,' I said as I passed him on the next-to-last round. 'Then on to Rome and down as far as Sicily. Sicily's in the Mediterranean, so I won't be able to walk any farther.' When I had completed the last round, I stopped and sat down beside him.

'Why not by way of the Balkans to Asia?' Hess asked.

'Everything there is Communist,' I replied. 'But maybe I could go by way of Yugoslavia to Greece. And from there through Salonika, Constantinople, and Ankara to Persia.'

Hess nodded. 'That way you could reach China.'

I shook my head. 'Communist too.'

'But then across the Himalayas to Tibet.'

I turned that route down too. 'Also Communist. But it would be possible to cross Afghanistan to India and Burma. The more interesting route would be through Aleppo, Beirut, Baghdad, and across the desert to Persepolis and Teheran. A long, hot tramp, lots of desert. I hope I'll find oases. At any rate, I have a good program now. It should do me for the time being: it's a distance of more than four thousand kilometers. You've helped me out of an embarrassing predicament. Many, many thanks, Herr Hess.'

With the hint of a bow, as though we were at a diplomatic reception, Hess replied, 'Most pleased to be of help, Herr Speer.'

Albert Speer, *Spandau: The Secret Diaries*, 1975
(trans. Richard and Clara Winston, 1976)

'THINK OF NOTHING IF THE GOING
GETS TOUGH'

I awoke at dawn, to the *didididididi* call of the Grey drongo
(probably); the chatterings and mutterings and babblings of
unseen Babblers (perhaps); the flutings and whistlings and
cat-calls of hidden pittas or bulbuls or cuckoo-shrikes or
laughing-thrushes (maybe); and the distant hoot of a gibbon
(certainly).

Dana, Leon and Inghai were already up, packing the supplies
into Iban carrying baskets.

'Empliau!' I said. 'Gibbons!'

The Iban laughed. 'No, no my friend,' said Leon with a grin,
'you tell that Mr Smythies in the book, it's not empliau, it's a
bird. The empliau – they called when you asleeps.'

'A bird?'

'Ruai. He very smarts. He make a little padi clearing in the
jungle and all his wives they come to see his tail.'

Checking the Iban against scientific and English names at
the back of Smythies, the mystery was soon solved: ruai was
Argusianus and *Argusianus* was the Great argus pheasant.

After breakfast, I awkwardly manoeuvred my Bergen on to
my back. It always seemed intolerably heavy until it was in
position, when the brilliantly designed strapping and cush-
ioning and webbing so balanced its frame on the back that it
was possible (on rare occasions) to forget that it was there. I
then buckled on my SAS belt with its attached compass-bag,
parang, and two water bottles in their canvas cases designed
to fit against either hip. I filled both from the stream and put
two water-purifying pills in each before screwing their tops
back on and slotting them into their holders.

James was similarly equipped, looking a little mournful,
smoking a cigarette, standing on the shingle and studying the
stones at his feet. Dana, Leon and Inghai finished hiding the

supplies we were to leave behind and securing the dugout well up a small creek, then hoisted long padi-carrying baskets on to their backs, and joined us. We waded across the Baleh and entered the jungle on the southern bank. Dana took the lead, holding his shotgun; I followed, James came behind me, then Inghai and then Leon, also with a shotgun.

'Why are we armed front and rear?' said James.

'For the wild Ukit men, they attack,' said Leon. 'This their land. They king of the jungle.'

'Heck,' said James, wheezing slightly under his Bergen.

'No, my very best friend,' said Leon after a pause, 'I jokes with you. They go away. They not disturb us. We leave messages. Our Tuai Rumah – he know what to do.'

The first hill, which I took to be just the river bank, was so steep that it was easiest to go up it on all fours, when not holding on to the saplings or tree trunks or creepers (and I quickly learnt to inspect each hand-hold for thorns or ants and, in general, snakes). The ridge at the top, however, to my great surprise, was only a pace or two across, and Dana's powerful tattooed-black calf muscles, on which my eyes were sweatily focused, suddenly disappeared from view, over the top and down the other side. I followed as best I could, picked up, it seemed, and hurled down the slope by the great weight of the Bergen, which nudged one in the back like a following bull. I slid over on to my chest and negotiated the steeper twists and turns as if descending a ship's rigging, holding on to the convoluted lattice of roots.

The heat seemed insufferable, a very different heat from the dazzling sunlight of the river-side, an all-enclosing airless clamminess that radiated from the damp leaves, the slippery humus, the great boles of the trees. Three hills in, the sweat towel round my forehead was saturated. My shirt was as wet as if I had worn it for a swim in the river. Dana, just ahead of me, however, appeared unaffected, his own shirt almost dry: and indeed the indigenous peoples of Borneo hardly sweat at all – with a humidity of 98 per cent there is nowhere for sweat to evaporate, no relief by cooling, just an added body-stocking of salt and slime and smell and moisture. I could feel a steady rivulet of sweat running down the centre of my chest, into my belly-button, and on into my pubic hairs, washing the precious crutch powder down my legs.

By hill five, I found it difficult to imagine how I could possibly sustain this pace, carrying this weight. Dana's hugely-muscled little legs were beginning to blur, two mad little pistons pumping up and down through the airless gloom of the forest. There were rare patches of light where a tree had fallen, brief snatches of sunlight and two-hundred-foot-long rotten trunks sprouting with fungi, heavy with moss and lichen, and surrounded by dense, springing vegetation, by thickets of ferns. But otherwise it was a creepered world of apparently endless twilight.

In the warm and scummy bathwater that seemed to slop from skullside to skullside in my head at every step, words of advice from the SAS Major in Hereford suddenly surfaced. It was the kind of comfort which he himself might have needed, I imagined, only after several months rather than several hours of this kind of walk, but it was a comfort, all the same: 'In those hills, lads, think of nothing if the going gets tough. Or, if you're young enough [he had seemed dubious], think of sex. Never, ever, think of the mountain that never gets any nearer. Think of nothing, and you'll survive to be a credit to the regiment.' I decided, in a *Boys' Own* sort of way, that yes, I very much wanted to be a credit to the regiment. So I thought of sex. But, just as I conjured the first pair of perky breasts and little brown nipples before my eyes and steamed-up glasses, the gully of the hill stream I was crossing went black with oncoming heatstroke. I dimly realised, with heat-hazy annoyance, that I really must be far too old to do it on the march.

Instead, a poem, all of my own, burst before me like a volcanic bubble in a mudpool. I went like this:

> Oh, fuck it,
> it's an Ukit.
> We're going to kick the bucket.

This was so brilliant, so obviously a poem of intrinsic interest, that it kept me amused, one word at a time, on the step, for the next three hills.

From a long, long way back we heard a shout. 'Stop!' it said. James had made the right decision.

Redmond O'Hanlon, Into the Heart of Borneo, 1984

STOP

The sun is beating down strongly and the pack seems heavier than it ought to be. The slope is tiring, and halfway up, the traveller, who is sweating freely, decides that it would be well to make a stop and recover his energy. An old shepherd is sitting in the sun, wrapped up in a blanket which covers all but his head.

The traveller approaches him.

'Good day to you.'

'God has given us a cool one today.'

'Cool?'

'Well, stop walking and you'll see.'

Camilo José Cela, Journey to the Alcarria, 1948
(trans. Frances M. Lopez Morillas, 1964)

EIGHT

You Walked?

When they first saw men walking for the pleasure of walking,
they thought they must be mad.

Strabo III

'I NAUSEATE WALKING'

Sir Wilfull: ... Yes, I made bold to see, to come and know if that how you were disposed to fetch a walk this evening; if so be that I might not be troublesome, I would have sought a walk with you.

Millamant: A walk? What then?

Sir Wilfull: Nay nothing – only for the walk's sake, that's all.

Millamant: I nauseate walking, 'tis a country diversion. I loathe the country and everything that relates to it.

William Congreve, *The Way of the World*, 1700

AGAINST LEG-STRETCHING

At our accustomed dismounting to recreate ourselves, and refresh the beasts, I would fetch a walk, to stretch my legs, that were stifled with a stumbling beast; wherewith the Turks were mightily disconcerted and in derision would laugh and mock me. For they cannot abide a man to walk in turnes.

William Lithgow, *The Totall Discourse of the Rare Adventures and painfull Peregrinations of long nineteene Yeares*, 1614

NO HORSE?

While [Parson] Adams was thus employed, Parson Trulliber, conceiving no great respect for the appearance of his guest, fastened the parlour door, and now conducted him into the kitchen, telling him he believed a cup of drink would do him no harm, and whispered his wife to draw a little of the worst ale. After a short silence Adams said, 'I fancy, sir, you already perceive me to be a clergyman' – 'Ay, ay,' cries Trulliber, grinning, 'I perceive you have some cassock; I will not venture to call it a whole one.' Adams answered, 'It was indeed none of the best, but he had the misfortune to tear it ten years ago in passing over a stile.' Mrs Trulliber, returning with the drink, told her husband, 'She fancied the gentleman was a traveller, and that he would be glad to eat a bit.' Trulliber bid her hold her impertinent tongue, and asked her, 'If parsons used to travel without horses?', adding, 'he supposed the gentleman had none by having his boots on.' – 'Yes, sir, yes,' says Adams; 'I have a horse, but I have left him behind me.' – 'I am glad you have one,' says Trulliber, 'for I assure you I don't love to see clergymen on foot; it is not seemly nor suiting the dignity of the cloth.' Here Trulliber made a long oration on the dignity of the cloth (or rather gown) not much worth relating, till his wife had spread the table and set a mess of porridge on it for his breakfast.

Henry Fielding, *The Adventures of Joseph Andrews*, 1742

PARIAH

Pedestrianism, in the estimate of the English landlords, carries with it the most awful shadow and shibboleth of the pariah.

Thomas De Quincey, *Confessions of an English Opium-Eater*, 1822

NO ROOM

'Madam, can you favour me with a bed?'
    She surveyed me with a small degree of surprize – 'No!'
    I took a seat.
    'I will pay whatever you desire.'

'I could spare one; but it will not suit me.'

'I have tried to procure one, but am unable. Pray, Madam, indulge me, it is drawing towards nine. – Do not suffer me to lie in the street.'

'You are a stranger to me!'

'So I am to every one else. If I must not sleep till I am known, I must walk one hundred and fifty miles for a bed.'

'What? are you on foot?'

'Yes; but if I am, I have not the appearance of a common tramper; neither would a horse be of use, except he could mount precipices, and climb over stone walls. Pray, Madam, favour me.'

'I am a single woman; and, to take in a stranger, may give rise to reflection.'

'Did you ever hear of a woman losing her character by a man of seventy-eight!' (I thought I perceived, pass through her mind, a small ray of pity.)

'I do not keep a public-house.'

'I ask pardon, Madam; I applied because I saw a sign over the door.'

'It has been a public-house; and the sign was forgot to be taken down.'

I retreated.

. William Hutton, *History of the Roman Wall*, 1802

NO CASH?

SONG

Bob

Let others travel far and wide,
To view each hill and valley
To see how different scenes appear,

And wherein 'tis they tally:
My purpose is where I begin
To see each country's produce,
To tell the merits of each inn,
And what I find of no use.

The ruin'd castle some admire
Which lets in wind and weather;
I like the snug and blazing fire,
When shelter'd altogether.
And though a lake is well enough
For sailing or for rowing,

Some ninnies go around the world
In search of fine adventures,
From port to port by weather hurl'd,
Till all their fortune's spent thus.
From port to port too I will go,
From Tenerife to Lisbon;
And so full of wine I get enough,
Why faith to me it is one.

Enter LANDLORD, *with first and second* PEDESTRIAN, *dressed in sailor's jackets and trousers, knapsacks at their backs, umbrellas etc.*

LANDLORD: Two gentlemen on foot, Sir. Your room will be ready immediately (exit).

BOB: Foot! Poor devils!

1ST PED: We do not interrupt you, I hope, Sir?

BOB: No. What, you've walked, have you? Why do you walk as sailors?

1ST PED: The dress is light, and well adapted for travelling.

BOB: But a'n't you afraid of being taken up?

2ND PED: No, Sir. We injure no one, why should anyone injure us?

BOB: You must be a little tired and foot-sore, I think?

1ST PED: Neither, Sir; we are used to it, and suffer no inconvenience whatsoever.

BOB: Used to it! What, you've come some way?

2ND PED: Some hundreds of miles, Sir.

BOB: What, going home? or going to see your friends?

2ND PED: Neither, Sir. Travelling for pleasure.

BOB: That's a good one! Travelling on foot for pleasure!

1ST PED: Yes, Sir.

BOB: Short of cash, perhaps? But then you might have stayed at home.

2ND PED: But not have seen the world there. My friend and myself, being anxious to see other places besides our own, and other men and other manners than those of our own confined circle, travel thus, at a light expense, in search of knowledge and amusement.

BOB: Why, they're crack'd. What then, if you had money, you wouldn't walk?

2ND PED: Not altogether, Sir. We might perhaps afford what others might esteem accommodations, but which would be none to us.

BOB: I wouldn't give a penny to travel without horses and servants!

James Plumptre, *The Lakers*, 1798

NO COACH?

Now, my friend, writing to you from here, I have already undergone so many hardships as a pedestrian that I am undecided whether to continue in this manner or not.

A pedestrian seems in this country to be a sort of beast of passage – stared at, pitied, suspected and shunned by everybody who meets him. So at least it has proved on my way from Richmond to Windsor.

My host at Richmond was greatly astonished at my declared intention to walk to Oxford, and even beyond; but he nevertheless sent his small son with me to put me on to the right road for Windsor.

At first I went along a very pleasant footpath by the side of the Thames, the Royal Garden lying on my right; on the opposite side of the river lay Isleworth, a spot distinguished by several fine houses and gardens. Here I was ferried across the river to reach the Oxford road, which passes through Windsor.

As soon as I was on the other side I went to a house and asked a man standing at the door if I was on the right road for Oxford.

'Yes,' he said, 'but you'll want a carriage to get you there.'

I answered that I intended to go there on foot, whereupon he gave me a look full of meaning, shook his head and went in the house.

I was now on a very fine, broad road, with many vehicles of all sorts. It was a hot day, so these sent up a heavy cloud of dust. As usual in this country, however, the highway was bordered by those lovely green hedges which contribute so greatly to its attraction, and when I was tired I would sit down occasionally in the shade of one of them and read my Milton. But it was soon evident to me that travellers riding and driving by all regarded me with surprise and made that same significant gesture, as if they took me to be someone not quite sane. So must anyone seem, apparently, who sits by a public road reading a book. I soon saw that if I wanted to rest and read I must find some lonely spot in a by-lane.

As I went on again every passing coachman called out to me: 'Do you want to ride on the outside?' If I met only a farm worker on a horse he would say to me companionably: 'Warm walking, sir', and when I passed through a village the old women in their bewilderment would let out a 'God Almighty!'

Karl Philipp Moritz, *Journeys of a German in England*, 1783
(trans. Reginald Nettel, 1965)

WHEN COACH PEOPLE EMBRACE PEDESTRIANISM

Before I came near to Loreto by tenne miles, I overtooke a Caroch, wherein two Gentlemen of Rome, and their two Concubines; who when they espied me, saluted me kindly, enquiring of what nation I was? whither I was bound? And what pleasure I had to travell alone? After I had to these demands given satisfaction, they intreated me to come up in the Caroch, but I thank-fully refused, and would not, replying the waye was faire, the weather seasonable, and my body unwearied. At last they perceiving my absolute refusall, presently dismounted on the ground, to re-create themselves in my company: and incontinently, the two young unmarried Dames came forth also, and would by no perswasion of me, nor their familiars mount againe; saying, they were all Pilgrimes, and bound to Loreto (for devotion sake) in pilgrimage, and for the pennance enjoyned to them by their Father Confessour. Truely so farre as I could judge, their pennance was smalle, being carried with the horses, and the appearance of their devotion much lesse; for lodging at Recanati, after supper, each youth led captive his dearest Darling to an unsanctified bed, and left me to my accustomed repose.

When the morning Starre appeared, we imbraced the way marching towards Loreto, and these vermillion nymphs, to let me understand they travelled with a cheerful stomacke, would oft runne races, skipping like wanton Lambes on grassie Mountaines, and quenching their follies in a sea of unquenchable fantasies. Approaching neare the gate of the Village, they pulled off their shoes and stockings and did walke barefoot through the lanes.

William Lithgow, *The Totall Discourse of the Rare Adventures and painfull Peregrinations of long nineteene Yeares*, 1614

THIS PEDESTRIAN DIDN'T

In these boots, and with this staff
Two hundred leaguers and a half –

(That means, two and a half hundred leagues. You follow? Not two hundred and one half league. Well –)

> *Two hundred leaguers and a half*
> *Walked I, went I, paced I, tripped I,*
> *Marched I, held I, skelped I, slipped I,*
> *Pushed I, panted, swung, dashed I;*
> *Picked I, forded, swam and splashed I,*
> *Strolled I, climbed I, crawled and scrambled,*
> *Dropped and dipped I, ranged and rambled;*
> *Plodded I, hobbled I, trudged and tramped I,*
> *And in lonely spinnies camped I,*
> *And in haunted pinewoods slept I,*
> *Lingered, loitered, limped and crept I,*
> *Clambered, halted, stepped and leapt I;*
> *Slowly sauntered, roundly strode I,*
> *And …*

> (Oh! Patron saints and Angels
>   That protect the four evangels!
>   And you Prophets vel majores
>   Vel incerti, vel minores
>   Virgines ac confessores
>   Chief of whose peculiar glories
>   Est in Aula regis stare
>   Atque orare et exorare
>   Et clamare et conclamare
>   Clamantes cum clamoribus
>   Pro nobis peccatoribus).
> *Let me not conceal it . . . . Rode I.*

Hilaire Belloc, *The Path to Rome*, 1902

SLOWER THAN THE SNAIL IN WOMAN SHAPE

We know there cannot be progression without retrogression, or gain with no corresponding loss; and often on my wheel, when flying along the roads at a reckless rate of very nearly nine miles an hour, I have regretted that time of limitations, galling to me then, when I was compelled to go on foot. I am a walker still, but with other means of getting about I do not feel so native to the earth as formerly. That is a loss. Yet a poorer walker it would have been hard to find, and on even my most prolonged wanderings the end of each day usually brought extreme fatigue. This, too, although my only companion was slow – slower than the proverbial snail or tortoise – and I would leave her half a mile or so behind to force my way through unkept hedges, climb hills, and explore the woods and thickets to converse with every bird and shy little beast and scaly creature I could discover. But mark what follows. In the late afternoon I would be back on the road or footpath, satisfied to go slow, then slower still, until the snail in woman shape would be obliged to slacken her pace to keep me company, and even to stand still at intervals to give me needful rest.

W. H. Hudson, *Afoot in England*, 1903

IT ROTS THE BRAIN

It is a fact that not once in all my life have I gone out for a walk. I have been taken out for walks; but that is another matter. Even while I trotted prattling by my nurse's side I regretted the good old days when I had, and wasn't a perambulator. When I grew up it seemed to me that the one advantage of living in London was that nobody ever wanted me to come out for a walk. London's very drawbacks – its endless noise and hustle, its smoky air, the squalor ambushed everywhere in it – assured this one immunity. Whenever I was with friends in the country, I knew that at any moment, unless rain was actually falling, some man might suddenly say, 'Come out for a walk!' in that sharp imperative tone which he would not dream of using in any other connection. People seem to think there is something inherently noble and virtuous in the desire to go for a walk. Any one thus desirous feels that he has a right to impose his will on whomever he sees comfortably settled in an arm-chair, reading. It is easy to say simply 'No' to an old friend. In the case of a mere acquaintance one wants some excuse. 'I wish I could, but' – nothing ever occurs to me except 'I have some letters to write.' This formula is unsatisfactory in three ways. (1) It isn't believed. (2) It compels you to rise from your chair, go to the writing-table, and sit improvising a letter to somebody until the walkmonger (just not daring to call you liar and hypocrite) shall have lumbered out of the room. (3) It won't operate on Sunday mornings. 'There's no post out till this evening' clinches the matter; and you may as well go quietly.

Walking for walking's sake may be as highly laudable and

exemplary a thing as it is held to be by those who practise it. My objection to it is that it stops the brain. Many a man has professed to me that his brain never works so well as when he is swinging along the high road or over hill and dale. This boast is not confirmed by my memory of anybody who on a Sunday morning has forced me to partake of his adventure. Experience teaches me that whatever a fellow-guest may have of power to instruct or to amuse when he is sitting on a chair, or standing on a hearth-rug, quickly leaves him when he takes one out for a walk. The ideas that came so thick and fast to him in any room, where are they now? where that encyclopaedic knowledge which he bore so lightly? where the kindling fancy that played like summer lightning over any topic that was started? The man's face that was so mobile is set now; gone is the light from his fine eyes. He says that A. (our host) is a thoroughly good fellow. Fifty yards further on, he adds that A. is one of the best fellows he has ever met. We tramp another furlong or so, and he says that Mrs. A. is a charming woman. Presently he adds that she is one of the most charming women he has ever known. We pass an inn. He reads vapidly aloud to me: 'The King's Arms. Licensed to sell Ales and Spirits.' I foresee that during the rest of the walk he will read aloud any inscription that occurs. We pass a 'Uxminster. 11 Miles.' We turn a sharp corner at the foot of a hill. He points at the wall, and says 'Drive Slowly.' I see far ahead, on the other side of the hedge bordering the high road, a small notice-board. He sees it too. He keeps his eye on it. And in due course 'Trespassers,' he says, 'Will Be Prosecuted.' Poor man! – mentally a wreck.

Luncheon at the A.'s, however, salves him and floats him in full sail. Behold him once more the life and soul of the party. Surely he will never, after the bitter lesson of this morning, go out for another walk. An hour later, I see him striding forth, with a new companion. I watch him out of sight. I know what he is saying. He is saying that I am rather a dull man to go a

walk with. He will presently add that I am one of the dullest men he ever went a walk with. Then he will devote himself to reading out the inscriptions.

How comes it, this immediate deterioration in those who go walking for walking's sake? Just what happens? I take it that not by his reasoning faculties is a man urged to this enterprise. He is urged, evidently, by something in him that transcends reason; by his soul, I presume. Yes, it must be the soul that raps out the 'Quick march!' to the body. – 'Halt! Stand at ease!' interposes the brain, and 'To what destination,' it suavely asks the soul, 'and on what errand, are you sending the body?' – 'On no errand whatsoever,' the soul makes answer, 'and to no destination at all. It is just like you to be always on the look-out for some subtle ulterior motive. The body is going out because the mere fact of its doing so is a sure indication of nobility, probity, and rugged grandeur of character.' – 'Very well, Vagula, have your own wayula! But I,' says the brain, 'flatly refuse to be mixed up in this tomfoolery. I shall go to sleep till it is over.' The brain then wraps itself up in its own convolutions, and falls into a dreamless slumber from which nothing can rouse it till the body has been safely deposited indoors again.

Even if you go to some definite place, for some definite purpose, the brain would rather you took a vehicle; but it does not make a point of this; it will serve you well enough unless you are going for a walk. It won't, while your legs are vying with each other, do any deep thinking for you, nor even any close thinking; but it will do any number of small odd jobs for you willingly – provided that your legs, also, are making themselves useful, not merely bandying you about to gratify the pride of the soul. Such as it is, this essay was composed in the course of a walk, this morning. I am not one of those extremists who must have a vehicle to every destination. I never go out of my way, as it were, to avoid exercise. I take it as it comes, and take it in good part. That valetudinarians are always chattering about it, and indulging in it to excess, is no reason for despising it. I am inclined to think that in moderation it is rather good for one, physically. But, pending a time when no people wish me to go and see them, and I have no wish to go and see any one, and there is nothing whatever for me to do off my own premises, I never will go out for a walk.

Max Beerbohm, *Going Out for a Walk*, 1918

THE GERMAN WALKING ROUND THE WORLD

I *left* Caceres on Sunday morning in a fury because the hall porter of the hotel – but that is too good a name for him: he was a weedy, spidery, hairy individual, who sat on the doorstep with a cigarette stuck to his lip, a man who had not seen soap, water, or razor for weeks – because this fellow accused me of running away without paying my bill. My flood of anger brought down a mass of eloquence with it: I do not recollect ever having had such a mastery of the Spanish tongue as I had at that moment. Subtle idioms and distinguished oaths poured from me. Skilfully, like a canoe, my tongue passed over the deeps and rapids of the majestic Castilian language. That moment of complete mastery was elating and magnificent. I marched into the streets triumphantly.

The stares of the populace did not worry me; if I had left in a pretty equable temper, I should have cringed before their gazes. The sight of a man in old tweeds and carrying a pack is enough to set a Spanish town agog for a week. On one occasion in the Asturias some friends and I were escorted into the town of Llanes by a mob of fifty yelling children and grown-ups who did not hesitate to throw stones at us and batter at the hotel door with sticks. In Spain one cultivates insensibility. One stares. One stares at men and women. Above all one disregards the feelings of women for they are there to be stared at, and they enjoy it. As

I marched out of Caceres in my anger, I gave back stare for stare, with all the contempt of the midlands and the south, East Anglia, and the Welsh mountains, Cornwall and the two bitter parts of Ireland in my eyes. At the end of the town I was stopped by two Guardias Civiles, handsome men in green, yellow, and red uniforms, the finest corps of gendarmerie in Europe.

I expected to be asked for my papers and to undergo a cross-examination. But the truth is the life of a Guardia Civil is a lonely one, and the poor men who police those deserted roads want some one to talk to; the Guardias wanted to know:

Was I the German who, according to the papers, was staying in Caceres and was walking round the world for a prize? They insisted that I must be that German. That I must be walking for a prize. For what other reasons could a man walk? Innocent smiles passed over the Guardias' faces like wind over golden corn. I said, to convince them, I would show them my passport, but they restrained me with the greatest courtesy.

'No!' they said, 'why should we wish to see your passport, for you are obviously a man of means and leisure who goes as he pleases, and not one of these begging malefactors.'

Ah, ha! thought I. Tell that to your pernicious, hairy, dirty, old spidery porter in the town.

My virtue thus publicly proclaimed by the police – for we were standing at a cross-roads and a little crowd had begun to gather – I continued my march.

V. S. Pritchett, *Marching Spain*, 1928

HIKAZ?

Mr Passenger did not immediately answer. He was holding back some branches so that they could pass into the next field. While he did this he stopped and listened. The noise which they had heard a few seconds before was becoming louder and now it could be recognized as the voices of people singing. As Mr Passenger paused, discordant chantings rasped towards them through the soft country air. All at once the afternoon was made hideous by an increasing volume of inharmonious sound.

'What is that?' Mr Passenger said.

'What can it be?'

They went through the brambles into the next field. From the gate opposite figures advanced across the plough. As they came nearer the figures revealed themselves as men and women, though which were which it was at first not easy to infer as both were dressed in shorts and bright coloured shirts without distinction as to sex. One at least had side-whiskers and one of the more uncompromising female members of the party wore plus-fours. The words which they were singing could now be distinguished.

> *Boney was a warrior!*
> *Ho! Hi! Ho!*

Mr Passenger said: 'Here, I say, what's all this?'

'Hikers.'

'Hikers?' said Mr Passenger. '*Hikaz?*'

The word was evidently unfamiliar to him and he pronounced it as if it belonged to some oriental language. But Zouch did not embark on an explanation of its meaning or derivation. He was wondering whether anything so horrible could be true.

Anthony Powell, *From a View to a Death*, 1933

NO CAR?

There was a fierce wind on the bridge across the Ishikari River, and it took me nearly twenty minutes to battle it. Ahead of me, against the haze of the mountains, I began to make out the distant high-rises of the city of Sapporo, site of the 1972 winter Olympics and the administrative capital of the island. The car cemeteries grew more and more frequent – acres of brightly colored metal, wheelless, impotent, still oddly condescending. It had taken me fifteen days to reach Sapporo – 370 kilometers from the start of my journey. It would have taken a motor car perhaps nine hours.

On the road into the city I was twice greeted in English. At a drive-in a young truck driver jumped out of his cab and said, 'You foot, yes, and good for walk, but sun day – rain day, oh, Jesus Christ!'

Further on, a businessman stopped his car to offer me a lift and, clearly puzzled by my refusal, said, 'Then what mode of transportation are you embarking?'

Japanese slipped out: *'Aruki desu.'*

'Aruki?'

'Aruki.'

A digestive pause.

'Do you mean to intend that you have pedestricized?'

I nodded. He drove away, shaking his head.

Martin Booth, *The Roads to Sata*, 1985

PEDESTRIANS WILL BE PERSECUTED

To enter out into that silence that was the city at eight o'clock of a misty evening in November, to put your feet upon that buckling concrete walk, to step over grassy seams and make your way, hands in pockets, through the silences, that was what Mr. Leonard Mead most dearly loved to do. He would stand upon the corner of an intersection and peer down long moonlit avenues of sidewalk in four directions, deciding which way to go, but it really made no difference; he was alone in this world of A.D. 2052, or as good as alone, and with a final decision made, a path selected, he would stride off, sending patterns of frosty air before him like the smoke of a cigar.

Sometimes he would walk for hours and miles and return only at midnight to his house. And on his way he would see the cottages and homes with their dark windows, and it was not unlike walking through a graveyard where only the faintest glimmers of firefly light appeared in flickers behind the windows. Sudden grey phantoms seemed to manifest upon inner room walls where a curtain was still undrawn against the night, or there were whisperings and murmurs where a window in a tomb-like building was still open.

Mr. Leonard Mead would pause, cock his head, listen, look, and march on, his feet making no noise on the lumpy walk. For long ago he had wisely changed to sneakers when strolling at night, because the dogs in intermittent squads would parallel his journey with barkings if he wore hard heels, and lights might click on and faces appear and an entire street be startled by the passing of a lone figure, himself, in the early November evening.

On this particular evening he began his journey in a westerly direction, toward the hidden sea. There was a good crystal frost in the air; it cut the nose and made the lungs blaze like a Christmas tree inside; you could feel the cold light going on and off, all the branches filled with invisible snow. He listened to the faint push of his soft shoes through autumn leaves with satisfaction, and whistled a cold quiet whistle between his teeth, occasionally picking up a leaf as he passed, examining its skeletal pattern in the infrequent lamplights as he went on, smelling its rusty smell.

'Hello, in there,' he whispered to every house on every side as he moved. 'What's up to-night on Channel 4, Channel 7, Channel 9? Where are the cowboys rushing, and do I see the United States Cavalry over the next hill to the rescue?'

The street was silent and long and empty, with only his shadow moving like the shadow of a hawk in mid-country. If he closed his eyes and stood very still, frozen, he could imagine himself upon the centre of a plain, a wintry, windless Arizona desert with no house in a thousand miles, and only dry river beds, the streets, for company.

'What is it now?' he asked the houses, noticing his wrist watch. 'Eight-thirty p.m.? Time for a dozen assorted murders? A quiz? A revue? A comedian falling off the stage?'

Was that a murmur of laughter from within a moon-white house? He hesitated, but went on when nothing more happened. He stumbled over a particularly uneven section of sidewalk. The cement was vanishing under flowers and grass. In ten years of walking by night or day, for thousands of miles, he had never met another person walking, not one in all that time.

He came to a cloverleaf intersection which stood silent where two main highways crossed the town. During the day it was a thunderous surge of cars, the gas stations open, a great insect rustling and a ceaseless jockeying for position as the scarab-beetles, a faint incense puttering from their exhausts, skimmed homeward to the far directions. But now these highways, too, were like streams in a dry season, all stone and bed and moon radiance.

He turned back on a side street, circling round toward his home. He was within a block of his destination when the lone car turned a corner quite suddenly and flashed a fierce white cone of light upon him. He stood entranced, not unlike a night moth, stunned by the illumination, and then drawn toward it.

A metallic voice called to him:

'Stand still. Stay where you are! Don't move!'

He halted.

'Put up your hands!'

'But –' he said.

'Your hands up! Or we'll shoot!'

The police, of course, but what a rare, incredible thing; in a city of three million, there was only *one* police car left, wasn't that correct? Ever since a year ago, 2052, the election year, the force had been cut down from three cars to one. Crime was ebbing; there was no need now for the police, save for this one lone car wandering and wandering the empty streets.

'Your name?' said the police car in a metallic whisper. He couldn't see the men in it for the bright light in his eyes.

'Leonard Mead,' he said.

'Speak up!'

'Leonard Mead!'

'Business or profession?'

'I guess you'd call me a writer.'

'Your profession,' said the police car, as if talking to itself. The light held him fixed, like a museum specimen, needle thrust through chest.

'You might say that,' said Mr. Mead. He hadn't written in years. Magazines and books didn't sell any more. Everything went on in the tomblike houses at night, he thought, continuing his fancy. The tombs, ill-lit by television light, where the people sat like the dead, the grey or multicoloured lights touching their faces, but never really touching *them*.

'No profession,' said the phonograph voice, hissing. 'What are you doing out?'

'Walking,' said Leonard Mead.

'Walking!'

'Just walking,' he said simply, but his face felt cold.

'Walking, just walking, walking?'

'Yes, sir.'

'Walking where? For what?'

'Walking for air. Walking to *see*.'

'Your address!'

'Eleven South Saint James Street.'

'And there is air *in* your house, you have an air *conditioner*, Mr. Mead?'

'Yes.'

'And you have a viewing screen in your house to see with?'

'No.'

'No?' There was a crackling quiet that in itself was an accusation.

'Are you married, Mr. Mead?'

'No.'

'Not married,' said the police voice behind the fiery beam. The moon was high and clear among the stars and the houses were grey and silent.

'Nobody wanted me,' said Leonard Mead with a smile.

'Don't speak unless you're spoken to!'

Leonard Mead waited in the cold night.

'Just *walking*, Mr. Mead?'

'Yes.'

'But you haven't explained for what purpose.'

'I explained; for air, and to see, and just to walk.'

'Have you done this often?'

'Every night for years.'

The police car sat in the centre of the street with its radio throat faintly humming.

'Well, Mr. Mead,' it said.

'Is that all?' he asked politely.

'Yes,' said the voice. 'Here.' There was a sigh, a pop. The back door of the police car sprang wide. 'Get in.'

'Wait a minute, I haven't done anything!'

'Get in.'

'I protest!'

'Mr. Mead.'

He walked like a man suddenly drunk. As he passed the front window of the car he looked in. As he had expected, there was no one in the front seat, no one in the car at all.

'Get in.'

He put his hand to the door and peered into the back seat, which was a little cell, a little black jail with bars. It smelled of riveted steel. It smelled of harsh antiseptic; it smelled too clean and hard and metallic. There was nothing soft there.

'Now if you had a wife to give you an alibi,' said the iron voice. 'But –'

'Where are you taking me?'

The car hesitated, or rather gave a faint whirring click, as if information, somewhere, was dripping card by punch-slotted card under electric eyes. 'To the Psychiatric Centre for Research on Regressive Tendencies.'

He got in. The door shut with a soft thud. The police car rolled through the night avenues, flashing its dim lights ahead.

They passed one house on one street a moment later, one house in an entire city of houses that were dark, but this one particular house had all of its electric lights brightly lit, every window a loud yellow illumination, square and warm in the cool darkness.

'That's *my* house,' said Leonard Mead.

No one answered him.

The car moved down the empty river-bed streets and off away, leaving the empty streets with the empty sidewalks, and no sound and no motion all the rest of the chill November night.

Ray Bradbury, *The Pedestrian*, 1953

NO ADVENTURER

It was raining hard the next day – too wet for walking: I was no adventurer – so I bought a one-way ticket on the fast train to Plymouth.

Paul Theroux, *The Kingdom by the Sea*, 1983

NINE

Walk With Me

'Good evening, Signorina,' the voice had murmured. 'Will you allow me to walk along with you?'

Giorgio Bassani

A WARNING – HIS 'BURNING LEG'

Mrs Mountstuart touched a thrilling chord. 'In spite of men's hateful modern costume, you see he has a leg.'

That is, the leg of the born cavalier is before you: and obscure it as you will, dress degenerately, there it is for ladies who have eyes. You see it: or, you see *he* has it. Miss Isabel and Miss Eleanor disputed the incidence of the emphasis, but surely, though a slight difference of meaning may be heard, either will do: many, with a good show of reason, throw the accent upon the *leg*. And the ladies knew for a fact that Willoughby's leg was exquisite; he had a cavalier court-suit in his wardrobe. Mrs Mountstuart signified that the leg was to be seen because it was a burning leg. There it is, and it will shine through! He has the leg of Rochester, Buckingham, Dorset, Suckling; the leg that smiles, that winks, is obsequious to you, yet perforce of beauty self-satisfied; that twinkles to a tender mid-way between imperiousness and seductiveness, audacity and discretion; between 'you shall worship me' and 'I am devoted to you'; is your lord, your slave, alternately and in one. It is a leg of ebb and flow and high-tide ripples. Such a leg, when it is done with pretending to retire, will walk straight into the hearts of women.

George Meredith, *The Egoist*, 1879

A WARNING – HER 'SOFT-STEPPING'

Another mark of industry is, a quick step, and a somewhat heavy tread, showing that the foot comes down with a heart good will; and if the body lean a little forward, and the eyes keep steadily in the same direction, while the feet are going, so much the better, for these discover earnestness to arrive at the intended point. *I do not like*, I never liked, your sauntering, soft-stepping girls, who move as if they were perfectly indifferent as to the result; and, as to the love of the story, whoever expects ardent and lasting affection from one of these sauntering girls, will, when too late, find his mistake: the character runs the same all the way through. And no man ever saw a sauntering girl, who did not, when married, make a mawkish wife and a cold-hearted mother.

William Cobbett, Advice to Young Men, 1830

FIRST ENCOUNTER

The heat had been painfully oppressive all day; and it was now a close and sultry night.

My mother and sister had spoken so many last words, and had begged me to wait another five minutes so many times, that it was nearly midnight when the servant locked the garden gate behind me. I walked forward a few paces on the shortest way back to London; then stopped and hesitated.

The moon was full and broad in the dark blue, starless sky; and the broken ground of the Heath looked wild enough in the mysterious light, to be hundreds of miles away from the great city that lay beneath it. The idea of descending any sooner than I could help into the heat and gloom of London repelled me. The prospect of going to bed in my airless chambers, and the prospect of gradual suffocation seemed, in my present restless frame of mind and body, to be one and the same thing. I determined to stroll home in the purer air, by the most roundabout way I could take; to follow the white winding paths across the lonely Heath; and to approach London through its most open suburb by striking into the Finchley Road, and so getting back, in the cool of the new morning, by the western side of the Regent's Park.

I wound my way down slowly over the Heath, enjoying the divine stillness of the scene, and admiring the soft alterations of light and shade as they followed each other over the broken ground on every side of me. So long as I was proceeding through this first and prettiest part of my night walk, my mind remained passively open to the impressions produced by the view; and I thought but little on any subject – indeed, so far as my own sensations were concerned, I can hardly say that I thought at all.

But when I had left the Heath, and had turned into the by-road, where there was less to see, the ideas naturally engendered by the approaching change in my habits and occupations gradually drew more and more of my attention exclusively to themselves. By the time I had arrived at the end of the road, I had become completely absorbed in my own fanciful visions of Limmeridge House, of Mr. Fairlie, and of the two ladies whose practice in the art of water-colour painting I was so soon to superintend.

I had now arrived at that particular point of my walk where four roads met – the road to Hampstead, along which I had returned; the road to Finchley; the road to West End, and the road back to London. I had mechanically turned in this latter direction, and was strolling along the lonely high-road – idly wondering, I remember, what the Cumberland young ladies would look like – when, in one moment, every drop of blood in my body was brought to a stop by the touch of a hand laid lightly and suddenly on my shoulder from behind me.

I turned on the instant, and my fingers tightening round the handle of my stick.

There, in the middle of the broad, bright high-road – there, as if it had that moment sprung out of the earth or dropped from the heaven – stood the figure of a solitary Woman, dressed from head to foot in white garments; her face bent in grave inquiry on mine, her hand pointing to the dark cloud over London, as I faced her.

I was far too seriously startled by the suddenness with which this extraordinary apparition stood before me, in the dead of night, and in that lonely place, to ask what she wanted. The strange woman spoke first.

'Is that the road to London?' she said.

I looked attentively at her, as she put that singular question to me. It was then nearly one o'clock. All I could discern distinctly by the moonlight, was a colourless, youthful face, meagre and sharp to look at about the cheeks and chin; large, grave, wistfully attentive eyes; nervous, uncertain lips; and light hair of a pale, brownish-yellow hue. There was nothing wild, nothing immodest in her manner; it was quiet and self-controlled, a little melancholy, and a little touched by suspicion; not exactly the manner of a lady, and, at the same time, not the manner of a woman in the humblest rank of life. The voice, little as I had yet heard of it, had something curiously still and mechanical in its tones, and the utterance was remarkably rapid. She held a small bag in her hand; and her dress – bonnet, shawl, and gown, all of white – was, so far as I could guess, certainly not composed of very delicate or very expensive materials. Her figure was slight, and rather above the average height – her gait and actions free from the slightest approach to extravagance. This was all that I could observe of her, in the dim light and under the perplexingly strange circumstances of our meeting. What sort of a woman she was, and how she came to be out alone in the high-road, an hour after midnight, I altogether failed to guess. The one thing of which I felt certain was that the grossest of mankind could not have misconstrued her motive in speaking, even at that suspiciously late hour and in that suspiciously lonely place.

'Did you hear me?' she said, still quietly and rapidly, and without the least fretfulness or impatience. 'I asked if that was the way to London.'

'Yes,' I replied, 'that is the way: it leads to St. John's Wood and the Regent's Park. You must excuse my not answering you before. I was rather startled by your sudden appearance in the road; and I am, even now, quite unable to account for it.'

'You don't suspect me of doing anything wrong, do you? I have done nothing wrong. I have met with an accident – I am very unfortunate in being here alone so late. Why do you suspect me of doing wrong?'

She spoke with unnecessary earnestness and agitation, and shrank back from me several paces. I did my best to reassure her.

'Pray don't suppose that I have any idea of suspecting you,' I said, 'or any other wish than to be of assistance to you, if I can. I only wondered at your appearance in the road, because it seemed to me to be empty the instant before I saw you.'

She turned, and pointed back to a place at the junction of the road to London and the road to Hampstead, where there was a gap in the hedge.

'I heard you coming,' she said, 'and hid there to see what sort of man you were, before I risked speaking. I doubted and feared about it till you passed; and then I was obliged to steal after you, and touch you.'

Steal after me, and touch me? Why not call to me? Strange, to say the least of it.

'May I trust you?' she asked. 'You don't think the worse of me because I have met with an accident?' She stopped in confusion; shifted her bag from one hand to the other, and sighed bitterly.

The loneliness and helplessness of the woman touched me. The natural impulse to assist her and to spare her got the better of the judgment, the caution, the worldly tact, which an older, wiser, and colder man might have summoned to help him in this strange emergency.

'You may trust me for any harmless purpose,' I said. 'If it troubles you to explain your strange situation to me, don't think of returning to the subject again. I have no right to ask you for any explanations. Tell me how I can help you; and if I can, I will.'

'You are very kind, and I am very, very thankful to have met you.' The first touch of womanly tenderness that I had heard from her trembled in her voice as she said the words; but no tears glistened in those large, wistfully-attentive eyes of hers, which were still fixed on me. 'I have only been in London once before,' she went on, more and more rapidly; 'and I know nothing about that side of it, yonder. Can I get a fly, or a carriage of any kind? Is it too late? I don't know. If you could show me where to get a fly – and if you will only promise not to interfere with me, and to let me leave you, when and how I please – I have a friend in London who will be glad to receive me – I want nothing else – will you promise?'

She looked anxiously up and down the road; shifted her bag again from one hand to the other; repeated the words, 'Will you promise?' and looked hard in my face, with a pleading fear and confusion that it troubled me to see.

What could I do? Here was a stranger utterly and helplessly at my mercy – and that stranger a forlorn woman. No house was near; no one was passing whom I could consult; and no earthly right existed on my part to give me a power of control over her, even if I had known how to exercise it. I trace these lines, self-distrustfully, with the shadows of after-events darkening the very paper I write on; and still I say, what could I do?

Wilkie Collins, *The Woman in White*, 1860

THE RITUAL OF A FIRST WALK

He moved with slow step and abstracted air towards a door in the wall bordering the orchard. I, supposing he had done with me, prepared to return to the house; again, however, I heard him call 'Jane!' He had opened the portal and stood at it, waiting for me.

'Come where there is some freshness, for a few moments,' he said; 'that house is a mere dungeon; don't you feel it so?'

'It seems to me a splendid mansion, sir.'

'The glamour of inexperience is over your eyes,' he answered; 'and you see it through a charmed medium; you cannot discern that the gilding is slime and the silk draperies cobwebs; that the marble is sordid slate, and the polished woods mere refuse chips and scaly bark. Now *here*' (he pointed to the leafy enclosure we had entered) 'all is real, sweet, and pure.'

He strayed down a walk edged with box, and apple-trees, pear-trees, and cherry-trees on one side, and a border on the other full of all sorts of old-fashioned flowers, stocks, sweet-williams, primroses, pansies, mingled with southernwood, sweet-briar, and various fragrant herbs. They were fresh now as a succession of April showers and gleams, followed by a lovely spring morning, could make them: the sun was just entering the dappled east, and his light illuminated the wreathed and dewy orchard-trees and shone down the quiet walks under them.

'Jane, will you have a flower?'

He gathered a half-blown rose, the first on the bush, and offered it to me.

'Thank you, sir.'

Charlotte Brontë, *Jane Eyre*, 1847

GETTING TO KNOW YOU

While wandering on in a slow manner, they were again surprised, and Elizabeth's astonishment was quite equal to what it had been at first, by the sight of Mr. Darcy approaching them, and at no great distance. The walk being here less sheltered than on the other side, allowed them to see him before they met. Elizabeth, however astonished, was at least more prepared for an interview than before, and resolved to appear and to speak with calmness, if he really intended to meet them. For a few moments, indeed, she felt that he would probably strike into some other path. This idea lasted while a turning in the walk concealed him from their view; the turning past, he was immediately before them. With a glance she saw, that he had lost none of his recent civility; and, to imitate his politeness, she began, as they met, to admire the beauty of the place; but she had not got beyond the words 'delightful' and 'charming' when some unlucky recollections obtruded, and she fancied that praise of Pemberley from her, might be mischievously construed. Her colour changed, and she said no more.

Mrs. Gardiner was standing a little behind; and on her pausing, he asked her, if she would do him the honour of introducing him to her friends. This was a stroke of civility for which she was quite unprepared; and she could hardly suppress a smile, at his now seeking the acquaintance of some of those very people, against whom his pride had revolted, in his offer to herself. 'What will be his surprise,' thought she, 'when he knows who they are! He takes them now for people of fashion.'

The introduction, however, was immediately made; and as she named their relationship to herself, she stole a sly look at him, to see how he bore it; and was not without the expectation of his decamping as fast as he could from such disgraceful companions. That he was surprised by the connexion was evident; he sustained it however with fortitude, and far from going away, turned back with them, and entered into conversation with Mr. Gardiner. Mrs. Gardiner, who was walking arm in arm with Elizabeth, gave her a look expressive of wonder. Elizabeth said nothing, but it gratified her exceedingly; the compliment must be all for herself. Her astonishment, however, was extreme, and continually was she repeating, 'Why is he so altered? From what can it proceed? It is impossible he should still love me.'

After walking some time in this way, the two ladies in front, the two gentlemen behind, on resuming their places, after descending to the brink of the river for better inspection of some curious water-plant, there chanced to be a little alteration. It originated in Mrs. Gardiner, who, fatigued by the exercise of the morning, found Elizabeth's arm inadequate to her support, and consequently preferred her husband's. Mr. Darcy took her place by her niece, and they walked on together.

Jane Austen, *Pride and Prejudice*, 1813

A DOGGED FRENZY OF PURSUIT

The sight of Miss Middleton running inflamed young Crossjay with the passion of the game of hare and hounds. He shouted a view-halloo, and flung up his legs. She was fleet; she ran as though a hundred little feet were bearing her onward smooth as water over the lawn and the sweeps of grass of the park, so swiftly did the hidden pair multiply one another to speed her. So sweet was she in her flowing pace, that the boy, as became his age, translated admiration into a dogged frenzy of pursuit, and continued pounding along, when far outstripped, determined to run her down or die. Suddenly her flight wound to an end in a dozen twittering steps, and she sank. Young Crossjay attained her, with just breath to say: 'You are a runner!'

'I forgot that you have been having your tea, my poor boy,' said she.

'And you don't pant a bit!' was his encomium.

George Meredith, *The Egoist*, 1879

WOULD YOU WALK WITH THIS MAN?

A long time ago there was a servant lassie, who worked for the minister at Little Dunkeld. She was a quiet lass, who had no mind for dances and such follies, and she liked fine to go for long walks on Birnham Hill.

After a time she told the minister that she had met a grand gentleman there, who used to walk and talk with her, and he was courting her. The minister said that a fine gentleman would be dangerous company for the lass, and he told her to bring him to the manse, and let him see what kind of a man he was.

The lassie was pleased enough, and next Saturday she brought in her jo.

He was a grand looking gentleman, sure enough, and pleasant spoken, but when the minister looked down at his feet, the blood ran cold in his veins, for he saw that he had cloven hoofs, and he knew that there was just one person who had that. So, when the stranger had gone, he said to the lassie: 'That's a braw man, yon, but did you see the feet of him?'

'Aye I did,' said the lass, 'and bonnie feet he has, with braw shining boots.'

'Take another look at them, when you walk with him again,' said the minister.

But nothing he could say made any difference. She was still terribly taken up with him.

K. M. Briggs, *Dictionary of British Folk Tales*, 1971

CHEEKED

On a Sunday morning two fellows came along on their shutter: they overtook a girl who was walking on the pavement, and one of them, more sallow and cheeky than his companion, began to talk to her. 'That's a nice nosegay, now – give us a rose. Come and ride – there's plenty of room. Won't speak? Now, you'll tell us if this is the road to London Bridge.' She nodded. She was dressed in full satin for Sunday; her class think much of satin. She was leading two children, one on each hand, clean and well-dressed. She walked more lightly than a servant does, and evidently lived at home; she did not go to service. Tossing her head, she looked the other way, for you see the fellow on the shutter was dirty, not 'dressed' at all, though it was Sunday, poor folks' ball-day; a dirty, rough fellow, with a short clay pipe in his mouth, a chalky-white face – apparently from low dissipation – a disreputable rascal, a monstrously impudent 'chap,' a true London mongrel. He 'cheeked' her; she tossed her head, and looked the other way. But by-and-by she could not help a sly glance at him, not an angry glance – a look as much as to say, 'You're a man, anyway, and you've the good taste to admire me, and the courage to speak to me; you're dirty, but you're a man. If you were well-dressed, or if it wasn't Sunday, or if it was dark, or nobody about, I wouldn't mind; I'd let you "cheek" me, though I have got satin on.' The fellow 'cheeked' her again, told her she had a pretty face, 'cheeked' her right and left. She looked away, but half smiled; she had to keep up her dignity, she did not feel it. She would have liked to have joined company with him. His leer grew leerier – the low, cunning leer, so peculiar to the London mongrel, that seems to say, 'I am so intensely knowing; I am so very much all there;' and yet the leerer always remains in a dirty dress, always smokes the coarsest tobacco in the nastiest of pipes, and rides on a barrow to the end of his life. For his leery cunning is so intensely stupid that, in fact, he is as 'green' as grass: his leer and his foul mouth keep him in the gutter to his very last day. How much more successful plain, simple straightforwardness would be! The pony went on a little, but they drew rein and waited for the girl again; and again he 'cheeked' her. Still, she looked away, but she did not make any attempt to escape by the side-path, nor show resentment. No; her face began to glow, and once or twice she answered him, but still she would not quite join company. If only it had not been Sunday – if it had been a lonely road, and not so near the village, if she had not had the two tell-tale children with her – she would have been very good friends with the dirty, chalky, ill-favoured, and ill-savoured wretch. At the parting of the roads each went different ways, but she could not help looking back.

Richard Jefferies, *The Open Air*, 1885

A CASE OF 'WON'T BITE'

Varenka with the white kerchief over her black hair, surrounded by the children and good-naturedly and cheerfully busy with them, and evidently excited by the possibility of an offer of marriage from a man she liked, looked very attractive. Koznyshev walked by her side and did not cease admiring her. Looking at her he remembered all the charming things he had heard her say, and all he knew of her that was good, and he grew more and more conscious that what he felt for her was something rare, something he had felt but once before, a long, long time ago, when he was very young. His sense of pleasure at her nearness went on increasing until it reached a point where, when placing in her basket an enormous wood mushroom with a thin stem and up-curling top, he looked into her eyes and, noting the flush of joyful and frightened agitation that suffused her face, he himself became embarrassed and gave her a smile that said too much.

'If it is so, I must think it over and come to a decision, and not let myself be carried away like a boy by the impulse of the moment,' he told himself.

'Now I will go and gather mushrooms quite on my own account, or else my harvest will not be noticeable,' said he, and went away from the skirts of the wood, where they were walking about on the short silky grass under sparsely growing old birches, and penetrated deeper into the wood, where among the white birch trunks grew grey-stemmed aspens and dark hazel bushes. When he had gone some forty paces he stepped behind a spindle bush with pink and red earring-shaped blossoms, and paused, knowing that he could no longer be seen. Around him everything was quiet. Only the hum of flies, like that of a swarm of bees, sounded continually high up in the birch trees beneath which he stood, and occasionally the children's voices reached him. Suddenly, from the skirts of the wood not far off, he heard Varenka's contralto voice calling to Grisha, and a smile of pleasure lit up her face. Conscious of that smile, Koznyshev shook his head disapprovingly at his own state and taking out a cigar began to light it. He was long unable to strike a match against the bark of a birch. The delicate white outer bark adhered to the phosphorus, and the light went out. At last one match did burn up, and the scented smoke of the cigar, like a broad swaying sheet definitely outlined, moved forwards and upwards over the bush under the overhanging branches of the birch-tree. Watching the sheet of smoke, he went on slowly, meditating on his condition of mind.

'Why not?' he thought. 'If it were just a sudden impulse or passion – if I only felt this attraction, this mutual attraction (it is mutual), but felt that it was contrary to the whole tenor of my life, and that by giving way to it I should be false to my vocation and duty … But it is nothing of the kind. The one thing I can find against it is that when I lost Marie I told myself that I would remain true to her memory. That is the only thing I can say against my feeling … That is important,' thought Koznyshev, conscious nevertheless that this consideration could not have any importance for him personally, although in the eyes of others it might spoil his poetic rôle. 'But, apart from that, however much I searched I could find nothing to say against my feeling. If I had chosen by reason alone, I could find nothing better!'

He recalled the women and girls he had known, but try as he would he could not recall one who united in herself to such a degree all, literally all, the qualities which he, thinking the matter over in cold blood, would desire in a wife. She had all the charm and freshness of youth but was no longer a child, and if she loved him, loved him consciously as a woman ought to love. That was one favourable consideration. The second one was: she was not only far from worldly, but evidently felt a repulsion from the world, yet she knew the world and had all the ways of a woman of good Society, without which a life-companion would be unthinkable for him. The third was: she was religious, not irresponsibly religious and kind-hearted like a child – like Kitty for instance – but her life was based on religious convictions. Even down to small details Koznyshev found in her all that he desired in a wife: she was poor and solitary, so that she would not bring into her husband's house a crowd of relations and their influence, as he saw Kitty doing. She would be indebted to her husband for everything, which was a thing he had always desired in his future family life. And this girl, uniting all these qualities, loved him. He was modest, but could not help being aware of this. And he loved her. One of the opposite arguments was his age. But he came of a long-lived race, he had not a single grey hair, no one thought he was forty, and he remembered that Varenka had said it was only in Russia that men of fifty considered themselves old, and that in France a man of fifty considered himself *dans la force de l'âge*, while one of forty was *un jeune homme*. And what was the use of counting by years, when he felt as young at heart as he had been twenty years ago? Was it not youth that he was experiencing now, when coming out again on the other side of the wood he saw, in the bright slanting sunbeams, the graceful form of Varenka in her yellow dress and with a basket on her arm, stepping lightly past the trunk of an old birch, and when the impression of Varenka merged into one with the view that had so struck him with its beauty: the view of the field of ripening oats bathed in the slanting sunbeams and the old forest beyond, flecked with yellow, fading away into the bluish distance. His heart leapt with joy. His feelings carried him away. He felt that the matter was decided. Varenka, who had bent to pick a mushroom, rose buoyantly and glanced round. Throwing away his cigar Koznyshev went toward her with resolute steps.

'Mlle Varenka! When very young I formed my ideal of the woman I should love and whom I should be happy to call my wife. I have lived many years, and now in you for the first time I have met what I was in search of. I love you, and offer you my hand.'

This was what Koznyshev said to himself when he was already within ten steps of Varenka. Kneeling and with outstretched arms defending some mushrooms from Grisha, she was calling little Masha.

'Come along, little ones! There are a lot here,' she cried in her delightful mellow voice.

On seeing Koznyshev approaching she did not move; yet everything told him that she felt his approach and was glad of it.

'Well, have you found anything?' she asked from beneath her white kerchief, turning her handsome face toward him, with a gentle smile.

'Not one,' said Koznyshev. 'And you?'

She did not reply, being busy with the children who surrounded her.

'There's another, near the branch,' she said, pointing to a

small mushroom cut across its firm pinkish crown by a dry blade of grass from beneath which it had sprung up. Varenka rose when Masha had picked the mushrooms, breaking it into two white pieces. 'It reminds me of my childhood,' she added, moving away from the children with Koznyshev.

They went a few paces in silence. Varenka saw that he wanted to speak, and guessing the subject she grew faint with joy and fear. They had gone far enough not to be overheard, but he still had not begun. It would have been better for Varenka to remain silent. It would have been easier after a silence to say what they wished to say than after talking about mushrooms; yet against her will, and as if by accident, she said:

'So you have not found anything? But of course deep in the wood there are always fewer.'

Koznyshev sighed and did not speak. He was vexed that she had spoken about mushrooms. He wished to bring her back to her first remark about her childhood; but without wishing to, after a pause, he replied to her last words:

'I have only heard that the white boleti grow chiefly on the outskirts, but I can't even tell which are the white ones.'

A few more minutes passed; they had gone still further from the children and were quite alone. Varenka's heart beat so that she seemed to hear it, and she felt herself growing red and then pale and red again.

To be the wife of a man like Koznyshev after her difficult life with Madame Stahl seemed to her the height of bliss. Besides, she was almost sure she loved him, and now in a moment it must be decided. She was frightened, frightened of what he might or might not say.

'He must make his declaration now or never'; Koznyshev also felt this. Everything – Varenka's look, her blush, her downcast eyes – betrayed painful expectation. He saw it and was sorry for her. He even felt that to say nothing now would be to offend her. His mind went rapidly over all the arguments in favour of his decision. He repeated to himself the words with which he had intended to propose; but instead of those words some unexpected thought caused him to say:

'What difference is there between the white boleti and the birch-tree variety?'

Varenka's lips trembled with emotion when she replied:

'There is hardly any difference in the tops, but only in the stems.'

And as soon as those words were spoken, both he and she understood that all was over, and that what ought to have been said would not be said, and their excitement, having reached its climax, began to subside.

'The stem of the birch-tree boletus reminds one of a dark man's beard two days old,' remarked Koznyshev calmly.

'Yes, that's true,' answered Varenka with a smile, and involuntarily the direction of their stroll changed. They began to return to the children. Varenka felt pained and ashamed, but at the same time she experienced a sense of relief.

Koznyshev when he got home and went again over all his reasons came to the conclusion that at first he had judged wrongly. He could not be unfaithful to Marie's memory.

'Gently, gently, children!' shouted Levin almost angrily, stepping in front of his wife to shield her, when the crowd of children came rushing at them with shrieks of delight.

Behind the children Koznyshev and Varenka came out of the wood. Kitty had no need to question Varenka: from the calm and rather shamefaced look on both faces she knew that her plan had not been realized.

'Well?' inquired her husband on their way home.

'Won't bite,' answered Kitty with a smile and manner of speaking like her father, which Levin often observed in her with pleasure.

'Won't bite? How do you mean?'

'Like this,' she said, taking her husband's hand, raising it to her mouth, and slightly touching it with her closed lips. 'As one kissed the bishop's hand.'

'Who won't bite?' said he, laughing.

'Neither! And it should have been like this ...'

'Mind, here are some peasants coming ...'

They didn't see!'

Leo Tolstoy, *Anna Karenina*, 1873–7
(trans. Louise and Aylmer Maude, 1939)

NO, THANK YOU

He began to rehearse what he considered another man in his place would do: pick up the threads at once: kiss her quite naturally, upon the mouth if possible, say, 'I've missed you,' no uncertainty. But his beating heart sent out its message of fear which drowned thought.

'It's Wilson at last,' Louise said. 'I thought you'd forgotten me,' and held out a hand. He took it like a defeat.

'Have a drink.'

'I was wondering whether you would like a walk.'

'It's too hot, Wilson.'

'I haven't walked up there, since ...'

'Up where?' He realised for those who do not love time never stands still.

'Up at the old station.'

She said vaguely with a remorseless lack of interest, 'Oh yes ... yes, I haven't been up there myself yet.'

Graham Greene, *The Heart of the Matter*, 1948

THINGS TAKE A TURN

She finally succeeded in making herself understood, and it was not without difficulty. We had arrived at Valence in time for dinner and, according to our excellent custom, we spent the rest of the day there. We had put up outside the town, at Saint-Jacques. I shall always remember that inn, and the room in it which Mme de Larnage occupied. After dinner she wanted to take a walk. She knew that the Marquis was no walker, and this was her way of contriving a *tête-à-tête*, which she had decided to make good use of, for there was no time to lose if any was to be left for enjoyment. We walked around the town by the side of the moat. There I resumed the long story of my illnesses, and she replied to me in so tender a tone, clasping my arm and sometimes pressing it to her heart, that only stupidity like mine could have prevented me from realizing that she meant what she said. The preposterous thing was that I was extremely moved myself. I have said that she was pleasing; love made her attractive, giving her back all the sparkle of her early youth; and she made her advances so cunningly that she would have seduced even a man on his guard. I was very ill at ease therefore, and always on the point of taking some liberty; but I was restrained by the fear of offending or displeasing, and by the still greater fear of being hissed and booed and ridiculed, of providing an after-dinner anecdote and of being congratulated on my enterprise by the pitiless Marquis. I was angry with myself for my stupid bashfulness, and for being unable to overcome it; but at the same time I reproached myself for it. I was in tortures. I had already abandoned my shy lover's language, of which I realized the full absurdity now that I was well on the road. But, not knowing what manner to adopt or what to say, I remained silent, and looked sulky. In fact I did everything in my power to court the treatment I had feared. Fortunately Mme de Larnage took a more humane line. She abruptly cut this silence short by putting her arm round my neck; and in a second her lips, pressed upon my own, spoke too clearly to leave me in doubt. The crisis could not have come at a happier moment.

I became charming. It was time. She had given me that confidence the lack of which almost always prevents me from being master of myself. For once I was myself.

Jean-Jacques Rousseau, *Confessions*, 1781 (trans. J. M. Cohen, 1953)

US

'You told her about our walk in the wood?'
  'I was only talking, you know.'
  'But that wood was where I kissed you.'

Elizabeth Bowen, *The Death of the Heart*, 1938

UNTHINKABLY NEAR

'You want to go?' he asked. 'Half a minute, I'll just have a horse put in –'

'No,' said Gudrun, 'I want to walk.'

He had promised to walk with her down the long, lonely mile of drive, and she wanted this.

'You might *just* as well drive,' he said.

'I'd *much rather* walk,' she asserted, with emphasis.

'You would? – Then I will come along with you. – You know where your things are? – I'll put boots on.'

He put on a cap, and an overcoat over his evening dress. They went out into the night.

'Let us light a cigarette,' he said, stopping in a sheltered angle of the porch. 'You have one too.'

So, with the scent of tobacco on the night air, they set off down the dark drive, that ran between close-cut hedges through sloping meadows.

He wanted to put his arm round her. If he could put his arm round her, and draw her against him as they walked, he would equilibrate himself. For now he felt like a pair of scales, the half of which tips down and down into an infinite void. He must recover some sort of balance. And here was the hope and the perfect recovery.

Blind to her, thinking only of himself, he slipped his arm softly round her waist, and drew her to him. Her heart fainted, feeling herself taken. But then, his arm was so strong, she quailed under its powerful close grasp. She died a little death, and was drawn against him as they walked down the stormy darkness. He seemed to balance her perfectly in opposition to himself, in their dual motion of walking. So, suddenly, he was liberated and perfect, strong, heroic.

He put his hand to his mouth and threw his cigarette away, a gleaming point, into the unseen hedge. Then he was quite free to balance her.

'That's better,' he said, with exultancy.

The exultation in his voice was like a sweetish, poisonous drug to her. Did she then mean so much to him? She sipped the poison.

'Are you happier?' she asked, wistfully.

'Much better,' he said, in the same exultant voice, 'and I *was* rather far gone.'

She nestled against him. He felt her all soft and warm, she was the rich, lovely substance of his being. The warmth and motion of her walk suffused through him wonderfully.

'I'm *so* glad if I help you,' she said.

'Yes,' he answered. 'There's nobody else could do it, if you wouldn't.'

'That is true,' she said to herself, with a thrill of strange, fatal elation.

As they walked, he seemed to lift her nearer and nearer to himself, till she moved upon the firm vehicle of his body. He was so strong, so sustaining, and he could not be opposed. She drifted along in a wonderful interfusion of physical motion, down the dark, blowy hillside. Across, shone the little yellow lights of Beldover, many of them, spread in a thick patch on another dark hill. But he and she were walking in perfect, isolated darkness, outside the world.

'But how much do you care for me?' came her voice, almost querulous. 'You see, I don't know, I don't understand.'

'How much!' His voice rang with a painful elation. 'I don't know either – but everything.' He was startled by his own declaration. It was true. So, he stripped himself of every safeguard, in making this admission to her. He cared everything for her – she was everything.

'But I can't believe it,' said her low voice, amazed, trembling. She was trembling with doubt and exultance. This was the thing she wanted to hear, only this. Yet now she heard it, heard the strange clapping vibration of truth in his voice as he said it, she could not believe. She could not believe – she did not believe. Yet she believed, triumphantly, with fatal exultance.

'Why not?' he said. 'Why don't you believe it? – It's true. It is true, as we stand at this moment –' he stood still with her in the wind; 'I care for nothing on earth, or in heaven, outside this spot where we are. And it isn't my own presence I care about, it is all yours. I'd sell my soul a hundred times – but I couldn't bear not to have you here. I couldn't bear to be alone. My brain would burst. It is true.'

He drew her closer to him, with definite movement.

'No,' she murmured, afraid. Yet this was what she wanted. Why did she so lose courage?

They resumed their strange walk. They were such strangers – and yet they were so frightfully, unthinkably near. It was like a madness. Yet it was what she wanted, it was what she wanted.

D. H. Lawrence, *Women in Love*, 1921

WHEN HE TURNS OUT TO BE A BOOTED BORE

It was a fresh, pleasant morning and she felt the more disposed to enjoy her walk because Mr Mybug (she could not learn to think of him as Meyerburg) was not with her. For the last three mornings he had been with her, but this morning she had said that he really ought to do some work. Flora did not see why, but one excuse was as good as another to get rid.

It cannot be said that Flora really enjoyed taking walks with Mr Mybug. To begin with, he was not really interested in anything but sex. This was understandable, if deplorable. After all, many of our best minds have had the same weakness. The trouble about Mr Mybug was that ordinary subjects, which are not usually associated with sex even by our best minds, did suggest sex to Mr Mybug, and he pointed them out and made comparisons and asked Flora what she thought about it all. Flora found it difficult to reply because she was not interested. She was therefore obliged merely to be polite, and Mr Mybug mistook her lack of enthusiasm and thought it was due to inhibitions. He remarked how curious it was that most Englishwomen (most young Englishwomen, that was, Englishwomen of about nineteen to twenty-four) were inhibited. Cold, that was what young Englishwomen from nineteen to twenty-four were.

They used sometimes to walk through a pleasant wood of young birch trees which were just beginning to come into bud. The stems reminded Mr Mybug of phallic symbols and the buds made Mr Mybug think of nipples and virgins. Mr Mybug pointed out to Flora that he and she were walking on seeds which were germinating in the womb of the earth. He said it made him feel as if he were trampling on the body of a great brown woman. He felt as if he were a partner in some mighty rite of gestation.

Flora used sometimes to ask him the name of a tree, but he never knew.

Yet there were few occasions when he was not reminded of a pair of large breasts by the distant hills. Then, he would stand looking at the woods upon the horizon. He would wrinkle up his eyes and breathe deeply through his nostrils and say that the view reminded him of one of Poussin's lovely things. Or he would pause and peer in a pool and say it was like a painting by Manet.

And, to be fair to Mr Mybug, it must be admitted he was sometimes interested by the social problems of the day. Only yesterday, while he and Flora were walking through an alley of rhododendrons on an estate which was open to the public, he had discussed a case of arrest in Hyde Park. The rhododendrons made him think of Hyde Park. He said that it was impossible to sit down for five minutes in Hyde Park after seven in the evening without being either accosted or arrested.

There were many homosexuals to be seen in Hyde Park. Prostitutes, too. God! those rhododendron buds had a phallic, urgent look!

Sooner or later we should have to tackle the problem of homosexuality. We should have to tackle the problem of Lesbians and old maids.

God! that little pool down there in the hollow was shaped just like somebody's navel! He would like to drag off his clothes and leap into it. There was another problem ... We should have to tackle that, too. In no other country but England was there so much pruriency about nakedness. If we all went about naked, sexual desire would automatically disappear. Had Flora ever been to a party where everybody took off all their clothes? Mr Mybug had. Once a whole lot of us bathed in the river with nothing on and afterwards little Harriet Belmont sat naked in the grass and played to us on her flute. It was delicious; so gay and simple and natural. And Billie Polswett danced a Hawaiian love-dance making all the gestures that are usually omitted in the stage version. Her husband had danced too. It had been lovely so warm and natural and *real*, somehow.

So, taking it all round, Flora was pleased to have her walk in solitude.

Stella Gibbons, *Cold Comfort Farm*, 1932

WITH VENUS ON WIMBLEDON COMMON

Each evening David and I met, generally on Wandsworth Common, where afar off I would recognize him by his long swinging stride, even though with my short sight I could distinguish nothing else about him. Sometimes on these evenings he would just walk with me as far as my gate, but sometimes we would go to Wimbledon Common. It was on one of these summer evenings we had been talking of Richard Jefferies and his love for the human body. We had just read his essay, 'Nature in the Louvre' and his description of the 'Venus Accroupi,' which he had admired so much. We were sitting in the undergrowth of a little copse in a remote part of the common. David had said that he had never seen a woman's body, and I do not remember quite how it came about, but I quite naturally and simply, without any feeling of shyness, knelt up in our secret bower and undid my clothes, and let them fall about my knees so that to the knees I was naked. I knew my body was pretty: my breasts were firm and round and neither too small nor too large, and my neck and shoulders made a pleasant line, and my arms were rounded and white, and though my hips were small, the line of the waist was lovely. I was proud of my body, and took the most innocent pleasure in its lines and health and strength. So we knelt in the grass and dead leaves of the copse opposite to each other, he silent and I laughing with joy to feel the air on my skin, and to see his enraptured gaze. For as he knelt he gazed wonderstruck and almost adoring, quite still, quite silent, looking now and then into my eyes with serious ecstatic look, his eyes full of tenderness and love, searching mine for any sign of regret or shyness. He did not touch me, but just knelt there letting his eyes take their fill of the beauty that was filling his soul with delight. When, without a word, I lifted my clothes about me, he helping me, he only then said, 'Jenny, I did not know there was such beauty.'

He told me as we walked home that no statue or picture of a nude woman had ever given him a true idea, and that it was a far more beautiful thing than he had thought. For though he loved the Greek statues, it seemed to him that my body was far lovelier.

Helen Thomas, *As It Was*, 1926

THEY JUST WALKED OFF TOGETHER

While we were marching along a young couple caught us up. They had come a long distance and, like us, were bound for Lhasa. They were glad to join the caravan and we fell into conversation with them. Their story was a remarkable one.

This pretty young woman with her rosy cheeks and thick black pigtails had lived happy and contented with her three husbands – three brothers they were – for whom she kept a house in a nomad tent in the Changthang. One evening a young stranger arrived and asked for lodging. From that moment everything was different. It must have been a case of love at first sight. The young people understood each other without saying anything and next morning walked off together. They made nothing of a flight over the wintry plain. Now they were happy to have arrived here, and meant to begin a new life in Lhasa.

Heinrich Harrer, *Seven Years in Tibet*, 1953 (trans. Richard Graves)

HER FOOTSTEPS IN HIS

They walked up a sheeptrack, in the rain. The hill was in cloud and tassels of white water came streaming out of the cloud-bank. He walked ahead, brushing aside the gorse and the bracken, and she planted her footsteps in his.

They rested by the rocks, and then followed the old drove road, arm in arm, talking with the ease of childhood friends. Sometimes she strained to catch a word of his Radnor dialect. Sometimes, he asked her to repeat a phrase. But both knew, now, that the barrier between them was down.

Bruce Chatwin, *On the Black Hill*, 1982

A WALK, A LOOK, A MARRIAGE

The Kirk, too, of next day I remember; and a certain tragical Countess of Rothes, – she had been a girl at school in London, fatherless; in morning walks in the Regent's Park she had noticed a young gardener, had transiently glanced into him, he into her, and had ended by marrying him; to the horror of Society, and ultimately herself, I suppose, for he seemed to be a poor commonplace creature, as he stood there beside her.

Thomas Carlyle, *Reminiscences*, 1881

ALL MAPPED OUT

She leaned over and touched his arm. It was their station. All at once, there they were, deep in the country, standing on a tiny platform in the startlingly clean sweet air. Once the train had gone it was very quiet. They both jumped at a scuttering noise, but it was only a dry leaf bowling along the tarmac. Then they embraced, swaying, until they were light-headed, giddy, drawing away from each other with enormous smiles, almost shyly.

Simon got his map out.

'I think it might be quite a way,' he said, starting to look worried. 'There don't seem to be any buses either. Or taxis.'

'Oh, taxis,' said Nicola, as if she were sick to death of taxis. 'You don't go to the country for taxis. You *walk* in the country.'

They examined the map together, and it could have meant anything since it was the first time either of them had tried to use one.

'Let's see where that leads,' he said, pointing to a green lane edged with hawthorn bushes, for no other reason than that he liked the look of it.

The first five miles or so were in daylight, or at least, dusk. They followed the single track road past flat tilting fields and hedgerows with little brown birds jumping in and out of them. A mistiness and moistness of rain in the air pressed coolness to their faces and blurred their hair with droplets. As they walked, they discussed life, death, and later on, when it became relevant, the weather.

Their voices piped away into the evening.

'Truth,' said Nicola.

'Not using other people,' they agreed solemnly.

'Love,' said Simon. 'Who you love.'

They stopped to hug each other. He squeezed her so hard that her breath came puffing out, her ribs creaked and her feet left the ground.

'I feel incredibly strong,' he marvelled. 'I feel I could lift you to the top of that tree with one hand.'

They compared notes on how, in each other's company, they felt full of power, flickering like flames, capable of tremendous effortless speed; and how this fading light was lovely and mysterious, seemingly criss-crossed with satiny threads of excitement. They made each other feel so alive, they agreed; all those other people on the train, they'd been dozy, half conscious in comparison.

She picked a blade of grass, stretched it between her thumbs and pursed her lips to blow. Kid's stuff, he pronounced this, copying her, and soon their piercing whistles split the air for half a mile around.

Time passed. It grew dark. The sky was a black meadow of silvered *petits moutons*; a gibbous moon backlit the scalloped border of each cloudlet. Some five or six fields away they could see a pub, a far-off gaudy box of rhythmic noise.

'We could ask there,' said Nicola.

'Too far,' said Simon. He peered at the map. 'Soon we hit a B-road, then we're laughing.'

'Can I have a look?' said Nicola. 'Ah. Mmm. I think we're here, look, that last church was marked. And, I see, that's where we're going. Yes. Quite a bit further.'

It started to rain.

*

By the time they reached the Meadowsweet Guest House it was nearly ten o'clock. They were drenched. Simon pressed the doorbell, and flashed her a desperate grin, like a plague victim. She returned a distant smile.

'We've got those chimes at home,' she said pensively. 'I didn't think they'd have them in the country.'

The door opened a crack and a suspicious bespectacled face peered at them over the guard-chain. Simon stepped forward.

'We booked,' he said, 'Simon Morrison.'

'It's ten o'clock,' said the face.

'It was a bit of a way from the station,' said Simon.

'You *walked*?' said the face disbelievingly. There was the scrabble and clink of various security measures being unfettered, then they were in, wiping their feet like a couple of children in the narrow hall.

'And you are Mr Morrison?' said their host, staring at Simon, who was looking his most half-baked.

'Thass right,' murmured Simon.

Their host's wife came to stare.

'I don't know,' she said at last. 'Come on, leave your wet shoes on the mat, then I'll bring you both a hot drink in the lounge.' She shook her head and bustled off, tutting, to the kitchen.

In the lounge, the leaping screen of the television was just one brightness among many. The room was small and savagely lit by a 150-watt bulb refracted through a complex chandelier which tinkled madly as Simon's head brushed it.

'Derek and Janet, I'd like you to meet our two strangers in the night,' said their host, who had decided to revert to jollity. 'Simon and, er.'

'Nicola,' said Nicola grimly. She and Simon stood awkwardly, sodden, in their socks. She glanced at him. He looked as though he wanted to hide behind the curtains. He looked, she thought, like a big child.

Derek and Janet gaped up at them from the settee.

'Raining, is it?' said Derek at last, gazing at Nicola's dripping elf-locks and rats-tails.

'Just a bit,' laughed their host, rubbing his hands. 'She looks like a little mermaid, doesn't she.' He put his arm matily round her shoulders. 'Sit ye down, Nicola, sit ye down.'

'Hot chocolate,' said his wife coldly from the door.

Up in their room at last, Nicola fell like a stone onto one of the twin beds.

'At least it's warm,' volunteered Simon. 'Clean. We can push the beds together.'

'No we can't,' snapped Nicola. 'I'd rather be under a haystack. This isn't the country. It's just like back at home.'

'It's the country outside, though,' said Simon, trying to draw her to him.

She shrugged him off.

'Nylon sheets,' she said bitterly. 'Horrible butterflies all over the duvet covers. Horrible little ornaments, rabbits in crinolines, mice on penny farthings.'

'But that sort of thing,' he said, amazed, 'it doesn't matter. I hadn't even noticed.'

'No, well,' she said. 'I thought, I thought at least there would be cotton sheets.'

'But that doesn't *matter*,' he persisted, earnest and gawky beneath another searchlight. 'Not at all. That's nothing.'

'Oh is it,' she sniffed.

'It sounded OK in the guide,' he said. '"Cosy and welcoming". We couldn't afford the ones with stars.'

'Don't,' she said, turning away from his boy's face. The caparisoned fairytale personage had reverted to plain lizard.

'You'd like me more if I was five years older. Ten. And my skin puts you off,' he said. 'Be honest.'

'Shut up,' she said, and started to cry. He sat down beside her and tried to draw her into his shoulder. She resisted. He swore. She cried harder.

'Please Nicola,' he said, pacing the room. 'It can't be just the duvet covers.'

'It's not!' she said wildly. 'It's life!'

'How do you mean?' he said. 'Life.'

'Look,' she snarled, 'can't you see it ahead? We're going to end up like them.'

'Never,' he soothed.

'Boring. Dead!'

She was restlessly beating her foot. A violent cyclonic mood would arrive like this sometimes, inexplicable, devastating, tearing through one or the other of them like a runaway freight train leaving maximum damage in its wake. She shuddered.

'Can't you see?' she said, trying to be calm. 'We'd struggle along for a bit but we'd never get beyond this. It's all mapped out.'

He held his arms out to her, trying to hug her, but she cackled like a witch and shrank away.

Helen Simpson, *Bed and Breakfast*, 1991

TWO AND TWO

'And then of course, when 'tis all over,' continued the tranter, 'we shall march two and two around the parish.'

'Yes sure,' said Mr Penny: 'two and two: every man hitched up to his woman, a believe.'

'I can never make a show of myself in that way!' said Fancy, looking at Dick to ascertain if he could.

'I'm agreed to everything you and the company like, my dear,' said Mr Richard Dewy heartily.

'Why we did when we were married, didn't we, Ann?' said the tranter, 'and so do everybody, my sonnies.'

Thomas Hardy, *Under the Greenwood Tree*, 1872

WALKING HOME AT NIGHT – HUSBAND TO WIFE

You then for me made up your mind
To leave your rights of home behind,
Your width of table-rim and space
Of fireside floor, your sitting place,
And all your claim to share the best
Of all the house with all the rest,
To guide for me my house, and all
My home, though small my home may be.

Come, hood your head; the wind is keen.
Come this side – here. I'll be your screen.

The clothes your mother put you on
Are quite outworn and wholly gone,
And now you wear from crown to shoe
What my true love has bought you new,
That now in comely shape is shown,
My own will's gift to deck my own;
And oh! I have to share.
For your true share a half is small.

Come, hood your head; wrap up, now do.
Walk close to me. I'll shelter you.

And now when we go out to spend
A frosty night with some old friend,
And ringing clocks may tell at last
The evening hours have fled too fast,
No forked roads, to left and right,
Will sunder us for night or light;
But all my woe's for you to feel,
And all my weal's for you to know.

Come, hood your head. You can't see out?
I'll lead you right, you need not doubt.

William Barnes, Walking Home at Night – Husband to Wife, 1868

NEVER LONELY

In and down we wandered,
Past many jeweled wonders,
And as the shadows tried us,
And as the nights grew longer,
The fireflies flew before us.
We lit bush fires to guide us,

We carried tall pine torches,
And the fireflies helped beside ...
And then new lights began to shine
On a phosphorescent tree,
That was our guide.

A tree like a giant aspen
That grew on a narrow roadway –
One side of each aspen leaf shone with silvery white;
Who had put the trees here
In the winding path transcendent
To guide us when the sun no more gave light?

The way was never lonely,
The way was never weary.
For we had one another and loved as now today.

Vachel Lindsay, 'The Journey to the Centre of the Earth –
The Forest Ranger's Honeymoon', 1925

HE IS SOMEWHERE ELSE

Then the breeze stirred rather more briskly overhead and the colour was flashed into the air above, into the eyes of the men and women who walk in Kew Gardens in July.

The figures of these men and women straggled past the flower-bed with a curiously irregular movement not unlike that of the white and blue butterflies who crossed the turf in zigzag flights from bed to bed. The man was about six inches in front of the woman, strolling carelessly, while she bore on with greater purpose, only turning her head now and then to see that the children were not too far behind. The man kept his distance in front of the woman purposely, though perhaps unconsciously, for he wanted to go on with his thoughts.

'Fifteen years ago I came here with Lily,' he thought. 'We sat somewhere over there by a lake, and I begged her to marry me all through the hot afternoon. How the dragon-fly kept circling round us; how clearly I see the dragon-fly and her shoe with the square silver buckle at the toe. All the time I spoke I saw her shoe and when it moved impatiently I knew without looking up what she was going to say: the whole of her seemed to be in her shoe. And my love, my desire, were in the dragon-fly; for some reason I thought that if it settled there, on that leaf, the broad one with the red flower in the middle of it, if the dragon-fly settled on the leaf she would say "Yes" at once. But the dragon-fly went round and round: it never settled anywhere – of course not, happily not, or I shouldn't be walking here with Eleanor and the children – Tell me, Eleanor. D'you ever think of the past?'

'Why do you ask, Simon?'

'Because I've been thinking of the past. I've been thinking of Lily, the woman I might have married ... Well, why are you silent? Do you mind my thinking of the past?'

'Why should I mind, Simon? Doesn't one always think of the past, in a garden with men and women lying under the trees? Aren't they one's past, all that remains of it, those men and women, those ghosts lying under the trees, ... one's happiness, one's reality?'

'For me, a square silver shoe-buckle and a dragon-fly –'

'For me, a kiss. Imagine six little girls sitting before their easels twenty years ago, down by the side of a lake, painting the water-lilies, the first red water-lilies I'd ever seen. And suddenly a kiss, there on the back of my neck. And my hand shook all the afternoon so that I couldn't paint. I took out my watch and marked the hour when I would allow myself to think of the kiss for five minutes only – it was so precious – the kiss of an old grey-haired woman with a wart on her nose, the mother of all my kisses all my life. Come Caroline, come Hubert.'

They walked on past the flower-bed, now walking four abreast, and soon diminished in size among the trees and looked half transparent as the sunlight and shade swam over their backs in large trembling irregular patches.

Virginia Woolf, *Kew Gardens*, 1927

COME WALK WITH ME

Come, walk with me,
   There's only thee
To bless my spirit now –
   We used to love on winter nights

To wander through the snow;
   Can we not woo back old delights?
The clouds rush dark and wild,
   They fleck with shade our mountain heights
The same as long ago
   And on the horizon rest at last
In looming masses piled;
   While moonbeams flash and fly so fast
We scarce can say they smiled.

Come walk with me – come, walk with me;
   We were not once so few,
But death has stolen our company
   As sunshine steals the dew.
He took them one by one and we
   Are left the only two;
So closer would my feelings twine
   Because they have no stay but thine.

Emily Brontë, 'Come Walk with Me', 1844

TEN

March Parade Procession

Quite a sight that tangle of humanity – all colours, shapes and sizes – as it straightened out. Then as one body it was time to move on.

Cable Street marcher

MARCH OF THE TEN THOUSAND

Cyrus marched onwards four stages – twenty parasangs – to the river Chalus. That river is a hundred feet broad, and is stocked with large tame fish which the Syrians regard as gods, and will not suffer to be injured – and so too the pigeons of the place. The villages in which they encamped belonged to Parysatis, as part of her girdle money. From this point he marched on five stages – thirty parasangs – to the sources of the river Dardas, which is a hundred feet broad. Here stood the palace of Belesys, the ruler of Syria, with its park – which was a very large and beautiful one, and full of the products of all the seasons in their course. But Cyrus cut down the park and burnt the palace. Thence he marched on three stages – fifteen parasangs – to the river Euphrates, which is nearly half a mile broad. A large and flourishing city, named Thapsacus, stands on its banks. Here they halted five days, and here Cyrus sent for the generals of the Hellenes, and told them that the advance was now to be upon Babylon, against the great king; he bade them communicate this information to the soldiers and persuade them to follow. The generals called an assembly, and announced the news to the soldiers. The latter were indignant and angry with the generals, accusing them of having kept secret what they had long known; and refused to go, unless a bribe of money were given them as had been given to their predecessors, when they went up with Cyrus to the court of his father, not as now to fight a battle, but on a peaceful errand – the visit of a son to his father by invitation. The demand was reported to Cyrus by the generals, and he undertook to give each man five silver minae as soon as Babylon was reached, and their pay in full, until he had safely conveyed them back to Ionia again. In this manner the Hellenic force were persuaded, – that is to say, the majority of them. Menon, indeed, before it was clear what the rest of the soldiers would do – whether, in fact, they would follow Cyrus or not – collected his own troops apart and made them the following speech: 'Men,' he said, 'if you will listen to me, there is a method by which, without risk or toil, you may win the special favour of Cyrus beyond the rest of the soldiers. You ask what it is I would have you to do? I will tell you. Cyrus at this instant is begging the Hellenes to follow him to attack the king. I say then: Cross the Euphrates at once, before it is clear what answer the rest will make; if they vote in favour of following, you will get the credit of having set the example, and Cyrus will be grateful to you. He will look upon you as being the heartiest in his cause; he will repay, as of all others he best knows how; while, if the rest vote against crossing, we shall all go back again; but as the sole adherents, whose fidelity he can altogether trust, it is you whom Cyrus will turn to account, as commandants of garrisons or captains of companies. You need only ask him for whatever you want, and you will get it from him, as being the friends of Cyrus.'

The men heard and obeyed, and before the rest had given their answers, they were already across. But when Cyrus perceived that Menon's troops had crossed, he was well pleased, and he sent Glus to the division in question, with this message: 'Soldiers, accept my thanks at present; eventually you shall thank me. I will see to that, or my name is not Cyrus.' The soldiers therefore could not but pray heartily for his success; so high their hopes ran. But to Menon, it was said, he sent gifts with lordly liberality. This done, Cyrus proceeded to cross; and in his wake followed the rest of the armament to a man. As they forded, never a man was wetted above the chest: nor ever until this moment, said the men of Thapsacus, had the river been so crossed on foot, boats had always been required; but these, at the present time, Abrocomas, in his desire to hinder Cyrus from crossing, had been at pains to burn. Thus the passage was looked upon as a thing miraculous; the river had manifestly retired before the face of Cyrus, like a courtier bowing to his future king. From this place he continued his march through Syria nine stages – fifty parasangs – and they reached the river Araxes. Here were several villages full of corn and wine; in which they halted three days, and provisioned the army.

v. – Thence he marched on through Arabia, keeping the Euphrates on the right, five desert stages – thirty-five parasangs. In this region the ground was one long level plain, stretching far and wide like the sea, full of absinth; whilst all the other vegetation, whether wood or reed, was sweet scented like spice or sweet herb; there were no trees; but there was wild game of all kinds – wild asses in greatest abundance, with plenty of ostriches; besides these, there were bustards and antelopes … The flesh of those they captured was not unlike venison, only more tender. No one was lucky enough to capture an ostrich. Some of the troopers did give chase, but it had soon to be abandoned; for the bird, in its effort to escape, speedily put a long interval between itself and its pursuers; plying its legs at full speed, and using its wings the while like a sail. The bustards were not so hard to catch when started suddenly; for they take only short flights, like partridges, and are soon tired. Their flesh is delicious.

As the army wended its way through this region, they reached the river Mascas, which is one hundred feet in breadth. Here stood a big deserted city called Corsote, almost literally environed by the stream, which flows round it in a circle. Here they halted three days and provisioned themselves. Hence they continued their march thirteen desert stages – ninety parasangs – with the Euphrates still on their right, until they reached the Gates. On these marches several of the baggage animals perished of hunger, for there was neither grass nor green herb, or tree of any sort; but the country throughout was barren … Some of the stages were very long, whenever they had to push on to find water or fodder; and once they found themselves involved in a narrow way, where the deep clay presented an obstacle to the progress of the men ...

Altogether it was plain that Cyrus was bent on pressing on the march, and averse to stoppages, except where he halted for the sake of provisioning or some other necessary object; being convinced that the more rapidly he advanced, the less prepared for battle would he find the king; while the slower his own progress, the larger would be the hostile army which he would find collected. Indeed, the attentive observer could see, at a glance, that if the king's empire was strong in its extent of territory and the number of inhabitants, that strength is compensated by an inherent weakness, dependent upon the length of roads and the inevitable dispersion of defensive forces, where an invader insists upon pressing home the war by forced marches.

Xenophon, Anabasis

ONE MAN'S ANABASIS

Xenophon, that warrior of ancient times, travelled through the whole of Asia Minor and got to God knows where without any maps at all. And the Goths of old too made their expeditions without any knowledge of topography. Marching forward all the time is what is called an anabasis: penetrating into unknown regions: being cut off by enemies who are waiting for the first convenient opportunity to wring your neck. If anyone has a good brain, like Xenophon or all those thieving tribes who came to Europe from God knows where in the Caspian or Sea of Azov, he can work real wonders on a march.

Caesar's Roman legions penetrated somewhere to the north by the Gallic Sea and they had no maps either. Once they said they would march back to Rome again by another route so that they could get more out of it. And they got there too. And it is obviously from that time that people say that all roads lead to Rome.

And all roads lead to České Budějovice too. The good soldier Švejk was fully convinced of this when instead of the Budějovice region he saw villages in the Milevsko region.

All the same he went steadily forward, for no good soldier can allow a Milevsko to stop him from getting to České Budějovice.

And so Švejk turned up west of Milevsko at Květov, after having rung all the changes in the repertoire of army songs which he knew from his various marches, and so just before Květov he was compelled to start again with the song:

'When we marched away,
All the girls began to cry ...'

An old woman who was returning from church on the way from Květov to Vráž, which was still in a westerly direction, hailed Švejk with the Christian greeting: 'Good morning, soldier, where are you bound for?'

'I'm going to my regiment at Budějovice, mother,' answered Švejk, 'to the war.'

'Then you're wrong, soldier,' said the old woman in a scared voice. 'You'll never get there this way through Vráž. If you go straight on you'll get to Klatovy.'

'I believe that a man can get to Budějovice even from Klatovy,' said Švejk resignedly. 'It's certainly a tidy walk, if a chap's hurrying to get to his regiment to avoid any trouble through not being punctual at his destination for all his goodwill.'

'We've already had a chap like you here. He had to go to Pilsen to the Landwehr. He was called Toníček Mašků,' the old woman said with a sigh. 'He was a relation of my niece and he went away. And a week later the gendarmerie were looking for him, because he hadn't reported to his regiment. After another week he turned up here in mufti saying he had been allowed home on leave. But the mayor went to the gendarmerie and they pulled him out of that "leave". Now he's written from the front that he's wounded and that he's lost a leg.'

The old woman looked pityingly at Švejk: 'You can wait in that spinney there, soldier. I'll bring you some of our potatoes. They'll warm you up a bit. You can see our cottage from here. It's just to the right behind the spinney. You mustn't go through our village of Vráž. The gendarmes there are like hawks. You can go afterwards from the spinney towards Malčín. But after that, soldier, avoid Čížová. The gendarmerie there would flay you and they always catch dissenters. Go straight through the wood to Sedlec by Horažd'ovice. There's a very good gendarme there who lets everybody through the village. Have you got any papers on you!'

'I haven't, mother!'

'Then don't go there. It's better you go to Radomyšl, but see that you get there by evening. Then all the gendarmes are in the pub. And there in the Lower Street behind St Florian you'll find a house painted blue below and you can ask for Farmer Melichárek. That's my brother. You can give him my love and he'll show you how to get to Budějovice from there.'

For over half an hour Švejk waited in the spinney for the old woman. When he had warmed himself with the potato soup which she had brought him in a pot covered with a pillow so as not to get cold, she took out of her kerchief a hunk of bread and a piece of bacon, stuck all of it into Švejk's pocket, made the sign of the cross on him and said that she had two grandsons in the army.

Then she repeated to him in detail through which villages he had to go and which he had to avoid. Finally she took a crown out of the pocket of her coat so that in Malčín he could buy some spirit for his journey, because Radomyšl was very far away.

Following the instructions of the old woman Švejk walked from Čížová towards Radomyšl to the east and thought to himself that he could not help getting to Budějovice from any point of the compass.

From Malčín he was accompanied by an old accordion player, whom he had found in a pub when he bought the spirit for that long journey to Radomyšl.

The accordion player took Švejk for a deserter and advised him to go with him to Horažd'ovice, where he had a married daughter whose husband was a deserter too. The accordion player had obviously had a drop too much in Malčín.

'She has been keeping her husband hidden in a stable for two months already,' he confided to Švejk, 'so she can hide you too and you'll be able to stay there until the end of the war. And if there are two of you it'll be jollier.'

When Švejk politely declined this invitation the accordion player suddenly got very angry and went off to the left over the fields, threatening Švejk that he would denounce him to the gendarmerie in Čížová.

Towards evening in Radomyšl in the Lower Street behind St Florian Švejk found Farmer Melichárek. When he conveyed greetings from his sister in Vráž it did not have any effect on the farmer.

He insisted repeatedly on seeing Švejk's papers. He was rather a prejudiced person, talking all the time about robbers, vagabonds and thieves, masses of whom were infesting the whole district of Písek.

'They run away from the army, they don't want to serve in it and then they roam about the whole district and steal,' he said with emphasis to Švejk, looking him straight in the eyes. 'And they all look as innocent as lambs.

'Yes, of course, people always get worked up when it's a

question of telling the truth,' he added, when Švejk got up from the bench. 'If a chap has a clean conscience, he sits still and lets his papers be examined. But if he hasn't got any ...'

'Well, goodbye to you, grandfather.'

'And goodbye to you too, and next time try and catch someone who isn't quite as sharp as me.'

When Švejk went off into the darkness, the old man still went on grumbling for quite a time: 'He says he's going to Budějovice to join his regiment. From Tábor. And the rascal goes first to Horažd'ovice and only then to Písek. Why, he's making a trip round the world.'

Švejk went on walking almost the whole night until somewhere near Putim he found a haystack in a field. As he was scratching the straw apart he heard a voice quite near him saying: 'What's your regiment? Where are you off to?'

'The 91st. I'm going to Budějovice.'

'Why should you be going there?'

'I've got my lieutenant there.'

He could hear close to him not just one person laughing but three. When the laughter died down Švejk asked what regiment they belonged to. He discovered that two of them were from the 35th and one from the artillery, also from Budějovice.

A month ago the 35th had deserted just before they should have marched to the front, and the artilleryman had been on the tramp from the day he was called up. He was from here at Putim and the haystack belonged to him. At night he always slept in the haystack. The day before he had found the other two in the wood and had taken them with him to his rick.

All cherished the hope that the war must be over in a month or two. They imagined that the Russians were already beyond Budapest and in Moravia. This was what people were saying everywhere in Putim. In the morning before dawn the dragoon's wife would bring them breakfast. After that the men of the 35th would go on to Strakonice, because one of them had an aunt there, and she again had a friend in the mountains beyond Sušice. He had a saw mill and they would find good shelter there.

'And you of the 91st can go with us too, if you like,' they offered Švejk. 'Shit on your lieutenant!'

'That won't be so easy,' answered Švejk and he squeezed and crawled deeper into the haystack.

When he woke up next morning they were all of them gone and one of them, obviously the dragoon, had placed at his feet a slice of bread for the journey.

Švejk walked through the forests and near Štěkno he met a tramp, an old gaffer, who welcomed him like an old friend with a nip of brandy.

'Don't walk about in that,' he told Švejk. 'That army uniform of yours could cost you hell. Now it's full of gendarmes everywhere and there's no chance of doing any begging in those clothes. Today, of course, it's not us the gendarmes chase like they did before. Now it's only you they're after.

'It's only you they're after,' he repeated in a tone of such conviction that Švejk thought it wiser not to tell him anything about the 91st regiment. Let him take him for what he thought him to be. Why destroy the good old fellow's illusions?

'And where are you bound for?' the tramp asked after a while, when they had both lit their pipes and were slowly walking round the village.

'To Budějovice.'

'For the love of Christ!' the tramp said in horror. 'They'll round you up there in a jiffy, before you can say Jack Robinson. You must wear mufti and be in rags. You must hobble about like a cripple.

'But don't be afraid. Now we'll go to Strakonice, Volyň, and Dub, and it'll be hellishly bad luck if we don't scrounge some mufti there. In Strakonice the people are still so idiotically honest that they often leave their doors open for you at night and in the

daytime they don't lock them at all. In winter when they go off
and have a chat with a neighbour you can pick up some mufti
straight away. What do you need? You have boots, so all you want
is something to put over you. Is your army greatcoat old?'

'Yes, it is.'

'Well, keep it. People go about in that in the country. You
need trousers and a jacket. When we get that mufti we'll sell
your army trousers and tunic to the Jew Herrman at Vodňany.
He buys everything that's army and sells it again in the villages.

'Today we'll go to Strakonice,' he unfolded his plan further.
'Four hours from here is the old Schwarzenberg sheep-fold.
The shepherd there is a friend of mine. He's an old gaffer too.
And so we'll stay the night there and in the morning we'll move
on to Strakonice to see if we can't scrounge some mufti some-
where in the neighbourhood.'

In the sheep-fold Švejk found the nice old gaffer, who
remembered how his grandfather used to tell him stories about
the French wars. He was about twenty years older than the old
tramp and called him 'lad' just as he did Švejk.

'Well, you see, lads,' he explained, when they sat round the
stove, on which potatoes were boiling in their jackets, 'at that
time my grandfather dissented too just like your soldier here
is doing. But they caught him in Vodňany and flogged his arse
so much that strips flew off it. But he had luck after all. Jareš's
son, the grandfather of old Jareš, the water bailiff from Ražice
near Protivín, got some powder and lead in him at Písek for
desertion. And before they shot him on the ramparts at Písek
he ran the gauntlet of the soldiers in the street and got six
hundred blows with sticks, so that when death came it was a
relief and redemption for him. But when did you run away?'
he turned to Švejk with tearful eyes.

'After call-up, when they took us away to the barracks,'
answered Švejk, realizing that a soldier must not shatter the
illusions of the old shepherd.

'Did you climb over the wall?' the shepherd asked curiously, obviously recalling how his grandfather used to tell of how he too climbed over the barrack wall.

'There was no other way, granddad.'

'And the guard was strong and they shot at you?'

'Yes, they did, granddad.'

'And where are you off to now?'

'He's off his head,' the tramp answered in place of Švejk. 'He insists on going to Budějovice. You know, he's a foolish young puppy and goes to his ruin. I must give him a few lessons. We'll try and scrounge some mufti for him and then everything'll be all right. We'll manage somehow until the spring and after that we'll go and take work with a farmer. This year there'll be a great shortage of labour, there'll be famine and they say all tramps will be rounded up and put on to farm work. And so I think it's better to go of your own accord. There won't be many farm workers. They'll all be wiped out.'

'You think that it won't be over this year?' asked the shepherd. 'Well, of course you're right, lad! There have been long wars in the past. There was the Napoleonic war and then the Swedish wars and the Seven Years' War, as they used to tell us. And people deserved these wars. The good Lord couldn't stand it any longer; people were getting so uppish, you see ...'

The water in which the potatoes were cooking on the stove began to bubble and after a short silence the old shepherd said in prophetic tones: 'And His Imperial Majesty won't win this war. There's no enthusiasm for it at all, because, as our school-master in Strakonice says, he wouldn't have himself crowned. Now he can talk as much soft soap as he likes. When you promised you'd be crowned you should have kept your word, you old bastard!'

'Perhaps he'll manage to do it now,' said the tramp.

'Nobody cares a hell any more about it now, lad,' the shepherd said irritably. 'You ought to be there when the neighbours get together down in Skočice. Everyone has a friend at the front and you should hear how they talk. After this war they say there'll be freedom and there won't be any noblemen's palaces or emperors, and the princes'll have their estates all taken away. The gendarmes already took off a chap called Kořínek because of talk like that. They said it was seditious. Yes, today it's gendarmerie law.'

'But so it was before,' replied the tramp. 'I remember how in Kladno there used to be a captain of the gendarmerie called Rotter. One fine day he began to breed those, what do you call them, police dogs, which are like wolves and follow everything when they're trained. And that captain at Kladno had his arse full with all those trainee dogs. He had a special little house for them, where they lived like lords. And one day he had the idea of experimenting with them on us poor tramps. So he gave orders that the gendarmerie in the whole Kladno district should round up the tramps, every man jack of them, and hand them all over to him. And once I was tramping from Lány and kept deep in the woods so that only a glimmer of me could be seen, but it was no good. I didn't get to the gamekeeper's lodge I was making for before they caught me and took me to the captain. And, chaps, you couldn't think or imagine what I had to go through with that captain and his dogs. First of all he made them all smell me, and then I had to climb up a ladder. And when I was on the top he set one of his monsters after me and the bloody brute pulled me down from the ladder on to the ground and kneeled on me, growling and snarling in my face. Then they took the brute away and told me to hide somewhere – anywhere I liked. I went into the woods towards the valley of Kačák, down into a ravine, and half an hour later two of those wolfhounds caught up with me, knocked me over and, while one of them held me by the throat, the other ran off to Kladno. An hour later Captain Rotter himself came with his gendarmes, shouted at the dogs, gave me five crowns and permission to beg in the Kladno region for two whole days ...'

And while the shepherd sieved the potatoes and poured into the dish sour sheep's milk the tramp continued to impart his memories of gendarmerie justice: 'In Lipnice there was a gendarmerie sergeant down underneath the castle. He lived in the gendarmerie station itself and I, being a simple old chap, was always under the impression that a gendarmerie station must be in some prominent place like in the square or some-where like that and certainly not somewhere in a side street. And so I kept to the side streets of that little country town and didn't look at the street signs. I took one house after the other until I got to the first floor of an ordinary cottage, opened the door and announced, "Have pity on a poor tramp." Good Lord, chaps, I could have dropped through the floor. It was the gendarmerie station. There were rifles along the wall, a crucifix on the table, a register on the chest and His Imperial Majesty looked down at me directly over the table. And before I could stammer anything, the sergeant jumped at me and gave me such a blow on the jaw at the door that I flew out down those wooden stairs to the very bottom and only stopped when I got to Kejžlice. That's gendarmerie law.'

They started to eat and soon went to sleep stretched out on the benches in the warm sitting-room.

In the night Švejk quietly dressed and went out. The moon was just rising in the east and in its waking light Švejk marched to the east, repeating: 'It's not possible for me not to get to Budějovice.'

And because when Švejk came out of the woods he saw on the right a town, he took a more northerly course and then turned to the south, where again there could be seen a town of some kind. (It was Vodňany.) And so he moved away in the opposite direction over the meadows and the early sun welcomed him on the snow-covered slopes above Protivín.

'Forward the brave!' said the good soldier Švejk to himself. 'Duty calls. I must get to Budějovice.'

But by an unfortunate chance instead of going from Protivin south to Budějovice Švejk directed his steps to the north towards Písek.

About noon Švejk saw a village in front of him. Coming down from a small hill he thought: 'It's no good going on like this. I'll ask how I can get to Budějovice.'

And going into the village he was very surprised when he saw its name marked on a post by the first house: 'Putim'.

'Jesus Christ,' sighed Švejk. 'Here I am back in Putim where I slept in the haystack.'

And so he was not the slightest bit surprised when he saw behind the little lake a white-washed house on which a 'chicken' was hanging (the name given in some places to the Austrian 'eaglet') and a gendarme walking out of it like a spider guarding its web.

The gendarme went straight up to Švejk and said nothing except, 'Where are you off to?'

'To my regiment at Budějovice.'

The gendarme smiled sarcastically: 'But you're going away from Budějovice. Your Budějovice is far behind you,' and he took Švejk into the gendarmerie station.

Jaroslav Hašek, *The Good Soldier Švejk*, 1921–3
(trans. Cecil Parrott, 1973)

LED BY THE SLINKY-HIPPED COLONEL

They started out without delay. A jeep, its headlamps lit, preceded them. The Colonel, in the lead, abreast of the Major and just ahead of Culver, plunged off into the deep dust of the road. He walked with a slinky-hipped, athletic stride, head down between his shoulders and slightly forward, arms bent and moving methodically; nothing broke the rhythm of his steps – ruts in the road or the deeply grooved tyre tracks – and Culver became quickly amazed, and rather appalled, at the pace he was setting. It was the pace of a trained hiker – determined, unhesitant, much closer to a trot now than a walk – and only a few minutes passed before Culver was gasping for breath. Sand lay thick in the road, hindering a natural step. They had not gone more than a couple of hundred yards; already he felt sweat trickling down his forehead and beneath his arms. For a moment fear surged up in him unnaturally, and a crazy panic. He had been afraid of the march before, but his fear had been abstract and hazy; now so quickly fatigued, in what seemed a matter of seconds, he felt surely (as Mannix had predicted) that he'd be unable to last the first hour. A panicky wash of blood came to his face and he struggled for breath, wanting to cry out – it passed. His mind groped for reason and the terror receded: once he adjusted to the shock of this pace, he realized, he'd be all right. Then the panic went away; as it did so, he found himself breathing easier, freed of that irrational fright. The Colonel pushed ahead in front of him with the absolute mechanical confidence of a wound-up, strutting tin soldier on a table top. Culver, panting a bit, heard his voice, as calm and unwinded as if he were sitting at a desk somewhere, addressed to the Major: 'We shoved off at nine on the dot, Billy. We should make the main road at ten and have a break.' 'Yes, sir,' he heard the Major say, 'we'll be ahead of the game.' Culver made a calculation then; by the operations map, which he knew so well, that was three and a half miles – a mile farther than the regulation distance for an hour's march. It was, indeed, like running. Pushing on through the sand, he felt a wave of hopelessness so giddy and so incomprehensible that it was almost like exhilaration – and he heard a noise – half-chuckle, half-groan – escape between his laboured breaths. Three and a half miles: the distance from Greenwich Village almost to Harlem.

In his mind he measured that giddy parade of city blocks, an exhausting voyage even on wheels. It was like twisting a knife in his side but he went on with the mental yardstick – to imagine himself plodding that stretch up the sandless comfortable receptive pavements of Fifth Avenue, past Fourteenth Street and the bleak vistas of the Twenties and the Thirties, hurrying onward north by the Library twenty blocks more to the Plaza, and pressing still onward along the green acres of the Park ... his thoughts recoiled. Three and a half miles. In an hour. With more than thirty-two still to go. A vision of Mannix came swimming back; Culver stumbled along after the dauntless Colonel, thinking, Christ on a crutch.

William Styron, *The Long March*, 1952

THE PRISON ROUND

Like ape or clown, in monstrous garb
With crooked arrows starred,
Silently we went round and round
The slippery asphalt yard;
Silently we went round and round,
And no man spoke a word.
Silently we went round and round
And through each hollow mind
The memory of dreadful things
Rushed like a dreadful wind,
And horror stalked before each man,
And terror crept behind.

Oscar Wilde, *The Ballad of Reading Gaol*, 1898

THE MARCH TO FREEDOM?

'*Antreten!*' the kapo shouts.

I finish tying up my strings, and we file slowly out. The dogs still aren't barking. We are counted again, and then we cross the brook and enter the meadow that rises toward the road we left yesterday. Still no sound of cannon. We hear that we've got to do twenty kilometers today. I'll probably make it. We have sat down in the meadow, and we eat some biscuits. We are even laughing. They'll surely overtake us; they'll surround us, and we won't make our destination. Where are they leading us? You say Buchenwald? Dachau? You must be joking ... It's a long way to Dachau; we'll be set free before that. No hypothesis holds water, or rather nothing supports it. There's no longer any way of knowing anything. The sentries are saying little, the kapos have been told nothing. 'Freed on the road': that's what Francis had read in the cards. A guy comes over to remind him of it, and Francis repeats what the cards said. 'A short trip ... we're freed on the road.' The guy doesn't say anything; he never believed in the cards, but then neither had he ever believed that he could fall over on the road and be shot where he lay. Now he no longer knows what he does and what he doesn't believe. We might be set free just like that; the Americans can move fast. But the SS will kill us first. Still, they can't kill us all, can they? But they did kill all the sick guys, without anything special having shown on their faces. The cards say we'll be freed on the road, after a short trip; they repeated that every time Francis dealt them out. However the cards are just a lot of shit. But, if it's a short trip, it could be tomorrow, tomorrow isn't far away. But nothing suggests it; something like that can be felt coming from a long way off, there are portents. But just the fact that we're on the road without anybody seeming to know where we're supposed to be taken, that after all is surely a sign. He gives up.

'*Der Krieg ist fertig! Der Krieg ist fertig!*'

It's the good old drunken kapo Alex who mumbles that as he goes by us. We know the war is over, we've been saying so for about two weeks, but nothing's over for us until they catch up with us and tear us away from the SS. The more defined the victory becomes, the clearer the danger we are in. The time will come when the very sight of us will become more intolerable to them with every passing minute, and our lives, depending less and less on circumstances, may soon depend on no more than someone's mood. In a state of harmlessness over the past several months, now the impending victory is rendering us questionable again. We reappear as animals with overly thick skins, as creatures out of a nightmare, indestructible. Hitherto, they only saw a mass whose liquidation you accelerate or which you let die on its own, depending on the orders they received; whereas now the skeletons with bent backs and hollow bellies are about to begin to topple them. Forerunners, maybe, of their soon to be conquerors. If, with the onset of the coming victory, the SS wavers, we are what they'll see first, and we'll pay for their downfall. Henceforth, rifle and machine pistol best express the nature of our relationship. They'll shoot or they won't shoot. Till now, their arrangement has been to have us live under conditions that let death come to us so to speak on its own. Now they're waiting for the occasion to finish us off swiftly, and there'll be plenty of such occasions on the road. Then the occasion will simply be the fact that we are still alive and that they just can't let go of us like that ...

We climb the steep slope towards the top of the meadow. The Poles and Russians, who were separated from us last night and spent the night somewhere else, are waiting for us on the road. We look down on the wooden house, with its red roof. The narrow purple column winds its way along over the grass. The sun is very faint, and the mist over the meadow clings low to the ground. It's beautiful. It's beautiful, and they may kill us in a little while. It's beautiful, and we're going to be hungry. I have seen the grass and the mist and the brown woods. Those are things that we too can see – which is what I try to hold on to. In a while I'll try to focus just on the trees, to apprehend their variety, to perceive the passage from dense forest to thinner growths, I shall even try to await with curiosity what the next turn of the road will bring. Can one be part of the column and only see the flowers at the wayside, only smell the wet leaves one walks upon? I was able to do this for a little while. But soon I was to see only the road and the backs like mine and hear only the kapo's yelling: 'Drücken, drücken!' 'Close ranks, close up!' It would be nice, for these twenty kilometers, to keep just this in my head: I'm going for a walk, the mountains are beautiful, I'm tired, but walking is tiring, that's only natural. The air feels cool on my face. Worn out, I may fall a little later on; it's nice to sink down when you're tired; I wouldn't hear anything, wouldn't see the kapo come running. A burst of shots. Finished. By the wayside. But I'll never be able even to begin saying 'I'm going for a walk.' From the heat of walking the lice wake up. The kapo's voice hounds us; the sun bakes us; the Polish block leader still carries his rifle. Where does our road end?

The war is ending. They don't know whether I am alive; but I'd like them to know that I am a part of this morning, that I've noticed it, that my presence in it leaves indisputable and transmittable traces.

Robert Antelme, *The Human Race*, 1947
(trans. Jeffrey Haight and Annie Mahler, 1992)

I PROTEST: COURAGE! DEATH OR FREEDOM!

'Shall we go straight toward the gate, or by a roundabout route to avoid the soldiers?' I was asked. I shouted huskily, 'No; straight through them. Courage! Death or Freedom!' and the crowd shouted in return, 'Hurrah!' We then started forward, singing in one mighty, solemn voice the Tsar's hymn, 'God Save the People'. But when we came to the line, 'Save Nicholas Alexandrovitch', some of the men who belonged to the Socialist Party were wicked enough to substitute the words 'Save George Appolonovich' [Gapon], while others simply repeated the words, 'Death or Freedom!' The procession moved on in a compact mass. In front of me were my two bodyguards and a young fellow with dark eyes from whose face his hard labouring life had not yet wiped away the light of youthful gaiety. On the flanks of the crowd ran the children. Some of the women insisted on walking in the first rows, in order, as they said, to protect me with their bodies, and force had to be used to remove them. I may mention also as a significant fact that at the start the police not only did not interfere with the procession, but moved with us with bared heads in recognition of the religious emblems. Two local police officers marched bareheaded in front of us, preventing any hindrance to our advance and forcing a few carriages that we met to turn aside in our favour. In this way we approached the Narva Gate, the crowd becoming denser as we progressed, the singing more impressive, and the whole scene more dramatic.

At last we reached within two hundred paces of where the troops stood. Files of infantry barred the road, and in front of them a company of cavalry was drawn up, with their swords shining in the sun. Would they dare to touch us? For a moment we trembled, and then started forward again.

Suddenly the company of Cossacks galloped rapidly towards us with drawn swords. So, then, it was to be a massacre after all! There was no time for consideration, for making plans, or giving orders. A cry of alarm arose as the Cossacks came down upon us. Our front ranks broke before them, opening to right and left, and down this lane the soldiers drove their horses, striking on both sides. I saw the swords lifted and falling, the men, women and children dropping to the earth like logs of wood, while moans, curses and shouts filled the air. It was impossible to reason in the fever of this crisis. At my order the front rows formed again in the wake of the Cossacks, who penetrated farther and farther, and at last emerged from the end of the procession.

Again we started forward, with solemn resolution and rising rage in our hearts. The Cossacks turned their horses and began to cut their way through the crowd from the rear. They passed through the whole column and galloped back towards the Narva Gate, where – the infantry having opened their ranks and let them through – they again formed line. We were still advancing, though the bayonets raised in threatening rows seemed to point symbolically to our fate. A spasm of pity filled my heart, but I felt no fear. Before we started, my dear friend, the workman K——, had said to me, 'We are going to give your life as a sacrifice.' So be it!

We were not more than thirty yards from the soldiers, being separated from them only by the bridge over the Tarakanovskii Canal, which here marks the border of the city, when suddenly, without any warning and without a moment's delay, was heard the dry crack of many rifle-shots. I was informed later on that a bugle was blown, but we could not hear it above the singing, and even if we had heard it we should not have known what it meant.

Vasiliev, with whom I was walking hand in hand, suddenly left hold of my arm and sank upon the snow. One of the workmen who carried the banners fell also. Immediately one of the two police officers to whom I had referred shouted out, 'What are you doing? How dare you fire upon the portrait of the Tsar?' This, of course, had no effect, and both he and the other officer were shot down – as I learned afterwards, one was killed and the other dangerously wounded. I turned rapidly to the crowd and shouted to them to lie down, and I also stretched myself out upon the ground. As we lay thus another volley was fired, and another, and yet another, till it seemed as though the shooting was continuous ...

At last the firing ceased. I stood up with a few others who remained uninjured and looked down at the bodies that lay prostrate around me. I cried to them, 'Stand up!' But they lay still. I could not at first understand. Why did they lie there? I looked again, and saw that their arms were stretched out lifelessly, and I saw the scarlet stain of blood upon the snow. Then I understood. It was horrible. And my Vasiliev lay dead at my feet.

Horror crept into my heart. The thought flashed through my mind, 'And this is the work of our Little Father the Tsar.' Perhaps this anger saved me, for now I knew in very truth that a new chapter was opening in the book of the history of our people. I stood up, and a little group of workmen gathered round me again. Looking backward, I saw that our line, though still stretching away into the distance, was broken and that many of the people were fleeing. It was in vain that I called to them, and in a moment I stood there, the centre of a few scores of men, trembling with indignation amid the broken ruins of our movement.

Father Gapon recalling St Petersburg, 22 January 1905

I PROTEST: STICKS IN THE AIR

From Scotland we are marching,
From ship-yard, mill and mine,
Our scarlet banners raise on high,
Now comes the day of reckoning,
No longer we'll endure
Starvation – we will conquer now,
Our victory is sure.
We are a strong determined band
Each with a weapon in his hand.

As the lines of the last verse were sung, the marchers would all raise their heavy walking sticks in the air, as a mark of defiance against the government.

Wal Hannington, *Unemployed Struggle*, 1919–1936

I PROTEST: WORKERS, STUDENTS, CHILDREN

The complexion of the march was much as it had been the year before, with greater quantities of everything. The bearded boys in blue jeans and long hair were along, and so were their thick-tressed girls, wearing heavy sweaters, tight slacks and tense, mascaraed expressions. One of these girls, a Chelsea Art student, began the march frivolously barefoot. She finished it grimly four days later, her blistered feet heavily bandaged. But she was still marching.

The bulk of the demonstrators were ordinary people from factories, offices, and shops, with many respectably dressed students and a surprising number of children, some of them very young. Invitations had gone out to several countries to send delegations to the march; sponsored groups from Sweden, Germany and France were there. Nationals from a myriad other countries walked under their respective banners: Australia, Spain, Norway, Denmark, Belgium, Cyprus, Tanganyika, Venezuela, Eire, Uganda, Iraq, and quite a few more. A number of Americans were marching, too, and their comments were varied: writer Clancy Sigal was uncharacteristically cagey about his views: 'There are strict rules about aliens mixing in the politics of this country; I'm here as an observer.' An ex-bomber pilot was less evasive: 'I'm here because I think bombs are bad; I've dropped enough of 'em to know.'

No Russian or Chinese banners were flying, though there were a few oriental faces among the marchers. One placard, written in Cyrillic letters, announced in bad Russian: 'Odessa govoreet nyet.' It proved to have been written by an Englishman. Other banners, signs, and cards peppered the column. One, crudely lettered and carried by a gaggle of schoolboys, read 6TH FORM PROTEST; another, neatly designed, said QUAKERS SAY NO TO ALL WAR. The Quakers appeared to be the largest religious group in the procession. Some signs were topical: BAN THE BOMB – NOT BANDA; others historical: DARTFORD – TOWN OF WAT TYLER; the Germans insisted Keine Atomwaffen in Deutschland, and Battersea declared itself against nuclear warfare. The Progressive League recalled darkly: THE POCOGNATHUS FAILED TO ADAPT – AND PERISHED. One placard displayed a quote from Einstein: 'If I had known, I would have become a locksmith.'

This time there were no meetings for speeches along the way, so the marchers were inundated only by the English clouds. The press, which by and large had sneered at the first march, covered this one with sympathy and occasional respect. So large a crowd of obviously respectable people was no longer a laughing matter.

The reactions of bystanders were generally tolerant, with a few exceptions. One man, when asked what he thought of it all, spat fiercely. Literally trembling with rage, he snarled, 'That's what I think of it, and if you're one of 'em, I want nothing to do with you!' After a moment it came out that his son worked at Aldermaston. Most onlookers were impressed by the size of the procession – never less than 2,500 and between 3,000 and 4,000 nearly all the way. Most also approved of the idea behind it. However, many also felt that the bomb was a political necessity. 'I think it's a good thing we're able to do this,' said an off-licence owner while marchers slogged by his shop in pouring rain; 'but if we didn't have the H-bomb, we wouldn't be able to do this.'

And what were 'we' doing? Protesting as before? Yes, but something else – another spirit – was rising out of the length of this long tramping rank. This spirit drifted over the march, suspended in a haze of banners and standards which stretched either way along the road as far as one could see. In all the four days the ends of the procession were never in sight of each other. One marcher followed the next, who in turn followed those in front of him – or her. All of them were more and more caught up in the surging stream of humanity.

By the fourth day levels were beginning to appear among the mass of demonstrators. A woman said at a lunch stop: 'I walked all the way, but she was given a lift when it rained.' The marchers were getting a taste for other kinds of prestige, too. They and their officials kept a bright eye out for the newsreel vans which toured up and down the march; and they were much more friendly to the photographers and journalists.

Word went round about TV coverage; and the respectful tone of certain newspapers was having its effect. Officials and marshals assumed an air of importance, and began to exaggerate the number of marchers less and less cautiously. They were rising above the scofflaw status of popular protest, approaching the moral apotheosis of righteous action. The press was backing them now; a six-wide rank of people stretching as far as the eye could see would not be sneered at any more, not even by those who disapproved of it. Aldermaston marchers were not to be ignored any more: they belonged.

Herb Greer, *Mud Pie*, 1964

FELLOW REVOLUTIONARIES

Jones! When from Calais southward you and I
Travell'd on foot together; then this Way,
Which I am pacing now, was like the May
With festivals of new-born Liberty
A homeless sound of joy was in the Sky:

The antiquated Earth as one might say,
Beat like the heart of Man: songs, garlands, play,
Banners and happy faces, far and nigh!
And now, sole register that these things were,
Two solitary greetings have I heard,
'*Good-morrow, Citizen!*' a hollow word,
As if a dead Man Spake it! Yet despair
I feel not: happy am I as a Bird:
Fair seasons yet will come and hopes as fair.

William Wordsworth, 'Composed near Calais,
on the Road Leading to Ardres', 1802

THE MECCAN BEAT

All the pilgrims hold it to be their great duty well to improve their time whilst they are at Mecca, not to do their accustomed duty and devotion in the temple, but to spend all their leisure time there, and as far as strength will permit to continue at Towoaf ie. walk round the Beat-Allah, which is about four and twenty paces square. At one corner of the Beat, there is a black stone fastened and framed in with silver plate, and every time they come to that corner, they kiss the stone; and having gone round seven times they perform two Erkaetsnomas, or prayers. The stone, they say, was formerly white, and then it was called Haggar Essaed ie. the White Stone. But by reason of the sins of the multitudes of the people, it has become black, and is now called Haggar Esswaed, or the Black Stone.

The place is so much frequented by people going round it, that the place of the Towoaf ie. the circuit which they take in going round it, is seldom void of people at any time of the day or night. Many have waited several weeks, nay months, for the opportunity of finding it so. For they say, that if any person is blessed with such an opportunity, that for his or her zeal in keeping up the honour of Towoaf, let they petition what they will at Beat-Allah, they shall be honoured. Many will walk round till they are quite weary, then rest, and at it again; carefully remembering at the end of every seventh time to perform two Erkaets. This Beat is in effect the object of their devotion, the idol which they adore: for, let them be never so distant from it, East or West, North, or South of it, they will be sure to bow down towards it; but when they are at the Beat, they may go on which side they please and pay their Sallah towards it. Sometimes there are several hundreds at Towoaf at once, especially after Acshamnomas, or fourth time of service, which is after candle-lighting, and these both men and women, but the women walk on the outside of the men, and the men nearest to the Beat.

In so great a resort as this, it is not to be supposed that every individual person can come to kiss the stone afore-mentioned; therefore, in such a case, the lifting up the hands towards it, smoothing down their faces, and using a short expression of devotion is sufficient. But when there are but few men at Towoaf, then the women get opportunity to kiss the said stone, and when they have gotten it, they close in with it as they come round, and walk as quick as they can to come to it again – and keep possession of it for a considerable time. The men, when they see that the women have got the place, will be so civil as to pass by and give them leave to take their fill, as I may say in their Towoaf or walking round, during which they are using some formal expressions. When the women are at the stone, then it is esteemed a very rude and abominable thing to go near them, respecting the time and place.

Richard Burton, *Personal Narrative of a Pilgrimage to El-Medinah and Meccah*, 1855–6

BURIED IN STYLE

Do you know I had the curiosity to go to the burying t'other night; I have never seen a royal funeral. Nay, I walked as a rag of quality, which I found would be, and so it was, the easiest way of seeing it. It is absolutely a noble sight. The Prince's Chamber hung with Purple and a quantity of silver lamps, the coffin under a canopy of purple velvet, and six vast chandeliers of silver on high stands had a very good effect: the ambassador from Tripoli and his son were carried to see that chamber. The procession through a line of foot-guards, every seventh man bearing a torch, the horse-guards lining the outside, their officers with drawn sabres and crape sashes, the drums muffled, the fifes, bells tolling and minute guns, all this was very solemn. But the charm was the entrance of the Abbey, where we were received by the Dean and Chapter in rich copes, the choir and almsmen all bearing torches; the whole Abbey so illuminated, that one saw it to greater advantage than by day; the tombs, long isles, and fretted roof all appearing distinctly and with the happiest chiaroscuro. There wanted nothing but incense, and little chapels here and there with priests saying mass for the repose of the defunct – yet one could not complain of its not being Catholic enough.

I had been in dread of being coupled with some boy of ten years old – but the heralds were not very accurate, and I walked with George Grenville, taller and older enough to keep me in countenance. When we came to the chapel of Henry VII all solemnity and decorum ceased – no order was observed, people sat or stood where they could or would, the yeomen of the guard were crying out for help, oppressed by the immense weight of the coffin, the Bishop read sadly, and blundered in the prayers. The fine chapter, *Man that is born of a woman*, was chanted not read, and the anthem besides being unmeasurably tedious, would have served as well for a nuptial.

Horace Walpole, 'The Burial of George II, 13th November 1760'

THE VIRGIN WENT BY

The processions continued as the week went on. Every time I ventured out I got caught up in the spectacle. On Wednesday evening I made my way to Bar Gonzalo near the cathedral. There were more tourists in the city now and everywhere I went there were crowds. As the Virgin and her crucified Son passed the bar on a platform the people at the outside tables stood up. The cross had two ladders reaching to the arms. It was all graphic and detailed, down to the red paint for blood on the wood of the cross. Then a man began to sing to the Virgin from a window. It sounded like a traditional Andalucian love song. His voice was high and strong, his hands outstretched, his tone full of longing and the sorrow of love.

Later, there was more singing. When another crying Virgin went by, her hands in front of her in a gesture of pain, a man and a woman sang to her from a window as well. The singing was passionate, notes rising to express infinite despair, as both singers gestured at the statue, and the crowds in the street stayed silent. 'Brava!' a woman roared as the bearers hoisted up the platform once more and carried it towards the cathedral. Just then forty guardia civiles, complete with machine-guns, marched by full of pomp and circumstance.

I went back to my L-shaped bar in the Barrio de Santa Cruz and started to ask the locals – they were mainly men – what they felt about the processions. No one could be exact or precise. They all agreed that they felt emotion – they pointed to their hearts – when they saw the statues and the flowers, especially if it was from their parish, but really no matter whose parish it was from they liked to see it done well: the flowers fresh, the cloth rich, the figures life-like. It was hard to describe the emotion you felt when you saw it going by, it wasn't exactly religious, it had more to do with who you were and your roots and your pride in Seville and your grandparents and your memories of childhood … it was hard to define. People shook their heads and narrowed their eyes and thought for a moment. No, they couldn't say what it was, but it existed and it was very powerful.

But you have not seen the *real* Holy Week, they said. Wait until midnight on Thursday. Then the *real* parade takes place. As midnight strikes, the gates of the church of the Virgin of the Macarena will open and the Virgin will appear and two thousand one hundred local men in traditional costume will accompany the Virgin through the streets; they will walk all night and all the next morning and they will not return to the church until one o'clock in the afternoon of the following day. And the people of Seville will stay up too, this is part of the tradition, and everybody must see the Virgin at least once as she is carried through the streets.

On Thursday night the sky was clear; the moon was almost full. At twelve o'clock the huge square in front of the Basilica of the Macarena held its breath as the doors of the church opened. It was like a medieval version of the gates of heaven, bright and golden. There were drums and a brass band. The people were spell-bound, children were lifted up to see, as this enormous platform, twelve feet by six, began to edge its way out of the doors of the church carrying nine life-size figures, led by more than a thousand men in uniforms and hoods, with another thousand waiting inside.

A woman sang from a window: she paid tribute to the

Virgin and lamented her sorrow. As the platform moved through the square people began to shout out to the Virgin: '*Guapa! Guapa!*', meaning beautiful, beautiful. They whistled and cheered as though the statue could hear them. '*Parece pálida,*' a woman behind me said, 'she looks pale.' It took hours for the procession to make its way to the crowded centre. At four in the morning there were still crowds in the streets, women wearing fur coats to keep out the cold. The procession spent an hour getting from the Corte Ingles to Plaza de San Francisco, at most a five-minute walk. A good number of the two thousand one-hundred strong confraternity were in bare feet. All along the route people sang to her from windows, telling of her beauty, her innocence and the cross she had to bear. At six in the morning the streets around the cathedral were full of the smell of incense. The procession was still moving slowly towards the cathedral – so slowly, indeed, that some of the confraternity could stop at a nearby bar, take their hoods off and have a beer, chatting and laughing.

Colm Tóibín, *The Sign of the Cross*, 1994

SIX HUNDRED THOUSAND MOVE ON

And he [Pharaoh] called for Moses and Aaron by night, and said, Rise up, and get you forth from among my people, both ye and the children of Israel; and go, serve the LORD, as ye have said ...

And the Egyptians were urgent upon the people, that they might send them out of the land in haste ...

And the children of Israel journeyed from Rameses to Succoth, about six hundred thousand on foot that were men, beside children.

And a mixed multitude went up also with them; and flocks, and herds, even very much cattle.

Exodus 12:31–38

THEY FOLLOWED HIM TO A JOYOUS LAND

Once more he stept into the street
   And to his lips again
   Laid his long pipe of smooth straight cane;
And ere he blew three notes (such sweet
Soft notes as yet musician's cunning
   Never gave the enraptured air)
There was a rustling that seemed like a bustling
Of merry crowds justling at pitching and hustling,
Small feet were pattering, wooden shoes clattering,
Little hands clapping and little tongues chattering,
And, like fowls in a farm-yard when barley is scattering,
Out came the children running.
   All the little boys and girls,
   With rosy cheeks and flaxen curls,
   And sparkling eyes and teeth like pearls,
   Tripping and skipping, ran merrily after
   The wonderful music with shouting and laughter.

The Mayor was dumb, and the Council stood
As if they were changed into blocks of wood,
Unable to move a step, or cry
To the children merrily skipping by,
– Could only follow with the eye
That joyous crowd at the Piper's back.
But how the Mayor was on the rack,
And the wretched Council's bosoms beat,
As the Piper turned from the High Street

To where the Weser rolled its waters
Right in the way of their sons and daughters!
However he turned from South to West,
And to Koppelberg Hill his steps addressed,
And after him the children pressed;
Great was the joy in every breast.
'He never can cross that mighty top!
'He's forced to let the piping drop,
'And we shall see our children stop!'
When, lo, as they reached the mountain-side,
A wondrous portal opened wide,
As if a cavern was suddenly hollowed;
And the Piper advanced and the children followed,
And when all were in to the very last,
The door in the mountain-side shut fast.
Did I say, all? No! One was lame,
   And could not dance the whole of the way;
And in after years, if you would blame
   His sadness, he was used to say, –
'It's dull in our town since my playmates left!
'I can't forget that I'm bereft
'Of all the pleasant sights they see,
'Which the Piper also promised me.
'For he led us, he said, to a joyous land,
'Joining the town and just at hand,
'Where waters gushed and fruit-trees grew
'And flowers put forth a fairer hue,
'And everything was strange and new;
'The sparrows were brighter than peacocks here,
'And their dogs outran our fallow deer,
'And honey-bees had lost their stings,
'And horses were born with eagles' wings:
'And just as I became assured
'My lame foot would be speedily cured,

'The music stopped and I stood still,
'And found myself outside the hill,
'Left alone against my will,
'To go now limping as before,
'And never hear of that country more!'

Robert Browning, 'The Pied Piper of Hamelin', 1842

MARCHING SONG

Along the streets came a trio – man, wife, child. The man, dressed in the blue cotton trousers of a working man, carries a bamboo pole across his shoulders and at each end of the pole hang bamboo baskets, heavily filled. As the man walks, he utters the rhythmical sing-song: 'Hai-ho, Hai-ho, Hai-ho!' Clinging to the basket in the back the child patters along, singing also in a childish high voice: 'Hai-ho, Hai-ho, Hai-ho.' The mother watches them and smiles.

Agnes Smedley, Chinese Destinies, 1934

WE ARE TAKING OVER THE STREET

A parade lets a little chaos into our strictly regulated lives; it is one of the few Dionysiac outlets still sanctioned by society as a whole. This is usually controlled, often highly patriotic chaos, but it does let in the wild. For a pre-determined time, on a chosen date, and along a set route, the city suddenly becomes filled with music, flowers, beasts, and fantasy.

Clowns caper about or rush up to spectators; they are descendants of the ancient satyr figures, and the medieval 'whifflers' who dressed as wild men brandishing sticks. Their job is to link the procession and the bystanders by making personal contact with the latter, and to keep the crowd not only entertained but off the parade route. They have always tended to bestow gifts; our clowns still dole out buttons, balloons, and candy to children.

Processional extravaganzas used to include famous precious objects carried along for all to see, and plenty of free wine. Giants have always been popular, especially if they can move about; an element of fright and wonder is essential to a good parade. Flowers covering the street are vegetation reclaiming the pavement; they also honour the parade that treads over them. Clothing may be flung down in the parade's path, or (for a short procession) a red carpet rolled out; a coloured line drawn on the road can mark out the parade's course.

Parades reify the ideals and the pride of a city; they also try to embody its past and its plans for the future. The floats which roll by are one of the oldest components of the parade. They are minitheatres (Dionysiac again) representing events or places, or city myths and institutions like the Fire Department or Our Hardy Pioneers. Modern North American parade floats tend to be singularly moralistic in tone, glorifying Road Safety or dedicated to 'Beating the Butt.'

The army and military bands are nearly always included in modern secular parades. The word *parade* itself is from a Spanish military term meaning 'a time and place where the army stops' (*parada*): during the rest period it wears its regalia and performs its drill for the townsfolk.

Exotic costumes, animals, floats representing distant places, or figures arriving 'from afar' – like Santa Claus – symbolically inject what is 'outside' into the city. Ritual reversals are another Dionysiac device. An extraordinary modern example of this is the corps of drum majorettes: women dressed as men, aggressively booted and helmeted, marching yet thereby displaying their legs, and tossing their batons in the air – *women*, actually *playing* with the symbols of power and attack.

Parades are not always cheerful celebrations: religious

processions can be very solemn, and funerals incorporate a form of parade. Political demonstrations almost invariably involve parading, but care is taken by participants to distinguish these from anything resembling pageantry. In tune with the puritanical modern attitude that anything involving costume or fantasy cannot be *serious*, people in political processions usually pretend to be eschewing ritual.

This they do ritually, by dressing in the toughest, most ordinary clothes they can find. ('Ordinary' is the root of the word 'ornery.') There may be banners, slogans, ritual gestures and cries, and sometimes flags. The message is that we are many, we have taken over the street and are moving ahead, and we mean business.

Margaret Visser, *The Way We Are*, 1995

THIS BROAD, SMILING RIVER OF LIFE

'Now let us walk,' muttered the lama, and to the click of his rosary they walked in silence mile upon mile. The lama, as usual, was deep in meditation, but Kim's bright eyes were open wide. This broad, smiling river of life, he considered, was a vast improvement on the cramped and crowded streets. There were new people and new sights at every stride – castes he knew and castes that were altogether out of his experience.

They met a troop of long-haired, strong-scented Sansis with baskets of lizards and other unclean food on their backs, their lean dogs sniffing at their heels. These people kept their own side of the road, moving at a quick, furtive jog-trot, and all other castes gave them ample room; for the Sansi is deep pollution. Behind them, walking wide and stiffly across the strong shadows, the memory of his leg-irons still on him, strode one newly released from the jail; his full stomach and shiny skin to prove that the Government fed its prisoners better than most honest men could feed themselves. Kim knew that walk well, and made broad jest of it as they passed. Then an Akali, a wild-eyed, wild-haired Sikh devotee in the blue-checked clothes of his faith, with polished-steel quoits glistening on the cone of his tall blue turban, stalked past, returning from a visit to one of the independent Sikh States, where he had been singing the ancient glories of the Khalsa to College-trained princelings in top-boots and white-cord breeches. Kim was careful not to irritate that man; for the Akali's temper is short and his arm quick. Here and there they met or were overtaken by the gaily dressed crowds of whole villages turning out to some local fair; the women, with their babes on their hips, walking behind the men, the older boys prancing on sticks of sugar-cane, dragging rude brass models of locomotives such as they sell for a half-penny, or flashing the sun into the eyes of their betters from cheap toy mirrors. One could see at a glance what each had bought; and if there were any doubt it needed only to watch the wives comparing, brown arm against brown arm, the newly purchased dull glass bracelets that come from the North-West. These merry-makers stepped slowly, calling one to the other and stopping to haggle with sweetmeat-sellers, or to make a prayer before one of the wayside shrines – sometimes Hindu, sometimes Mussalman – which the low-caste of both creeds share with beautiful impartiality. A solid line of blue, rising and falling like the back of a caterpillar in haste, would swing up through the quivering dust and trot past to a chorus of quick cackling. That was a gang of *changars* – the women who have taken all the embankments of all the Northern railways under their charge – a flat-footed, big-bosomed, strong-limbed, blue-petticoated clan of earth-carriers, hurrying north on news of a job, and wasting no time by the road. They belong to the caste whose men do not count, and they walked with squared elbows, swinging hips, and heads on high, as suits women who carry heavy weights. A little later a marriage procession would strike into the Grand Trunk with music and shoutings, and a smell of marigold and jasmine stronger even than the reek of the dust. One could see the bride's litter, a blur of red and tinsel, staggering through the haze, while the bridegroom's bewreathed pony turned aside to snatch a mouthful from a passing fodder-cart. Then Kim would join the Kentish-fire of good wishes and bad jokes, wishing the couple a hundred sons and no daughters, as the saying is. Still more interesting and more to be shouted over it was when a strolling juggler with some half-trained monkeys, or a panting, feeble bear, or a woman who tied goats' horns to her feet, and with these danced on a slack-rope, set the horses to shying and the women to shrill, long-drawn quavers of amazement.

The lama never raised his eyes. He did not note the money-lender on his goose-rumped pony, hastening along to collect the cruel interest; or the long-shouting, deep-voiced little mob – still in military formation – of native soldiers on leave, rejoicing to be rid of their breeches and puttees, and saying the most outrageous things to the most respectable women in sight. Even the seller of Ganges-water he did not see, and Kim expected that he would at least buy a bottle of that precious stuff. He looked steadily at the ground, and strode as steadily hour after hour, his soul busied elsewhere. But Kim was in the seventh heaven of joy. The Grand Trunk at this point was built on an embankment to guard against winter floods from the foothills, so that one walked, as it were, a little above the country, along a stately corridor, seeing all India spread out to left and right. It was beautiful to behold the many-yoked grain and cotton wagons crawling over the country roads: one could hear their axles, complaining a mile away, coming nearer, till with shouts and yells and bad words they climbed up the steep incline and plunged on to the hard main road, carter reviling carter. It was equally beautiful to watch the people, little clumps of red and blue and pink and white and saffron, turning aside to go to their own villages, dispersing and growing small by twos and threes across the level plain. Kim felt these things, though he could not give tongue to his feelings, and so contented himself with buying peeled sugar-cane and spitting the pith generously about his path. From time to time the lama took snuff, and at last Kim could endure the silence no longer.

'This is a good land – the land of the South!' said he. 'The air is good; the water is good. Eh?'

'And they are all bound upon the Wheel,' said the lama. 'Bound from life after life. To none of these has the Way been shown.' He shook himself back to this world.

Rudyard Kipling, *Kim*, 1901

ELEVEN

Final Steps

When we die, the wind blows away our footprints, and that
is the end of us.

Kalahari Bushmen

I WANT TO GO WANDERING

I want to go wandering. Who shall declare
I will regret if I dare?

    To the rich days of age –
        To some mid-afternoon –
    A wide fenceless prairie,
        A lonely old tune,
    Ant-hills and sunflowers,
        And sunset too soon.

    Behind the brown mountain
        The sun will go down:
    I shall climb, I shall climb,
        To the sumptuous crown;
    To the rocks of the summit,
        And find some strange things: –
    Some echo of echoes
        When the thunder-wind sings;
    Old Spanish necklaces,
        Indian rings,
    Or a feeble old eagle
        With great, dragging wings.
    He may leave me and soar;
        But if he shall die,
    I shall bury him deep
        While the thunder-winds cry.

And there, as the last of my earth-nights go:
What is the thing I shall know?
With a feather cast off from his wings
I shall write, be it revel or psalm,
Or whisper of redwood, or cypress, or palm, -

The treasure of dream that he brings.

The soul of the eagle will call,
Whether he lives or he dies: –
The cliff and the prairie call,
The sagebrush and starlight sing,
And the songs of my far-away Sangamon call
From the plume of the bird of the Rockies,
And midnight's omnipotent wing –
The last of my earth-nights will ring
With cries from a far haunted river,
And all of my wandering,
    Wandering,
    Wandering
    Wandering ...

Vachel Lindsay, 'I Want to go Wandering', 1904

A LAST WALK FOR TESS

They then walked on under the trees, Tess turning her head every now and then to look at him. Worn and unhandsome as he had become, it was plain that she did not discern the least fault in his appearance. To her he was, as of old, all that was perfection, personally and mentally. He was still her Antinous, her Apollo even ...

With an instinct as to possibilities he did not now, as he had intended, make for the first station beyond the town, but plunged still farther under the firs, which here abounded for miles. Each clasping the other round the waist they promenaded over the dry bed of fir-needles, thrown into a vague intoxicating atmosphere at the consciousness of being together at last, with no living soul between them; ignoring that there was a corpse. Thus they proceeded for several miles till Tess, arousing herself, looked about her, and said, timidly –

'Are we going anywhere in particular?'

'I don't know, dearest. Why?'

'I don't know.'

'Well, we might walk a few miles further, and when it is evening find lodgings somewhere or other – in a lonely cottage, perhaps. Can you walk well, Tessy?'

'O yes! I could walk for ever and ever with your arm round me!'

Upon the whole it seemed a good thing to do. Thereupon they quickened their pace, avoiding high roads, and following obscure paths tending more or less northward. But there was an unpractical vagueness in their movements throughout the day; neither one of them seemed to consider any question of effectual escape, disguise, or long concealment. Their every idea was temporary and unforefending, like the plans of two children.

At mid-day they drew near to a roadside inn, and Tess would have entered it with him to get something to eat, but he persuaded her to remain among the trees and bushes of this half-woodland, half-moorland part of the country, till he should come back. Her clothes were of recent fashion; even the ivory-handled parasol that she carried was of a shape unknown in the retired spot to which they had now wandered; and the cut of such articles would have attracted attention in the settle of a tavern. He soon returned, with food enough for half-a-dozen people and two bottles of wine – enough to last them for a day or more, should any emergency arise.

They sat down upon some dead boughs and shared their meal. Between one and two o'clock they packed up the remainder and went on again.

'I feel strong enough to walk any distance,' said she.

'I think we may as well steer in a general way towards the interior of the country, where we can hide for a time, and are less likely to be looked for than anywhere near the coast,' Clare remarked. 'Later on, when they have forgotten us, we can make for some port ... We shall soon get out of this district altogether. We'll continue our course as we've begun it, and keep straight north ...'

Having thus persuaded her the plan was pursued, and they kept a bee line northward. Their long repose at the manor-house lent them walking power now; and towards mid-day they found that they were approaching the steepled city of Melchester, which lay directly in their way. He decided to rest her in a clump of trees during the afternoon, and push onward under cover of darkness. At dusk Clare purchased food as usual, and their night march began, the boundary between Upper and Mid-Wessex being crossed about eight o'clock.

To walk across country without much regard to roads was not new to Tess, and she showed her old agility in the performance. The intercepting city, ancient Melchester, they were obliged to pass through in order to take advantage of the town bridge for crossing a large river that obstructed them. It was about midnight when they went along the deserted streets, lighted fitfully by the few lamps, keeping off the pavement that it might not echo their footsteps. The graceful pile of cathedral architecture rose dimly on their left hand, but it was lost upon them now. Once out of the town they followed the turnpike-road, which after a few miles plunged across an open plain.

They had proceeded thus gropingly two or three miles further when on a sudden Clare became conscious of some vast erection close in his front, rising sheer from the grass. They had almost struck themselves against it.

'What monstrous place is this?' said Angel.

'It hums,' said she. 'Hearken!'

He listened. The wind, playing upon the edifice, produced a booming tune, like the note of some gigantic one-stringed harp. No other sound came from it, and lifting his hand and advancing a step or two, Clare felt the vertical surface of the structure. It seemed to be of solid stone, without joint or moulding. Carrying his fingers onward he found that what he had come in contact with was a colossal rectangular pillar; by stretching out his left hand he could feel a similar one adjoining. At an indefinite height overhead something made the black sky blacker, which had the semblance of a vast architrave uniting the pillars horizontally. They carefully entered beneath and between; the surfaces echoed their soft rustle; but they seemed to be still out of doors. The place was roofless. Tess drew her breath fearfully, and Angel, perplexed, said –

'What can it be?'

Feeling sideways they encountered another tower-like pillar, square and uncompromising as the first; beyond it another and another. The place was all doors and pillars, some connected above by continuous architraves.

'A very Temple of the Winds,' he said.

The next pillar was isolated; others composed a trilithon; others were prostrate, their flanks forming a causeway wide enough for a carriage; and it was soon obvious that they made up a forest of monoliths grouped upon the grassy expanse of the plain. The couple advanced further into this pavilion of the night till they stood in its midst.

'It is Stonehenge!' said Clare.

'The heathen temple, you mean?'

'Yes. Older than the centuries; older than the d'Urbervilles! Well, what shall we do, darling? We may find shelter further on.'

But Tess, really tired by this time, flung herself upon an oblong slab that lay close at hand, and was sheltered from the wind by a pillar. Owing to the action of the sun during the preceding day the stone was warm and dry, in comforting contrast to the rough and chill grass around, which had damped her skirts and shoes.

'I don't want to go any further, Angel,' she said stretching out her hand for his. 'Can't we bide here?'

'I fear not. This spot is visible for miles by day, although it does not seem so now.'

'One of my mother's people was a shepherd hereabouts, now I think of it. And you used to say at Talbothays that I was a heathen. So now I am at home.'

He knelt down beside her outstretched form, and put his lips upon hers.

'Sleepy are you, dear? I think you are lying on an altar.'

'I like very much to be here,' she murmured. 'It is so solemn and lonely – after my great happiness – with nothing but the sky above my face. It seems as if there were no folk in the world but we two ...'

Clare thought she might as well rest here till it should get a little lighter, and he flung his overcoat upon her, and sat down by her side.

... In the far north-east sky he could see between the pillars a level streak of light. The uniform concavity of black cloud was lifting bodily like the lid of a pot, letting in at the earth's edge the coming day, against which the towering monoliths and trilithons began to be blackly defined.

'Did they sacrifice to God here?' asked she.

'No,' said he.

'Who to?'

'I believe to the sun. That lofty stone set away by itself is in the direction of the sun, which will presently rise behind it.'

'This reminds me, dear,' she said. 'You remember you never would interfere with any belief of mine before we were married? But I knew your mind all the same, and I thought as you thought – not from any reasons of my own, but because you thought so. Tell me now, Angel, do you think we shall meet again after we are dead? I want to know.'

He kissed her to avoid a reply at such a time.

'O, Angel – I fear that means no!' said she, with a suppressed sob. 'And I wanted so to see you again – so much, so much!

What – not even you and I, Angel, who love each other so well?' …

In a minute or two her breathing became more regular, her clasp of his hand relaxed, and she fell asleep. The band of silver paleness along the east horizon made even the distant parts of the Great Plain appear dark and near; and the whole enormous landscape bore that impress of reserve, taciturnity, and hesitation which is usual just before day. The eastward pillars and their architraves stood up blackly against the light, and the great flame-shaped Sun-stone beyond them; and the Stone of Sacrifice midway. Presently the night wind died out, and the quivering little pools in the cup-like hollows of the stones lay still. At the same time something seemed to move on the verge of the dip eastward – a mere dot. It was the head of a man approaching them from the hollow beyond the Sun-stone. Clare wished they had gone onward, but in the circumstances decided to remain quiet. The figure came straight towards the circle of pillars in which they were.

He heard something behind him, the brush of feet. Turning, he saw over the prostrate columns another figure; then before he was aware, another was at hand on the right, under a trilithon, and another on the left. The dawn shone full on the front of the man westward, and Clare could discern from this that he was tall, and walked as if trained. They all closed in with evident purpose. Her story then was true! Springing to his feet, he looked around for a weapon, loose stone, means of escape, anything. By this time the nearest man was upon him.

'It is no use, sir,' he said. 'There are sixteen of us on the Plain, and the whole country is reared.'

'Let her finish her sleep!' he implored in a whisper of the men as they gathered round.

When they saw where she lay, which they had not done till then, they showed no objection, and stood watching her, as still as the pillars around. He went to the stone and bent over her, holding one poor little hand; her breathing now was quick and small, like that of a lesser creature than a woman. All waited in the growing light, their faces and hands as if they were silvered, the remainder of their figures dark, the stones glistening green-gray, the Plain still a mass of shade. Soon the light was strong, and a ray shone upon her unconscious form, peering under her eyelids and waking her.

'What is it, Angel?' she said, starting up. 'Have they come for me?'

'Yes, dearest,' he said. 'They have come.'

'It is as it should be,' she murmured. 'Angel, I am almost glad – yes, glad! This happiness could not have lasted. It was too much. I have had enough; and now I shall not live for you to despise me!'

She stood up, shook herself, and went forward, neither of the men having moved.

'I am ready,' she said quietly.

Thomas Hardy, *Tess of the D'Urbervilles*, 1891

THE ONE DARK PATH

I felt the need to lie down somewhere, and since a friendly, cosy little place by the lakeside was nearby, I made myself comfortable, somewhat tired as I was, on the soft ground under the artless branches of a tree. As I looked at earth and air and sky the melancholy unquestioning thought came to me that I was a poor prisoner between heaven and earth, that all men were miserably imprisoned in this way, that for all men there was only the one dark path into the other world, the path down into the pit, into the earth, that there was no other way into the other world than that which led through the grave. 'So then everything, everything, all this rich life, the friendly, thoughtful colours, this delight, this joy and pleasure in life, all these human meanings, family, friend, and beloved, this bright tender air full of fathers, houses of mothers, and dear gentle roads, must one day pass away and die, the high sun, the moon, and the hearts and eyes of men.'

Robert Walser, *The Walk*, 1917
(trans. Christopher Middleton, 1957)

TO SEEK OBLIVION THROUGH THE FAR-OFF GATE

I wandered in a suburb of the north,
    And reached a spot whence three close lanes led down
Beneath thick trees and hedgerows winding forth
    Like deep brook channels, deep and dark and lown:
The air above was wan with misty light,
The dull grey south showed one vague blur of white.

I took the left-hand lane and slowy trod
    Its earthen footpath, brushing as I went
The humid leafage; and my feet were shod
    With heavy languor, and my frame downbent,
With infinite sleepless weariness outworn,
So many nights I thus had paced forlorn.

After a hundred steps I grew aware
    Of something crawling in the lane below;
It seemed a wounded creature prostrate there
    That sobbed with pangs in making progress slow,
The hind limbs stretched to push, the fore limbs then
To drag, for it would die in its own den.

But coming level with it I discerned
    That it had been a man; for at my tread

It stopped in its sore travail and half-turned,
   Leaning upon its right, and raised its head,
And with the left hand twitched back as in ire
Long grey unreverend locks befouled with mire.

A haggard filthy face with bloodshot eyes,
   An infamy for manhood to behold.
He gasped all trembling, What, you want my prize?
   You leave, to rob me, wine and lust and gold
And all that men go mad upon, since you
Have traced my sacred secret of the clue?

You think that I am weak and must submit;
   Yet I but scratch you with this poisoned blade,
And you are dead as if I clove with it
   That false fierce greedy heart. Betrayed! betrayed!
I fling this phial if you seek to pass,
And you are forthwith shrivelled up like grass

And then with sudden change, Take thought! take thought!
   Have pity on me! it is mine alone.
If you could find, it would avail you naught;
   Seek elsewhere on the pathway of your own:
For who of mortal or immortal race
The lifetrack of another can retrace?

Did you but know my agony and toil!
   Two lanes diverge up yonder from this lane;
My thin blood marks the long length of their soil;
   Such clue I left, who sought my clue in vain:
My hands and knees are worn both flesh and bone;
I cannot move but with continual moan.

But I am in the very way at last

To find the long-lost broken golden thread
Which reunites my present with my past,
    If you but go your own way. And I said,
I will retire as soon as you have told
Whereunto leadeth this lost thread of gold.

And so you know it not! he hissed with scorn;
    I feared you, imbecile! It leads me back
From this accursèd night without a morn,
    And through the deserts which have else no track,
And through vast wastes of horror-haunted time,
To Eden innocence in Eden's clime:

And I become a nursling soft and pure,
    An infant cradled on its mother's knee,
Without a past, love-cherished and secure;
    Which if it saw this loathsome present Me,
Would plunge its face into the pillowing breast,
And scream abhorrence hard to lull to rest.

He turned to grope; and I retiring brushed
    Thin shreds of gossamer from off my face,
And mused, His life would grow, the germ uncrushed;
    He should to antenatal night retrace,
And hide his elements in that large womb
Beyond the reach of man-evolving Doom.

And even thus, what weary way were planned,
    To seek oblivion through the far-off gate
Of birth, when that of death is close at hand!
    For this is law, if law there be in Fate:
What never has been, yet may have its when;
The thing which has been never is again.

James Thomson, 'The City of Dreadful Night', 1874

THE END OF A STROLLER

Whenever Richard Cory went down town,
We people on the pavement looked at him;
He was a gentleman from sole to crown,
Clean favored, and imperially slim.

And he was always quietly arrayed,
And he was always human when he talked;
But still he fluttered pulses when he said,
'Good morning', and glittered when he walked.

And he was rich – yes, richer than a king –
And admirably schooled in every grace:
In fine, we thought that he was everything
To make us wish we were in his place.

So on we worked, and waited for the light,
And went without the meat and cursed the bread;
And Richard Cory, one calm summer night,
Went home and put a bullet through his head.

Edward Arlington Robinson, 'Richard Cory', 1937

AUNT MATILDE'S UNEXPLAINED OUTINGS

My father and uncles didn't seem to notice any change at all. The dog was quiet, and abandoning its street manners it seemed to acquire Aunt Matilde's somewhat dignified mien; but it preserved all the impudence of a female whom the vicissitudes of life have not been able to shock, as well as its good temper and its liking for adventure. It was easier for the men to accept than reject it since the latter would at least have meant speaking, and perhaps even an uncomfortable revision of their standards of security.

One night, when the pitcher of lemonade had already made its appearance on the library credenza, cooling that corner of the shadows, and the windows had been opened to the air, my father stopped abruptly at the entrance to the billiard room.

'What is this?' he exclaimed, pointing at the floor.

The three men gathered in consternation to look at a tiny round puddle on the waxed floor.

'Matilde!' Uncle Gustavo cried.

She came over to look and blushed with shame. The dog had taken refuge under the billiard table in the next room. Turning toward the table, my father saw it there, and suddenly changing course he left the room, followed by his brothers, heading toward the bedrooms, where each of them locked himself in, silent and alone.

Aunt Matilde said nothing. She went up to her room followed by the dog. I stayed in the library with a glass of lemonade in my hand, looking out at the summer sky and listening, anxiously listening to distant foghorns and the noise of the unknown city, terrible and at the same time desirable, stretched out under the stars.

Then I heard Aunt Matilde descend. She appeared with her hat on and her keys jingling in her hand.

'Go to bed,' she said. 'I'm taking her for a walk on the street so she can take care of her business there.'

Then she added something that made me nervous: 'The night's so pretty ...'

And she went out.

From that night on, instead of going upstairs after dinner to turn down her brothers' beds, she went to her room, put on her hat, and came down again, her keys jingling. She went out with the dog, not saying a word to anybody. My uncles and my father and I stayed in the billiard room, or, as the season wore on, sat on the benches in the garden, with the rustling elm and the clear sky pressing down on us. These nightly walks of Aunt Matilde's were never mentioned, there was never any indication that anybody knew anything important had changed in the house; but an element had been introduced there that contradicted all order.

At first Aunt Matilde would stay out at most fifteen or twenty minutes, returning promptly to take coffee with us and exchange a few commonplaces. Later, her outings inexplicably took more time. She was no longer a woman who walked her dog for reasons of hygiene; out there in the streets, in the city, there was something powerful attracting her. Waiting for her, my father glanced furtively at his pocket watch, and if she was very late, Uncle Gustavo went up to the second floor, as if he had forgotten something there, to watch from the balcony. But they never said anything. Once when Aunt Matilde's walk had taken too long, my father paced back and forth along the path between the hydrangeas, their flowers like blue eyes watching the night. Uncle Gustavo threw away a cigar he couldn't light satisfactorily, and then another, stamping it out under his heel. Uncle Armando overturned a cup of coffee. I watched, waiting for an eventual explosion, for them to say something, for them to express their anxiety and fill those endless minutes stretching on and on without the presence of Aunt Matilde. It was half past twelve when she came home.

'Why did you wait up for me?' she said smiling.

She carried her hat in her hand and her hair, ordinarily so neat, was disheveled. I noted that daubs of mud stained her perfect shoes.

'What happened to you?'

'Nothing,' was her answer, and with that she closed forever any possible right her brothers might have had to interfere with those unknown hours, happy or tragic or insignificant, which were now her life.

I say they were her life, because in those instants she

remained with us before going to her room, with the dog, muddy too, next to her, I perceived an animation in her eyes, a cheerful restlessness like the animal's, as if her eyes had recently bathed in scenes never before witnessed, to which we had no access. These two were companions. The night protected them. They belonged to the noises, to the foghorns that wafted over docks, dark or lamplit streets, houses, factories, and parks, finally reaching my ears.

Her walks with the dog continued. Now she said good night to us right after dinner, and all of us went to our rooms, my father, Uncle Gustavo, Uncle Armando, and myself. But none of us fell asleep until we heard her come in, late, sometimes very late, when the light of dawn already brightened the top of our elm tree. Only after she was heard closing her bedroom door would the paces by which my father measured his room stop, and a window be closed by one of her brothers to shut out the night, which had ceased being dangerous for the time being.

Once after she had come in very late, I thought I heard her singing very softly and sweetly, so I cracked open my door and looked out. She passed in front of my door, the white dog cuddled in her arms. Her face looked surprisingly young and perfect, although it was a little dirty, and I saw there was a tear in her skirt. This woman was capable of anything; she had her whole life before her. I went to bed terrified that this would be the end.

And I wasn't wrong. Because one night shortly afterwards, Aunt Matilde went out for a walk with the dog and never came back.

We waited up all night long, each one of us in his room, and she didn't come home. The next day nobody said anything. But the silent waiting went on, and we all hovered silently, without seeming to, around the windows of the house, watching for her. From that first day fear made the harmonious dignity of the three brothers' faces collapse, and they aged rapidly in a very short time.

'Your aunt went on a trip,' the cook told me once, when I finally dared to ask.

But I knew it wasn't true.

Life went on in our house as if Aunt Matilde were still living with us. It's true they had a habit of gathering in the library, and perhaps locked in there they talked, managing to overcome the wall of fear that isolated them, giving free rein to their fears and doubts. But I'm not sure. Several times a visitor came who didn't belong to our world, and they would lock themselves in with him. But I don't believe he had brought them news of a possible investigation; perhaps he was nothing more than the boss of a longshoremen's union who was coming to claim damages for some accident. The door of the library was too thick, too heavy, and I never knew if Aunt Matilde, dragged along by the white dog, had got lost in the city, or in death, or in a region more mysterious than either.

José Donoso, *The Walk*, 1971 (trans. Andre Conrad, 1971)

BOOTS REQUIRE NEW OWNER

'They are his new boots,' she pursued;
'They have not been worn at all:
They stay there hung on the wall,
And are getting as stiff as wood.
He bought them for the wet weather,
And they are of waterproof leather.'

'Why does her husband,' said I,
'Never wear those boots bought new?'
To a neighbour of hers I knew;

Who answered: 'Ah, those boots. Aye,
He bought them to wear whenever
It rained. But there they hang ever.

'"Yes," he laughed, as he hung them up,
"I've got them at last – a pair
I can walk in anywhere
Through rain and slush and slop.
For many a year I've been haunted
By thoughts of how much they were wanted."

'And she's not touched them or tried
To remove them ... Anyhow,
As you see them hanging now
They have hung ever since he died
The day after gaily declaring:
"Ha-ha! Now for wet wayfaring.
They're just the chaps for my wearing."'

Thomas Hardy, 'The New Boots', 1928

GOODBYE TO 'THE BOYS'

Bruce had summoned Werner Herzog because he thought the director had healing powers. When they had first met in Melbourne in 1984, shortly after Bruce's visit to Swartkrans, their talks had begun with a discussion on the restorative powers of walking. 'He had an almost immediate rapport with me,' says Herzog, 'when I explained to him that tourism was a mortal sin, but walking on foot was a virtue, and that whatever went wrong and makes our civilisation something doomed is the departure from the nomadic life.' Herzog had written a short prose book, *Of Walking in Ice*, which illustrated this theory and which Bruce loved.

Herzog had brought with him to Seillans a documentary he had made on the Wodaabe nomads of the Niger, 'Herdsmen of the Sun'. These were Bruce's Bororo Peuls, 'a people obsessed by the horizons and their own beauty'. Bruce was eager to see the film. 'I showed it to him only in bits of ten minutes,' says Herzog, 'and then he would just pass out, or become delirious, and then he would ask me to go on showing him the film. He was a skeleton, there was nothing left of him, and all of a sudden he would shout at me: "I've got to be on the road again, I've got to be on the road again." And I said to him, "Yes, that's where you belong." And he said: "Can you come with me?" And I said: "Yes, sure, we will walk together." And then he said: "My rucksack is so heavy." And I said: "Bruce, I carry it." And we spoke about where we were walking and had a walk together and he all of a sudden had a lucid moment when his blanket was off him and every few minutes I turned him around because his bones were aching and he called his legs "the boys". He said: "Can you put the left boy around to this side and the right boy?" And he looked down at himself and he saw the legs were only spindles and he looked at me in this very lucid moment and he said: "I'm never going to walk again." He said: "Werner, I'm dying." And I said, "Yes, I am aware of that." And then he said: "You must carry my rucksack, you are the one who must carry it." And I said: "Yes, I will proudly do that." And I have his rucksack and it's such a dear thing to me. Let's say if my house was on fire, I would throw my children out of the window, but of all my belongings it would be the rucksack that I would save.'

Nicholas Shakespeare, *Bruce Chatwin*, 1999

GOOD BYE TO THE ROAD

(i)

No matter where I fall
On the road
Fall will I to be buried
Among flowering bush-cloves.

Bashō (Matsuo Munefusa), *The Narrow Road
to the Deep North*, 1702 (trans. Nobuyuki Yuasa, 1966)

(ii)

But whether or no
The world is round
And he must still go
Through depths profound,
O'er heights of snow,
On virgin ground
To find a grave
To find a grave.

John Davidson, 'The Pioneer', 1891

TOWARDS THE BIG SLEEP

Day had broken cold and grey, exceedingly cold and grey, when
the man turned aside from the main Yukon trail and climbed
the high earth bank, where a dim and little-travelled trail led
eastward through the fat spruce timberland. It was a steep bank,
and he paused for breath at the top, excusing the act to himself
by looking at his watch. It was nine o'clock. There was no sun
or hint of sun, though there was not a cloud in the sky. It was

a clear day, and yet there seemed an intangible pall over the face of things, a subtle gloom that made the dark, and that was due to the absence of sun. The fact did not worry the man. He was used to the lack of sun. It had been days since he had seen the sun, and he knew a few more days must pass before that cheerful orb, due south, would just peep above the skyline and dip immediately from view.

The man flung a look back along the way he had come. The Yukon lay a mile wide and hidden under three feet of ice. On top of this ice were as many feet of snow. It was all pure white, rolling in gentle undulations where the ice jams of the freeze-up had formed. North and south, as far as his eye could see, it was unbroken white, save for a dark hairline that curved and twisted from around the spruce-covered island to the south, and that curved and twisted away into the north, where it disappeared behind another spruce-covered island. This dark hairline was the trail – the main trail – that led south five hundred miles to the Chilcoot Pass, Dyea, and salt water; and led north seventy miles to Nulato, and finally to St. Michael, on Bering Sea, a thousand miles and a half thousand more.

But all this – the mysterious, far reaching hairline trail, the absence of the sun from the sky, the tremendous cold, and strangeness and weirdness of it all – made no impression on the man. It was not because he was long used to it. He was a newcomer in the land, a *chechaquo*, and this was his first winter. The trouble with him was he was without imagination. He was quick and alert in the things of life, but only in the things and not the significances. Fifty degrees below zero meant eighty odd degrees of frost. Such fact impressed him as being cold and uncomfortable, and that was all.

As he turned to go on he spat speculatively. There was a sharp explosive crackle that startled him. He spat again. And again, in the air, before it could fall to the snow, the spittle crackled. He knew that at fifty below, spittle crackled in the snow, but this spittle had crackled in the air. Undoubtedly it was colder than fifty below – how much colder he did not know. But the temperature did not matter. He was bound for the old claim on the left fork of Hendersen Creek, where the boys were already. They had come over across the divide from the Indian Creek country, while he had come the roundabout way to look at the possibilities of getting out logs in the spring from the islands in the Yukon.

He would be in camp by six o'clock; a bit after dark, it was true, but the boys would be there, a fire would be going, and a hot supper would be ready. As for lunch, he pressed his hand against the protruding bundle under his jacket. It was also under his shirt, wrapped up in a handkerchief and lying against the naked skin. It was the only way of preventing the biscuits from freezing. He smiled agreeably to himself as he thought of those biscuits, each cut open and sopped in bacon grease, and each enclosing a slice of fried bacon.

He plunged in among the big spruce trees. The trail was faint. A foot of snow had fallen since the last sled had passed over, and he was glad he was without a sled, travelling light.

At the man's heels trotted a dog, a big native husky, the proper wolf-dog, grey-coated and without any visible or temperamental difference from its brother, the wild wolf. The animal was depressed by the tremendous cold. It knew it was no time for travelling. Its instinct told it a truer tale than was told to the man by the man's judgment. It experienced a vague but menacing apprehension that subdued it and made it slink along at the man's heels, and that made it question eagerly every unwonted movement of the man as if expecting him to go into camp or to seek shelter somewhere and build a fire, or else to burrow under the snow and cuddle its warmth away from the air.

The man held on through the level stretch of woods for several miles, crossed a wide flat of nigger heads, and dropped down a bank to the frozen bed of a small stream. This was Hendersen's Creek, and he knew he was ten miles from the forks. He looked at his watch. It was ten o'clock. He was making four miles an hour, and he calculated that he would arrive at the forks at half-past twelve. He decided to celebrate that event by eating his lunch there.

The dog dropped in again at his heels, with a tail drooping discouragement, as the man swung along the creek bed. The furrow of the old sled trail was plainly visible, but a dozen inches of snow covered up the marks of the last runners. In a month no man had come up or down that silent creek. The man held steadily on. He was not much given to thinking, and just then particularly he had nothing to think about save he would eat lunch at the forks and that at six o'clock he would be in camp with the boys.

Once in a while the thought reiterated itself that it was very cold and that he had never experienced such cold. As he walked along he rubbed his cheekbones and nose with the back of his mittened hand. He did this automatically, now and again changing hands. But, rub as he would, the instant he stopped his cheekbones went numb, and the following instant the end of his nose went numb. He was sure to frost his cheeks; he knew that, and experienced a pang of regret that he had not devised a nose strap of the sort Bud wore in cold snaps.

Empty as the man's mind was of thoughts, he was keenly observant, and he noticed the changes in the creeks, the curves and bends and timber jams, and always he sharply noted where he placed his feet. Once, coming round a bend, he shied abruptly, like a startled horse, curved away from the place where he had been walking, and retreated several paces back along the trail. The creek he knew was frozen clear to the bottom – no creek could contain water in that arctic winter – but he knew also that there were springs that bubbled out from the hillsides and ran along under the snow and on top of the ice of the creek.

He knew that the coldest snaps never froze those springs and he knew likewise their danger. They were traps. They hid pools of water under the snow that might be three inches deep. That was why he shied in panic. He had felt the give in his feet and heard the crackle of a snow-hidden ice skin. And to get his feet wet in such a temperature meant trouble and danger. At the very least it meant delay, for he would be forced to stop and build a fire, and under its protection to bare his feet while he dried his socks and moccasins. He stood and studied the creek bed and its banks, and decided that the flow of water came from the right. He reflected awhile, rubbing his nose and cheeks, then skirted to the left, stepping gingerly and testing the footing for each step. Once clear of the danger, he took a fresh chew of tobacco and swung along at his four-mile gait.

In the course of the next two hours he came upon several similar traps. Usually the snow above the hidden pools had a sunken, candied appearance that advertised the danger. Once again, however, he had a close call; and once, suspecting danger, he compelled the dog to go in front. The dog did not want to go. It hung back till the man shoved it forward, and then it went quickly across the white, unbroken surface. Suddenly it broke through, floundering to one side, and got away to firmer footing. It had wet its forefeet and legs, and almost immediately the water that clung to it turned to ice. It made quick efforts to lick the ice off its legs, then dropped down in the snow and began to bite out the ice that had formed between the toes. To permit the ice to remain would mean sore feet. It did not know this. It merely obeyed the mysterious prompting that arose from the deep crypts of its being. But the man knew, having achieved a judgment on the subject, and he removed the mitten from his right hand and helped to tear out the ice particles. He did not expose his fingers more than a minute, and was astonished at the swift numbness that smote them. It certainly was cold. He pulled on the mitten hastily, and beat the hand savagely across his chest.

At twelve o'clock the day was at its brightest. Yet the sun was too far south on its winter journey to clear the horizon. The bulge of the earth intervened between it and Hendersen Creek, where the man walked under a clear sky at noon and cast no shadow. At half past twelve, to the minute, he arrived at the forks of the creek. He was pleased at the speed he had made. If he kept it up, he would certainly be with the boys by six. He unbuttoned his jacket and shirt and drew forth his lunch. The action consumed no more than a quarter of a minute, yet in that brief moment the numbness laid hold of the exposed fingers. He did not put the mitten on, but, instead, struck the fingers a dozen sharp smashes against his leg. Then he sat down on a snow-covered log to eat. The sting that followed upon the striking of his fingers against his leg ceased so quickly that he was startled. He had had no chance to take a bite of biscuit. He struck the fingers repeatedly and returned them to the mitten, baring the other hand for the purpose of eating. He tried to take a mouthful, but the ice muzzle prevented. He had forgotten to build a fire and thaw out. He chuckled at his foolishness, and as he chuckled he noticed the numbness creeping into the exposed fingers. Also, he noted that the stinging which had first come to his toes when he sat down was already passing away. He wondered whether the toes were warm or numb. He moved them inside the moccasins and decided they were numb.

He pulled the mitten on hurriedly and stood up. He was a bit frightened. He stamped up and down until the stinging returned into the feet. It certainly was cold, was his thought. There was no mistake about it, it *was* cold. He strode up and down, stamping his feet and threshing his arms, until reassured by the returning warmth. Then he got out matches and proceeded to make a fire. From the undergrowth, where high water of the previous spring had lodged a supply of seasoned twigs, he got his firewood. The dog took satisfaction in the fire, stretching out close enough for warmth and far enough away to escape being singed.

When the man had finished his biscuits, he filled his pipe and took his comfortable time over a smoke. Then he pulled on his mittens, settled the ear-flaps of his cap firmly about his ears, and took the creek trail up the left fork. The dog was disappointed and yearned back towards the fire. This man did not know cold. Possibly all the generations of his ancestry had been ignorant of cold, of real cold. But the dog knew; all its ancestry knew, and it had inherited the knowledge. And it knew that it was not good to walk abroad in such fearful cold.

The man's moist breath quickly powdered with white his moustache, eyebrows, and lashes. There did not seem to be so many springs on the left fork of the Hendersen, and for half an hour the man saw no signs of any. And then it happened. At a place where there were no signs, where the soft, unbroken snow seemed to advertise solidity beneath, the man broke through. It was not deep. He wet himself half-way to the knees before he floundered out to the firm crust.

He was angry, and cursed his luck out loud. He had hoped to get into the camp with the boys at six o'clock, and this would delay him an hour, for he would have to build a fire and dry out his footgear. This was imperative at that low temperature – he knew that much; and he turned aside to the bank, which he climbed. On top, tangled about in the underbrush about the trunks of several small spruce trees, was a high water deposit of dry firewood – sticks and twigs, principally, but also larger portions of seasoned branches and fine, dry, last year's grasses. He threw down several pieces on the top of the snow. The flame he got by touching a match to a small thread of birch bark that he took from his pocket. This burned even more readily than paper. Placing it on the foundation, he fed the young flame with wisps of dry grass and the tiniest dry twigs.

He worked slowly and carefully, keenly aware of his danger. Already all sensation had gone out of his feet. To build the fire he had been forced to remove his mittens, and the fingers had quickly gone numb. His pace of four miles an hour had kept his heart pumping blood to the surface of his body and to all extremities. But the instant he stopped, the action of the pump eased down. The extremities were the first to feel its absence. His wet feet froze the faster, and his exposed fingers numbed the faster. But he was safe. Toes and nose and cheek would be only touched by the frost, for the fire was beginning to burn with strength. He was feeding it with twigs the size of his finger. In another minute he would be able to feed it with branches the size of his wrist, and then he could remove his wet footgear, and, while it dried, he could keep his naked feet warm by the fire, rubbing them at first, of course, with snow. The fire was a success. He was safe. He started to untie his moccasins. For a moment he tugged with his numb fingers, then, realizing the folly of it, he drew his sheath knife.

But before he could cut the strings, it happened. It was his own fault, or, rather, his mistake. He should not have built the fire under the spruce tree. He should have built it in the open. Now the tree under which he had done this carried a weight of snow on its boughs. No wind had blown for weeks, and each bough was fully freighted. Each time he had pulled a twig he had communicated a slight agitation to the tree. High up in the tree one bough capsized its load of snow. This fell on the boughs beneath, capsizing them, and it descended without warning upon the man and the fire. Where it had burned was a mantle of fresh and disordered snow.

The man was shocked. It was as though he had just heard his own sentence of death. For a moment he sat and stared at the spot where the fire had been. Then he grew very calm. It was up to him to build the fire over again, and this second time there must be no failure. Even if he succeeded, he would most likely lose some toes. His feet must be badly frozen by now, and there would be some time before the second fire was ready.

Such were his thoughts, but he did not sit and think them. He was busy all the time they were passing through the mind. He made a new foundation for a fire, this time in the open, where no treacherous tree could blot it out. And all the while the dog sat and watched him, a certain yearning wistfulness in its eyes, for it looked upon him as the fire provider, and the fire was slow in coming.

When all was ready, the man reached in his pocket for a piece of birch bark. He knew the bark was there, and, though he could not feel it with his fingers, he could hear its crisp rustling as he fumbled for it. Try as he would, he could not clutch hold of it. And all the time, in his consciousness, was the knowledge that each instant his feet were freezing. This thought tended to put him in panic, but he fought against it and kept calm. He pulled on his mittens with his teeth, and threshed his arms back and forth, beating his hands with all his might against his sides. He did this sitting down, and he stood up to do it; and all the while the dog sat in the snow, watching the man.

After a time he was aware of the first faraway signals of sensation in his beaten fingers. The faint tingling grew stronger until it evolved into a stinging ache that was excruciating, but which the man hailed with satisfaction. He stripped the mitten from his right hand and fetched forth the birch bark. The exposed fingers were quickly going numb again. Next he bought out his bunch of sulphur matches. But the tremendous cold had already driven the life out of his fingers. In his effort to separate one match from the others, the whole bunch fell into the snow. He tried to pick it out of the snow but failed. The dead fingers could neither touch nor clutch. He was very careful.

He drove the thought of his frozen feet, and nose, and cheeks, out of his mind, devoting his whole soul to the matches. He watched, using the sense of vision in place of that of touch, and when he saw his fingers on each side of the bunch, he closed them – that is, he willed to close them, for the wires were down, and the fingers did not obey. He pulled the mitten on the right hand, and beat it fiercely against his knee. Then with both mittened hands, he scooped the bunch of matches, along with much snow, into his lap. Yet he was no better off.

After some manipulation he managed to get the bunch between the heels of his mittened hands. In this fashion he carried it to his mouth. He drew the lower jaw in, curled the upper lip out of the way, and scraped the bunch with his upper teeth in order to separate a match. He succeeded in getting one, which he dropped on his lap. He was no better off. He could not pick it up. Then he devised a way. He picked it up in his teeth and scratched it on his leg. Twenty times he scratched before he succeeded in lighting it. Then the match fell into the snow and went out. Suddenly he bared both hands, removing the mittens with his teeth. He caught the whole bunch between the heels of his hands. His arm muscles not being frozen enabled him to press the hand heels tightly against the matches. Then he scraped the bunch along his leg. It flared into flame, seventy sulphur matches at once! There was no wind to blow them out. He kept his head to one side to escape the strangling fumes, and held the blazing bunch to the birch bark. As he so held it, he became aware of sensation in his hand. His flesh was burning. He could smell it.

When he could endure no more, he jerked his hands apart. The blazing matches fell sizzling into the snow, but the birch bark was alight. He began laying dry grasses and the tiniest twigs on the flame. He could not pick and choose, for he had to lift the fuel between the heels of his hands. Small pieces of rotten wood and green moss clung to the twigs, and he bit them off as well as he could with his teeth. He cherished the flame carefully and awkwardly. It meant life, it must not perish. But each twig gushed a puff of smoke and went out. The fire provider had failed. As he looked about him, his eyes chanced on the dog, sitting across the ruins of the fire before him. The sight of the dog put a wild idea into his head. He remembered the tale of the man, caught in a blizzard, who killed a steer and crawled inside the carcass, and so was saved. He would kill the dog and bury his hands in the warm body until the numbness went out of them. Then he could build another fire. He spoke to the dog, calling to him; but in his voice there was a strange note of fear that frightened the animal. Then the man got to his hands and knees and crawled towards the dog. This unusual posture again excited suspicion, and the animal sidled away.

The man sat up in the snow for a moment and struggled for calmness. Then he pulled on his mittens, by means of his teeth, and got to his feet. He glanced down at first in order to assure himself he was really standing up, for the absence of sensation in his feet left him unrelated to the earth.

A certain fear of death, dull and oppressive, came to him. This fear quickly became poignant as he realized that it was no longer a mere matter of freezing his fingers and toes, or of losing his hands and feet, but it was a matter of life and death with the chances against him. This threw him into a panic, and he turned and ran up the creek bed along the old, dim trail. The dog joined in behind him and kept up with him. He ran blindly without intention, in fear such as he had never known in his life. Slowly, as he ploughed and floundered through the snow, he began to see things again – the banks of the creek, the old timber jams, the leafless aspens, and the sky. The running made him feel better. He did not shiver. Maybe his feet would thaw out; and anyway, if he went far enough, he would reach camp and the boys. Without doubt he would lose some fingers and toes and some of his face; but the boys would take care of him, and save the rest of him when he got there.

Several times he stumbled, and finally he tottered, crumpled up, and fell. When he tried to rise, he failed. He must sit and rest, he decided, and next time he would merely walk and keep on going. As he sat and regained his breath, he noted he was feeling warm and quite comfortable. He was not shivering, and it even seemed that a warm glow had come to his chest and trunk. And yet, when he touched his nose or cheeks, there was no sensation. Running would not thaw them out. Nor would it thaw out his hands and feet. Then the thought came to him that the frozen portions of his body must be extending. This was too much, and he made another wild run along the trail. Once he slowed down to a walk, but the thought of the freezing extending itself made him run again. And all the time the dog ran with him, at his heels. When he fell down a second time, it curled its tail over its forefeet and sat in front of him, facing him, curiously eager and intent. The warmth and security of the animal angered him, and he cursed it till it flattened down its ears appeasingly. He was losing his battle with the frost. The thought of it drove him on, but he went no more than a hundred feet, when he staggered and pitched headlong. It was his last panic. When he had recovered his breath and control, he sat up and entertained in his mind the conception of meeting death with dignity. He pictured the boys finding his body the next day. Suddenly he found himself with them, coming along the trail looking for himself. And, still with them, he came around a turn in the trail and found himself lying in the snow. He did not belong with himself anymore, for even then he was out of himself, standing with the boys and looking at himself in the snow. It certainly was cold, was his thought. When he got back to the States he could tell the folks what real cold was.

Then the man drowsed off into what seemed to him the most comfortable and satisfying sleep he had ever known. The dog sat facing him and waiting. The brief day drew to a close in a long, slow twilight. There was no sign of a fire to be made, and besides, never in the dog's experience had it known a man to sit like that in the snow and make no fire. As the twilight drew in, its eager yearning for the fire mastered it, and with a great lifting and shifting of forefeet, it whined softly, then flattened its ears in anticipation of being chidden by the man. But the man remained silent. Later the dog whined loudly. And still later it crept closer to the man and caught the sense of death. Then it turned and trotted up the trail in the direction of the camp it knew, where there were other food providers and fire providers.

Jack London, 'To Build a Fire', 1910

WALKING FURIOUS HEADLONG

Nor will I go out of my way to avoid such things, when avoidable, no, I simply will not go out of my way, though I have never in my life been on my way anywhere, but simply on my way. And in this way I have gone through great thickets, bleeding, and deep into bogs, water too, even the sea in some moods and been carried out of my course, or driven back, so as not to drown. And that is perhaps how I shall die at least if they don't catch me, I mean drowned, or in fire, yes, perhaps that is how I shall do it at last, walking furious headlong into fire and dying burnt to bits.

Samuel Beckett, *From an Abandoned Work*, 1958

'I'D RATHER WALK,' HE SAID

When three milestones had loitered past, the tramp overtook a boy who was stooping to light a cigarette. He wore no overcoat, and looked unspeakably fragile against the snow. 'Are you on the road, guv'nor?' asked the boy huskily as he passed.

'I think I am,' the tramp said.

'Oh! then I'll come a bit of the way with you if you don't walk too fast. It's a bit lonesome walking this time of day.' The tramp nodded his head, and the boy started limping along by his side.

'I'm eighteen,' he said casually. 'I bet you thought I was younger.'

'Fifteen, I'd have said.'

'You'd have backed a loser. Eighteen last August, and I've been on the road six years. I ran away from home five times when I was a little 'un, and the police took me back each time. Very good to me, the police was. Now I haven't got a home to run away from.'

'Nor have I,' the tramp said calmly.

'Oh, I can see what you are,' the boy panted; 'you're a gentleman come down. It's harder for you than for me.' The tramp glanced at the limping, feeble figure and lessened his pace.

'I haven't been at it as long as you have,' he admitted.

'No, I could tell that by the way you walk. You haven't got tired yet. Perhaps you expect something the other end?'

The tramp reflected for a moment. 'I don't know,' he said bitterly, 'I'm always expecting things.'

'You'll grow out of that,' the boy commented. 'It's warmer in London, but it's harder to come by grub. There isn't much in it really.'

'Still, there's the chance of meeting somebody there who will understand –'

'Country people are better,' the boy interrupted. 'Last night I took a lease of a barn for nothing and slept with the cows, and this morning the farmer routed me out and gave me tea and toke because I was little. Of course, I score there; but in

London, soup on the Embankment at night, and all the rest of the time coppers moving you on.'

'I dropped by the roadside last night and slept where I fell. It's a wonder I didn't die,' the tramp said. The boy looked at him sharply.

'How do you know you didn't?' he said.

'I don't see it,' the tramp said after a pause.

'I tell you,' the boy said hoarsely, 'people like us can't get away from this sort of thing if we want to. Always hungry and thirsty and dog-tired and walking all the time. And yet if any one offers me a nice home and work my stomach feels sick. Do I look strong? I know I'm little for me age, but I've been knocking about like this for six years, and do you think I'm not dead? I was drowned bathing at Margate, and I was killed by a gipsy with a spike; he knocked my head right in, and twice I was froze like you last night, and a motor cut me down in this very road, and yet I'm walking along here now, walking to London to walk away from it again, because I can't help it. Dead! I tell you we can't get away if we want to.'

The boy broke off in a fit of coughing and the tramp paused while he recovered.

'You'd better borrow my coat for a bit,' he said, 'your cough's pretty bad.'

'You go to hell!' the boy said fiercely, puffing at his cigarette; 'I'm all right. I was telling you about the road. You haven't got down to it yet, but you'll find out presently. We're all dead, all of us who're on it, and we're all tired, yet somehow we can't leave it. There's nice smells in the summer, dust and hay and the wind smack in your face on a hot day; and it's nice waking up in the wet grass on a fine morning. I don't know, I don't know –' he lurched forward suddenly, and the tramp caught him in his arms.

'I'm sick,' the boy whispered – 'sick.'

The tramp looked up and down the road, but he could see

no houses or any sign of help. Yet even as he supported the boy doubtfully in the middle of the road a motor-car suddenly flashed in the middle distance, and came smoothly through the snow.

'What's the trouble?' said the driver quietly as he pulled up. 'I'm a doctor.' He looked at the boy keenly and listened to his strained breathing.

'Pneumonia,' he commented. 'I'll give him a lift to the infirmary, and you, too, if you like.'

The tramp thought of the workhouse and shook his head. 'I'd rather walk,' he said.

The boy winked faintly as they lifted him into the car.

'I'll meet you beyond Reigate,' he murmured to the tramp. 'You'll see.' And the car vanished along the white road.

All the morning the tramp splashed through the thawing snow, but at midday he begged some bread at a cottage door and crept into a lonely barn to eat it. It was warm in there, and after his meal he fell asleep among the hay. It was dark when he woke, and started trudging once more through the slushy roads.

Two miles beyond Reigate a figure, a fragile figure, slipped out of the darkness to meet him.

'On the road, guv'nor?' said a husky voice. 'Then I'll come a bit of the way with you if you don't walk too fast. It's a bit lonesome walking this time of day.'

'But the pneumonia!' cried the tramp aghast.

'I died at Crawley this morning,' said the boy.

Richard Middleton, *The Brighton Road*, 1912

ON TO WHERE THE EARTH MEETS THE SKY

They walked slowly, at a good distance from each other, along the narrow climbing path. To their right, boulders and shale, steep and dazzling. Before them, a barrier of rocks and snow, thrust into an enamel sky. There were six of them plus a dog. Five brothers, their common wife, the dog. The long and lanky Yudhiṣṭhira led the way, followed by the black mongrel that they had found wandering around the western slopes and that had followed them ever since. They called the animal Dharma, because it was always at Yudhiṣṭhira's feet.

They never spoke and rarely stopped. They had trudged along interminable beaches, then headed for the highest peaks, crossed the Himālaya and the desert that stretches beyond, and now were climbing again toward Mount Meru, which joins the earth to the sky, toward Indra's paradise. They were wearing faded rags held together with strips of bark. But their steps were warriors' steps. Their minds met in memory and mourning. They counted the dead of that single family that had fought against itself to the point of extinction. The appalling carnage of Kurukṣetra was the central vortex. It was there that the chains of earlier events converged, from there that the chains of future events emerged. The links were welded together with boons and curses that went far, far back, intertwining with other stories that distracted them as they tried, sometimes in vain, to reconstruct their every twist and turn. 'Time! Time!' were the only words that Arjuna answered when Yudhiṣṭhira in a tone of sober acknowledgement told him that everything was over now. 'It is time that cooks each creature in its pot,' said Yudhiṣṭhira. And now it was time to leave the world. The others had agreed with a nod of their heads. And as they stubbornly climbed on and up like tiny parasites hugging the world's back, everything that had happened, the shame and the glory, the rancors and the spells, seemed to level out and break up, blending their colours in one knotted, worn-out drape.

The still beautiful Draupadī brought up the rear. As always she emanated a scent of lotus, mixed with sweat. Every so often she would raise her head and narrow her proud, bright eyes, a delicate embroidery of wrinkles forming on the burnished skin at their corners, to look at the strong shoulders of those five men among whom her body had been equally shared. She dwelled just a little longer on Arjuna, who, with his strange, high cheekbones, still looked like a boy and a foreigner. From the depths of the silence came the roar of a distant stream, hidden in a gorge. The occasional muffled thud. Ice breaking up. No birds in the air here. No animals on their path. No one noticed when Draupadī missed her footing and fell. But the brothers turned together and saw something dark, like a bundle of rags, rolling down through the boulders till it disappeared. They said nothing, gathering around Yudhiṣṭhira. 'You know why it happened? Because in her secret heart Draupadī always preferred Arjuna to the rest of us,' said Yudhiṣṭhira. No one answered. They set off again. Every day the sun followed its obsessive course, ever nearer. Sometimes they would be beset by fogs. Then even their feet were lost to them. One by one they fell, even Arjuna. Each time, with a few terse words, Yudhiṣṭhira would explain why. When Bhīma fell, and he was the last, as he lay dying he managed to ask: 'Why?' 'Because you were too greedy, when you were eating you never asked yourself whether there was enough for others,' said Yudhiṣṭhira. Then he walked on along the path, without turning back. Now there was only the dog behind him.

Roberto Calasso, Ka, 1996 (trans. Tim Parks, 1998)

ACKNOWLEDGEMENTS

For the anthologist it is never a walk alone, so my thanks go to the friends, family and colleagues who helped along the way.

To Caroline Michel for commissioning the idea and to Arzu Tahsin for her editorial work; to Mitzi Angel and Ali Reynolds for their administrative support. And most recently to Vintage, to Áine Mulkeen and Rachel Cugnoni who were responsible for re-issuing the book with its new title.

To: Justin Arnold, Paul Bailey, Daisy Breen, Rachel Calder, Mungo Campbell, Clive Davis, Richard Holmes, Christopher Hope, Robert Macfarlane, David Miller, Ray Minshull, Mimi Nyle, Chris Paling, Helen Simpson, Iain Sinclair, Sarah Spankie and D. J. Taylor.

And I am grateful to staff at the British Library, the BBC Library, and Boston Public Library for their efforts in locating titles familiar and unfamiliar.

The editor and publishers gratefully acknowledge permission to reprint copyright material from the following:

Robert Antelme: from *The Human Race*, 1957 (trans. Jeffrey Haight and Annie Mahler, 1992) by permission of South

Western University Press; Paul Bailey: from *An Immaculate Mistake*, (Bloomsbury, 1990) by permission of the author c/o Rogers, Coleridge & White Ltd; Julian Barnes: from *England, England* (Jonathan Cape, 1998) by permission of Random House Inc.; from *Metroland* (Jonathan Cape, 1980) by permission of Random House; Matsuo Bashō: from *The Narrow Road to the Deep North* (trans. Nobuyuki Yuasa, 1966) by permission of Penguin Books Ltd; Samuel Beckett: from *An Abandoned Work*, 1958, and *The End*, 1967, by permission of the estate of Samuel Beckett and John Calder Books Ltd; Max Beerbohm: from *On Going for A Walk*, 1918 by permission of the estate of Max Beerbohm and London Management and Representation Ltd; Hilaire Belloc: 'Final Song', (from *The Path To Rome*, 1902) by permission of Peters, Fraser & Dunlop on behalf of the estate of Hilaire Belloc; Walter Benjamin; from *Charles Baudelaire: A Lyric Poet in the High Era of Capitalism* (trans. Harry Zohn, 1983) by permission of Verso; Alan Booth: from *The Road to Sata*, (Viking, 1986) by permission of Penguin Books Ltd; William Boyd: from 'Not Yet, Jayette', (from the collection *On the Yankee Station*, 1981) by permission of the author c/o Rogers, Coleridge & White Ltd; Daniel Boulanger: from *Pinceloup the Shoebreaker*, 1963, (trans. Penny Pucelik and Marijo Despereaux Schneider, 1989), by permission of Editions de la Table Ronde Ltd and the translators; Ray Bradbury: 'The Pedestrian', 1953, from *The Golden Apples of the Sun*, (Rupert Hart Davis) by permission of Simon and Schuster Ltd and Abner Stein Ltd; John Buchan: from *The Scholar Gypsies*, 1896, by permission of A. P. Watt Ltd on behalf of the Lord Tweedsmuir and Jean, Lady Tweedsmuir; Roberto Calasso: from *Ka*, 1996 (trans. Tim Parks, 1998) by permission of Random House; Camilo José Cela: from *Journey to the Alcarria*, 1948, (trans. Frances M. Lopez Morillas, 1964) by permission of Granta Books and Atlantic Monthly Press, New York; Louis-Ferdinand Céline: from *Guignol's Band*, 1954, by permission of New Directions Publishing; Bruce Chatwin: from *The Songlines*, (Jonathan Cape, 1987), by permission of Putnams US, Penguin Inc. and Rogers, Coleridge & White Ltd; G. K. Chesterton: from *The Queer Feet*, (*The Innocence of Father Brown*, 1910) by permission of A. P. Watt Ltd, on behalf of The Royal Literary Fund; Merle Collins: *The Walk*, (from *Rain Darling*, 1990) by permission of The Women's Press Ltd; Nicholas Crane: from *Clearwaters Rising: A Mountain Walk Across Europe*, 1996, by permission of Penguin Books Ltd; Dante Alighieri: from *Il Purgatorio*, (trans. Dorothy L. Sayers, 1949) by permission of David Higham Assoc; José Donoso: from *The Walk*, 1971 (trans. Andre Conrad, 1971), by permission of the heirs of José Donoso and Agencia Literaria Carmen Balcells, Barcelona; Patrick Leigh Fermor: from *A Time of Gifts*, 1977, by permission of John Murray Publishers; Stella Gibbons: from *Cold Comfort Farm*, 1932, by permission of Curtis Brown Ltd; Stephen Graham: from *The Gentle Art of Tramping*, 1927, by permission of A & C Black; Graham Greene: from *The Heart of The Matter*, 1948, by permission of the estate of Graham Greene and David Higham Assoc.; Herb Greer: from *Mud Pie*, 1964, by permission of the author; Jaroslav Hasek: from *The Good Soldier Švejk*, 1923 (trans. Cecil Parrott, 1973) by permission of Random House Inc.; Werner Herzog: from *Of Walking in Ice*, (Jonathan Cape, 1978), (trans. Alan Greenberg and Martje Herzog, 1980) by permission of Random House, Carl Hanser Verlag and Tanam Press; John Hillaby: from *Journey to the Jade Sea*, 1964, *Journey Through Britain*, by permission of Constable Publishers; Richard Holmes: from *Footsteps*, 1985, by permission of Hodder and Stoughton Ltd; Christopher Hope: from *Hanoi Hug*, 1998, by permission of the author; Miles Jebb: from *Walkers*, 1985, by permission of Constable Publishers; Søren Kierkegaard: from *Kierkegaard's Writing: Letters and Documents*, (trans. Henrik Rosenmeier, 1978) by Princeton University Press; Rudyard Kipling: from *Kim*, 1901, by permission of A. P. Watt Ltd, on behalf of The National Trust for Places of Historical Interest and Natural Beauty; D. H. Lawrence: from *Women in Love*, 1921 and *Lady Chatterly's Lover*, 1928, by permission of Laurence Pollinger Ltd, and the estate of Freida Lawrence Ravagli; Laurie Lee: from *I Walked Out One Midsummer's Morning*, 1969, by permission of Penguin Books Ltd, and Peters, Fraser & Dunlop; Bernard Levin: from *Enthusiasms*, (Jonathan Cape, 1985), by permission of the author c/o Curtis Brown Ltd and Random House; Nicholas Luard: from *The Field of the Star*, 1998, by permission of Penguin Books Ltd; Richard Mabey: from *The Unofficial Countryside*, (Harper Collins, 1973) by permission of Anthony Sheil Assoc.; Thomas Mann: from *Death in Venice*, 1912, (Secker & Warburg, 1928), (trans. H. T. Loweby), by permission of Alfred Knopf Inc.; Maurice Marples: from *Shank's Pony*, (Dent, 1959), by permission of The Orion Publishing Group Ltd; Guy de Maupassant: 'Bed 29', from *A Day in the Country and Other Stories*, (trans. David Coward, 1990), by permission of Oxford University Press; Giuliana Morandini: from *Angelo a Berlino* (Edizioni Bonipiani, 1987), (trans. Liz Heron, 1993), by permission of Virago Books Ltd; Carl Phillip Moritz: from *Journeys of a German in England*, 1782, (trans. Reginald Nettel, Jonathan Cape, 1983); Jan Neruda: from *The Ritual of My Legs* (*50 Poems*), 1931 (trans. Ben Belitt) by permission of Grove Atlantic, Inc.; Eric Newby: from *A Short Walk in the Hindu Kush*, 1972, by permission of Harper Collins; Robert Orledge: from *Satie Remembered*, 1995, (trans. Roger Nichols), by permission of Faber & Faber, and Amadeus Press; Redmond O'Hanlon: from *Into the Heart of Borneo*, 1984, by permission of Random House Inc. and Peters, Fraser & Dunlop; Tim Parks: *Glory*, from: *Adultery and Other Diversions*, 1998, by permission of Gillon Aitken Associates; Harold Pinter: from *The Caretaker*, 1960, by permission of Faber & Faber, and Grove Atlantic Inc.; V. S. Pritchett: *RH* from: *Marching Spain*, 1928 by permission of

Random House; Anthony Powell: from *A View To a Death*, 1933, by permission of the author and David Higham Assoc.; John Cowper Powys: from *Autobiography*, 1934, by permission of the estate of John Cowper Powys and Christopher Sinclair-Stevenson; Marcel Proust: from *Swann's Way*, 1913, (trans. C. K. Scott Moncrieff, Chatto and Windus, 1922) by permission of Random House and Random House Inc.; Edwin Arlington Robinson; Richard Cory, from the *Collected Poems* by permission of Simon and Schuster Inc.; Jean Jacques Rousseau: from *The Confessions* (Penguin Classics, 1953), (trans. J. M. Cohen), by permission of Penguin Books Ltd; Nicholas Shakespeare: from *Bruce Chatwin*, 1999, by permission of Doubleday Inc. and The Harvill Press with Jonathan Cape; George Bernard Shaw: from *The Star*, 1890, by permission of The Society of Authors on behalf of the estate of Bernard Shaw; Iain Sinclair: from *Lights Out for the Territory*, 1997, by permission of the author and Granta Books; Helen Simpson: from *Bed and Breakfast*, 1991, by permission of the author and Peters, Fraser & Dunlop; Agnes Smedley: from *Chinese Destinies*, 1934, by permission of Laurence Pollinger Assoc. and the estate of Agnes Smedley; Albert Speer: from *Spandau, the Secret Diaries*, 1975, (trans. Winston and Clara Winston, 1976) by permission of Simon and Schuster Inc. and Harper Collins; Dr Benjamin Spock and Stephen J. Parker: from *Dr Spock's Baby and Child Care* by permission of Pocket Books, a division of Simon and Schuster Ltd and The Benjamin Spock Trust; William Styron: from *The Long March*, (Hamish Hamilton, 1952), by permission of Tessa Sayle Agency; Patrick Suskind: from *The Story of Mr Sommer*, 1991 (trans. Michael Hoffman, 1992) by permission of Bloomsbury Ltd and Diogenes Verlag A. G. Zurich; Rabindranath Tagore: from *Glimpses of Bengal*, 1921, (trans. Andrew Robinson, Krishna Dutta, 1991) by permission of Macmillan and Visva-Bharati University, Calcutta; Colm Tóibín: from *The Sign of the Cross*, 1994 by permission of

INDEX

Minutes later upon the path, I found what looked like a large jay feather, far bigger than any I'd seen in England. 'There's a Spanish saying,' Miguel said with a broad smile, 'Caminar es atesorar: To walk is to gather treasure.'

Robert Macfarlane

He was in his oldest clothes, striding with the tough easy stride of thousands of miles of walking – walking all through his life.

Christina Stead

www.vintage-books.co.uk